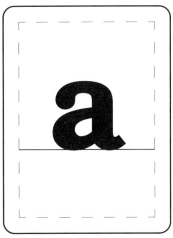

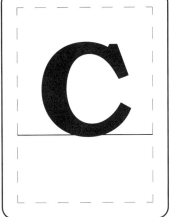

This Book Belongs To

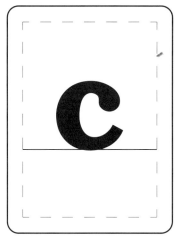

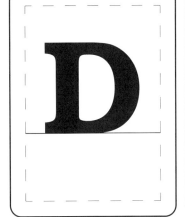
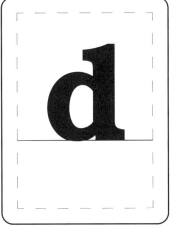

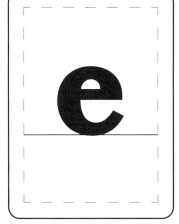

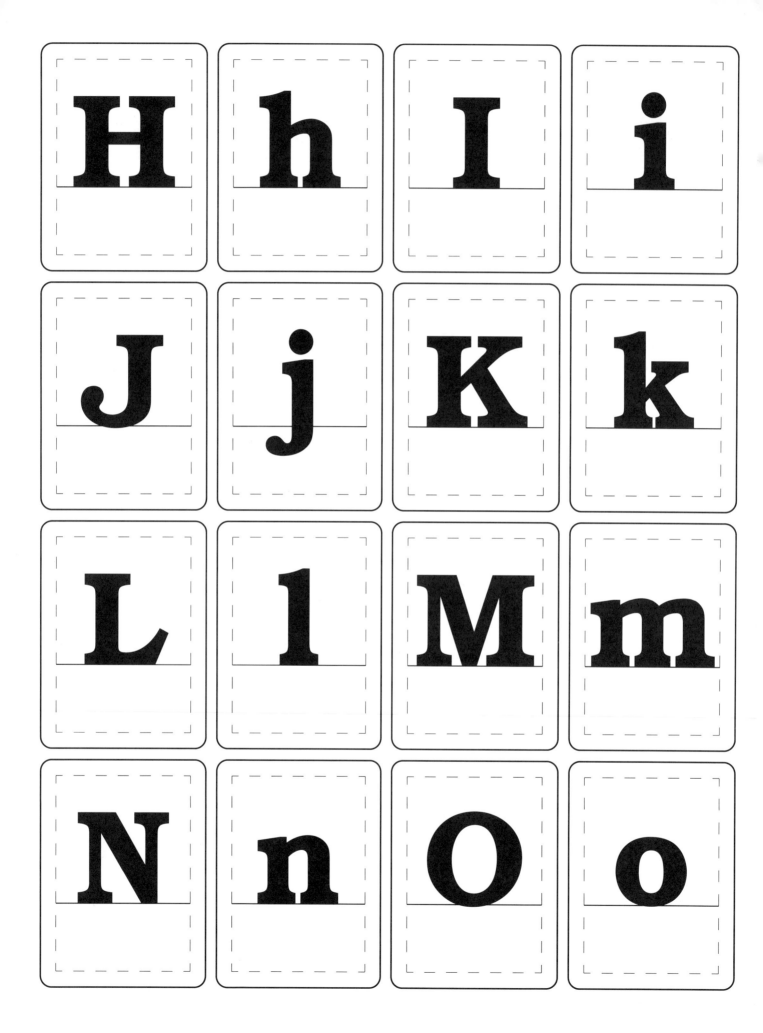

Soft Toys for Babies

Birth to 18 Months

By

Judi Maddigan

Open Chain Publishing, Inc.
Menlo Park, CA

Copyright

Published in Menlo Park, CA, by Open Chain Publishing, Inc., PO Box 2634-B, Menlo Park, CA 94026.

phone (415)366-4440
fax (415)366-4455

ISBN 0-932086-29-2 softbound

ISBN 0-932086-30-6 hardbound

Library of Congress Catalog Card Number 91-061651

Photographs by
Lee Phillips

Designed and composed by
Rosalyn Carson

Line drawings by
Pamela S. Poole

Patterns, charts, and diagrams by
Judi Maddigan

Computer aid by
Tony Fanning

Editor:
Robbie Fanning

Production Coordinator:
Cate Keller

Printed in MEXICO

The publisher wishes to thank Monica Spilker, for lending Amy's crib; Draeger's in Menlo Park, CA, for lending the grocery cart; and the parents of the following children, pictured on the color pages: Tara Harrison (back cover), Sean Pacheco, Vikramjit Kohli, Hana Raftery (front cover), Taylor and Sean Sieling, Kyle Sparks, and Anne Thompson.

ACKNOWLEDGMENTS

Many sewers contributed to this book by testing patterns and producing additional samples for photography. Most are talented needlework artists and teachers in their own right; all adjusted their own busy schedules to meet mine. Thanks to Lauri Realini, for machine piecing and quilting the AlphaPet Quilt and for her construction suggestions; to Charlene Nakamura, for the Teethe-n-Clutch; to Carol Garliepp, for Chapter 8's machine appliqué on challenging fabrics; to Juanita Schubel for machine appliqué and for her training and advice; and to Barbara Maddigan, for cross stitching the 26 quilt animals—twice.

I credit the following persons and companies for their assistance: Laura Loeffler, The DMC Corporation; Jane Schenck, the Pellon Division of Freudenberg Nonwovens; Maggie Johnston, Delta/ Shiva; Fred Drexler, Sulky of America; Fran Fuller, Tomorrow's Treasures; Richard Gannon, JoAnn Pugh, and Bernina of America.

I recognize the contributions of Esther Seehof, Ph.D., who assisted with the child development aspects of this text.

Thanks also to Louise Vernon, for her expert coaching; to Judie Underwood, for listening; to the members of Cupertino Writers for their insightful critiques; and to my dad, Ben Bogdan, for proofreading the original manuscript and its countless revisions.

I owe much to Open Chain Publishing for transforming my computer disks into this handsome form; to Tony Fanning, for managing multiple computer text and graphics programs—without glitches; to Mary Lee Cole, for knowing how to reach more readers; to Cate Keller, for taming the multitude of details; to Kaarli Bowers, for expediting all the extras; to Jonathan Batchelor, for cheerfully implementing every correction to the text; to Rosalyn Carson, for the inviting book design; and to Pamela Poole, for her patience and talent in refining the illustrations.

I appreciate the skill of photographer Lee Phillips in capturing our adorable babies.

In addition, I have many personal gifts to be grateful for. To Joe, for 22 years of loving me because of—and in spite of—my artistic temperament; to Laura and Brandon, for their interest; to Mom and Dad, for teaching me I could accomplish whatever I set my mind to; and to my sister, Joan, for producing my niece, Tara, at just the right time.

Lastly, to Robbie Fanning, with respect and affection. I relish the time we spend together. After a day with Robbie, I come home exhilarated and overflowing with ideas. Her inborn love of sewing reminds me of all the remarkable, earth-changing things we can accomplish with a few remnants of fabric and thread.

TABLE OF CONTENTS

The right toys introduced at the right times can promote a child's development.

By choosing the proper supplies and techniques, you can sew better toys than you can buy.

Check this glossary for terms and techniques.

Understanding child development will help you decide which toys would most benefit your baby, and when.

This changeable mobile will delight your child—it was designed from a baby's point of view.

If you make this quilt, your baby may form a special attachment to it.

Even before your baby can reach out and grasp, this mitten can help him discover his hands.

These crib toys are perfect for your baby because they're soft, safe, adorable, and wonderfully noisy.

Your baby will return again and again to finger the variety of rich textures in these appliquéd pads.

This ball delivers color and sound for your young baby; later, it promotes physical coordination.

You can help your child discuss difficult issues with this toy's eight expressive teddy bear faces.

Quilt this special seat for your baby's comfort and safety.

When you give a handmade educational toy, you start your child on the path toward a lifetime of learning.

FOREWORD

Like any new mother-to-be, I hit the books when I got pregnant: Spock, Brazelton, Dodson, and others all gave me silent lessons in child development.

But the experts left out subtle details. One day I had left my baby under the mobile in the living room while I washed the dishes. Suddenly, I heard soft noises, like distant pigeons. My baby was cooing! Obviously, I knew that someday my child would talk, but nobody told me that the first non-wailing sounds would be cooing.

Now my "baby" is in her twenties. Of all my motherly gifts to her, I'm most proud that we had a lot of fun together from Day 1.

Today I see parents being earnestly correct with their youngsters. They speak in carefully modulated tones and explain why every little thing is important to learn. I always want to say what nobody wrote in the books: "Carpe diem: seize the day. Play with your kid today; tomorrow she'll be in college."

I sewed a lot when my daughter was young, she nestling in a carrier on my back. I made her toys from patterns in women's magazines and appliquéd whales and flowers on her jumpers. How I wish I'd had Judi Maddigan's patterns then. My daughter would have loved the Chit-chat Mitt and the Peek-a-Pocket and the Rainbow Cubs Mobile.

But now I see the grander scheme. That's what grandparents, aunts and uncles, and neighbors are for: a second chance to play-more-with-a-baby.

You will enjoy making and playing with these toys, whether or not the giftee is your baby or someone else's.

It was especially interesting for me when I watched the photography of the children for the color pages. They responded to the toys with instant fascination and cooing. Several of the parents had brought along older children to the photography session and they, too, loved the toys, even those for the youngest baby, such as the Mobile. The Peek-a-Pocket, with its eight expressive faces, was a hit with all ages.

These toys, along with their Play Guides, will add richness to a child's environment. But most of all, they add to the fun of playing with babies.

Carpe diem. Play today.

—**Robbie Fanning**
co-author, **Get It All Done and Still Be Human/A Personal Time-Management Workshop**

Preface

Writing a book is a little like giving birth. A book, like a baby, starts with the germ of an idea. You nurture and protect that grain of a thought, carrying it with you wherever you go. You feel it grow and develop. It affects your family and friends. It makes you anxious, excited, apprehensive, and profoundly happy—all at once. It even wakes you up at night. Your hopes and dreams are tied up in it. You sweat and labor to deliver it into the world. And when it's finally born, you have the joy of saying hello, and a hard time saying goodbye.

Like an elephant, I feel as though I just went through a very long pregnancy. This book was conceived when I couldn't find many up-to-date instructions on sewing educational toys. In the last decade, with toy manufacturers developing so many fascinating new playthings, I thought surely there would be equally exciting patterns for home sewers. When I couldn't find many, my ideas for a book of age-graded, heirloom-quality toys started to evolve.

I dove into research, drafting, designing, testing, and more research. From the start, safety became the primary concern. Once each new design satisfied the safety issues, I examined durability, educational value, and appeal to various age groups. Next, I analyzed how to make the construction easier. Finally, I pondered the *cute* factor. When I had a toy that looked "cute as a button" and still satisfied the other requirements, I knew the project was sound and healthy and could mature into one of this book's chapters.

Along the way, researching the stages of child development suggested appropriate toys. A child's first two years are a magical, miraculous time. (I learned things I wish I had known earlier, when my daughter was only 17 days old instead of 17 years.) The more I read, the more I saw a common thread. This book includes child development information so that you can help your baby gain the most from a particular toy.

I hope you will enjoy this first book of the *Stitch & Enrich* series. I'm eager to show you how your sewing skills can help a special baby in your life.

Above all, I encourage you to enjoy and appreciate your child. If you sew, you already have the perfect skill to enrich his development. This book's toys were designed to teach basic concepts and to develop abilities, but when you make one of these projects, you contribute much more to a child's well-being. You help him feel good about himself. I believe the care and concern you stitch into each toy are communicated through your finished product. Your talents, your pride, and your efforts are why these toys are extraordinary.

—**Judi Maddigan**

San Jose, California

A Matter of Convention

The English words "baby," "infant," and "child" apply to either sex. Unfortunately, our language does not also provide singular pronouns appropriate for either boy or girl. To avoid cumbersome constructions like "(s)he" or "his/her," in most cases I have opted for the simpler "he" and "his." This is solely a matter of convention and does not mean that boys are my favorite. Both girls and boys will enjoy these toys.

Whether you're a parent or grandparent, aunt, cousin, or friend, you'll discover that sewing toys for "your" baby will make your time together even more precious. Eighteen months—that's all you've got. Babies don't stay babies for long. Think of what a child needs to learn in such a short time. It's a wondrous series of firsts.

- The first time Baby focuses on a toy, it can be the **Rainbow Cubs Mobile**—the one you made from Chapter 4.

- The first time Baby swipes at a rattle, it can be a friendly bear named **Squiggles**, **Wiggles**, or **Giggles**, from Chapter 7.

- The first time Baby realizes his hands are a part of himself, you've helped him learn with the **Chit-chat Mitt** in Chapter 6.

Baby has a lot of questions during those first 18 months. How do different textures feel? The **Texture Pads** in Chapter 8 tell him. Can he pass something from one hand to the other? He'll find out with the **Teethe-n-Clutch** in Chapter 9. Does a peeka-boo face cease to exist when he can't see it? Only the **Peek-a-Pocket** in Chapter 10 knows for sure.

CHAPTER 1

INTRODUCTION

I'm going to show you how to sew exciting toys for your baby. You have probably sewn many projects in the past—pants, blouses, throw pillows, whatever—but none of them were as important to your baby as what you will sew from this book. Sewing a skirt won't make your child a better person, but the right types of toys introduced at the right stages can make a remarkable difference in how a child grows, develops, and matures. But when you barely have time for your current sewing projects, **why would you want to sew toys?**

- **Because children aren't picky.** They love whatever you make, even if in your eyes it's less than perfect. We could learn from our kids. They love unconditionally. And they will adore the toys you make.

- **Because toys are always the right size.** Maybe you haven't tried craft sewing. Maybe you've only done fashion sewing. What's the part of fashion sewing most people hate? Fitting, right? With toys we don't need to bother.

- **Because making toys saves money.** Have you priced educational toys lately?

- **Because it's fun.** Imagine starting out with a few scraps of fabric and ending up with a toy having a personality of its own.

All the prior motives are valid, but there are more important reasons. Let's look at toys the way a baby sees them. A baby sees colors in glorious shades and hues for the first time. Tranquil, rhythmic melodies enthrall him. As he reaches out, soft and tender feelings tingle his fingertips. Wonder and excitement fill him, and he can't wait to explore more.

All healthy babies are born with an equally healthy need to explore and learn. Adults don't need to teach babies curiosity. We don't need to teach the desire to explore. All we must do is nurture that inborn thirst to discover, to keep it alive and thriving.

It's a tall order. Anyone who has tried to entertain a baby for just one hour knows that a child devours new toys with stunning speed. That's where this book can help.

These soft toys celebrate the basics. They feature washable, durable fabrics. Their themes revolve around teddy bears, universal symbols of comfort, security, and dependability. They stress the time-honored traditions of care in handwork and craftsmanship. Multi-purposed and interactive, they serve in as many capacities as your child invents.

Several of this book's toys have multiple uses—some your child can try now; some he can grow into. Other toys will coordinate with projects in future volumes of the *Stitch & Enrich* series (see page 182 for more information).

Through these pages, I want to guide you and help you make playthings that your child and the entire family will cherish. I hope the toys that spring from this book will become your child's favorites, the ones picked up day after day, the ones grabbed for reassurance, the ones snuggled at night—maybe even the ones saved for "my kids someday."

These are the things childhood is made of—the quilt dragged to day care, or the teddy bear rattle clutched during thumb sucking. These are the rewards of a carefully sewn, beautifully constructed gift, a gift you handcrafted with love.

How to Use This Book

Browse through this book because it's different from other sewing texts. You'll notice Chapter 2 lists toy-making supplies, discusses sewing methods, and explains techniques like counted cross stitch and machine appliqué. You can refer to that chapter in detail later.

Chapter 2 also features the **HelpLine**. Here's a place for a bookmark or paper clip, so that you can snap the book open to review the details when needed. We've also shaded the edges so you can find it more easily. Even if you're eager to start sewing, take a few minutes to skim those pages for useful tips and information. Some of the HelpLine's information is not covered elsewhere.

The third chapter discusses child development topics relating to play and playthings. It can help you choose which toys to make and can suggest ways to maximize purchased toys, too. However, that chapter is not meant to serve as your sole source of child development information. (The Bibliography, on page 172, recommends excellent child-care books beyond the scope of this book.)

Chapters 4 through 11 present the sewing projects, complete with patterns and illustrated, step-by-step instructions. These chapters appear according to the toy's suggested age range, and can be explored in any order.

As you read this book, watch for type like this. It points out my tips and suggestions. I hope you'll find them helpful.

Play Guides

Any of these toys would make thoughtful gifts. But if you give the toy to a family that doesn't have this book, how can you pass along important tips and suggestions? That's where each chapter's Play Guide comes in. By photocopying one page, you can share age guidelines, skills development, safety information, and ways for parent and child to play and learn together. And if you're making the toys for your own family, all the reference material is organized in one place for each toy.

Safety Foremost

The overriding concern in designing these toys has been *safety*. Even so, there is no such thing as a toy guaranteed 100% safe at all times, for all children, under all circumstances. Adults must exercise sound judgment in deciding which toys are appropriate for their children, and when—regardless of generalized age recommendations. This book helps you make an educated choice.

Chapters 2 and 3 include child safety issues for babies under 18 months of age. In addition, each Play Guide reviews safety concerns specific to its corresponding toy. Also check the Bibliography for free or inexpensive pamphlets and booklets regarding toy safety.

I think you will enjoy making these toys. Readers who still doubt that they have time to start a new sewing project should sneak a peek at the Conclusion. Otherwise, let's start with a look at the basic techniques.

Metric Conversion Chart

While the measurements in this book are given in imperial, they are easy to convert—if you must. Most of the patterns show the seamline. If you will copy the seamline, as well as the cutting line, you will be able to construct most toys with little trouble.

Here are common measurements I use in the book, with their metric equivalent:

1/4"	6mm
3/8"	1cm
1/2"	1.3cm
5/8"	1.5cm
3/4"	2cm
1"	2.5cm
1-1/4"	3cm
1-1/2"	4cm
2"	5cm

You need to know only two equivalents to convert any measurement:

1" = 2.5cm or 25mm
1 yd = 0.9 meters

Now use a calculator to convert imperial to metrics and round off.

Example:

12" x 2.5cm = 30cm
3-1/2 yd x 0.9m = 3.2m

CHAPTER 2

GENERAL INSTRUCTIONS

The right supplies can turn a drudgery into a delight. The right techniques can turn handwork into handpleasure. That's what this chapter's about. It has its own table of contents for quick reference. (You might add a bookmark or stick a paper clip on this page so it's easy to find.)

Study the directions before you start cutting or sewing. Every sewer hates mistakes. What's the best way to prevent mess-ups? Preparation. Gather all materials and supplies. Figure out the construction sequence first, and you'll save time in the long run.

Squiggles the Bear

Throughout this book you'll notice a friendly little guy named Squiggles. His job is to help explain stitch diagrams, making them fun and easy. He spends much of his time in the HelpLine.

Toddlers will enjoy snooping through this book with you, page by page. Ask them to find Squiggles, and talk about what he is doing in each figure. Older pre-schoolers will be able to match the Squiggles in later chapters to the same drawings in the HelpLine. (Make the game easier by finding the correct pages first.) Sharing moments like these can include children in your sewing. Who knows? You might plant the seeds for your children's future love of sewing.

To make your own Squiggles, see Chapter 7, page 99.

Numbers and Abbreviations

Before we look at sewing supplies, I should explain the numbering conventions. In this text, a hyphen separates full numerals from fractions. So, in case you're confused, 3-3/4" reads "three and three-fourths inches." Stitch width is straightforward, since most machines measure it in millimeters from 0 to 5. But the method of specifying stitch length varies from machine to machine. So you will find references for stitch length like 2.5 – 3mm (8 – 10spi). This means a stitch length of 2.5 to 3 millimeters, or 8 to 10 *stitches per inch.*

Fig. 2.1 Introducing Squiggles the Bear

Toymaking Supplies

Most of the supplies for toymaking are the same as for general sewing. Here's what you'll need:

The Basics

Throughout the book, specific brand names for products I have used are included in parentheses. Mail-order suppliers are listed on page 174.

Sewing machine. Although you could make these projects completely by hand, you'll probably want to do as much as possible by machine. In addition to saving time, the machine makes strong, durable seams (important for safety, which we'll discuss shortly). Machine appliqué usually requires a zigzag machine.

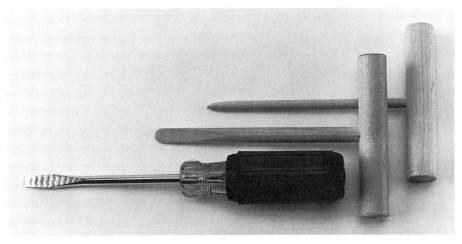

Fig. 2.3 Use a screwdriver or special stuffing stick to pack fiberfill into stuffed toys.

A computerized machine is a boon, but you can still produce first-rate toys with a less-than-state-of-the-art machine.

Fabric shears. Choose a top quality pair, like Gingher.

Straight pins. You'll need both regular pins and quilting pins. My favorite fine pins are 1-3/8" long with glass heads.

Assorted needles. In addition to regular hand needles, you'll also use a 3-1/2" dollmaking needle.

Fabric markers. Both disappearing and water-soluble fabric marking pens work well for transferring pattern markings. On heirloom projects like the quilt, I prefer to use a silver pencil (Berol). Tailor's chalk is another safe alternative.

Tape measure. In addition to my 60" tape, I also like a 6" seam gauge.

Screwdriver. For stuffed toys, you'll need a screwdriver or other stuffing tool (see Suppliers listing on page 174).

Handy Extras

Although not mandatory, the following supplies will save time and effort:

Awl for separating the fabric's threads when inserting safety eyes and noses.

Wash-A-Way Wonder Tape (double-sided transparent tape) for positioning zippers and fastener tapes.

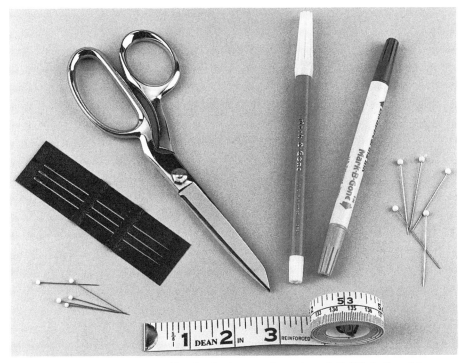

Fig. 2.2 Toymaking supplies include regular pins, 3-1/2" dollmaking needles, good shears, fabric markers, quilting pins, tape measure.

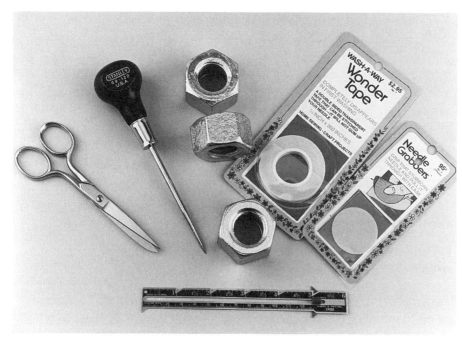

Fig. 2.4 Optional supplies: 5" sewing scissors, awl, pattern weights, double-sided tape, Needle Grabbers, seam gauge.

5" sewing scissors for snipping threads and light trimming.

Needle Grabbers (small rubber circles) for pulling doll-making needles through stubborn areas.

Pattern weights for holding pattern pieces, without pins, during cutting.

Rotary cutter, ruler, and mat (Fig. 2.5) for strip and rectangle cutting.

Serger (overlock machine) for serging and seam finishes.

Fabrics

Each project's yardage requirements serve as a guide for purchasing the minimum amount of yardage. Many toys take considerably less than the full fabric width and can often be made from remnants in your fabric stash.

Bright, vivid colors and patterns attract babies. You'll want to select strong, durable yardage, generally medium- to heavy-weight.

For practicality, you can't go wrong with 100% cotton. It was used for most of the book's samples (except for the textured fabrics). Corduroy, denims, poplin-weight, and quilt-weight cottons are all serviceable.

Although you might be tempted to use felt, avoid it. Felt disintegrates with multiple washings or rough handling. Good substitutes are coat-weight woolens (which ravel) or imitation suedes (which don't).

Many untreated fabrics, especially cotton, flame quickly. This is one reason **you should remove this book's projects from the crib before putting a baby down for a nap or to sleep at night**. (The next chapter mentions additional reasons.)

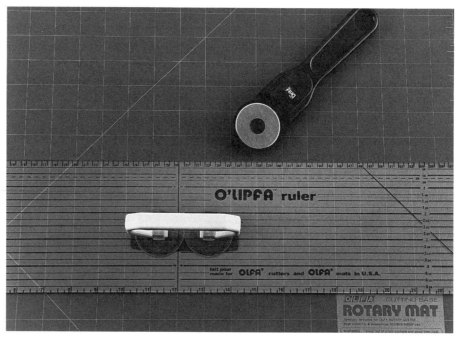

Fig. 2.5 Slice precise strips and rectangles with a rotary cutter and mat. A plexiglass ruler, complete with a suction lift (handle), streamlines the process.

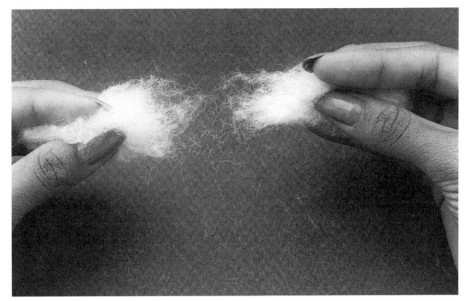

Fig. 2.6 *When you pull apart cheap fiberfill, tiny particles separate, drift into the air, and can be inhaled into your lungs. Select a better quality.*

Materials treated with fire retardants are generally available to home sewers only in children's sleepwear fabrics.

Fiberfill

For stuffed toys, you should choose the filling as carefully as you choose the fabrics. Polyester fiberfill makes a smart choice. It handles easily, stays where you put it, and doesn't lump. It's also washable and non-allergenic, making it perfect for babies.

A top-quality fiberfill has long fibers that do not disintegrate into tiny, airborne fragments. Many brands meet this criterion. Since they handle differently, buy small bags of several and find your own favorite. These good fiberfills can cost three times the so-called "bargain"

brands, but they're worth the difference.

One more point while we're on the subject of stuffing: Don't attempt to stuff with only your hands. A stuffing tool such as a screwdriver or stuffing stick packs the fiber-

fill solidly into the nooks and crannies and produces a toy that will hold its shape through years of play.

Thread

In addition to fabric, fiberfill, and notions listed in each project's materials list, you'll need all-purpose sewing thread for your machine. Although I use large, less expensive cones of polyester thread on my serger, I choose small spools of good quality polyester or cotton-covered polyester for my conventional sewing machine (Fig. 2.8). Rayon thread, extra-fine thread, and 100% cotton thread are not strong enough for seams, but they are excellent for decorative touches.

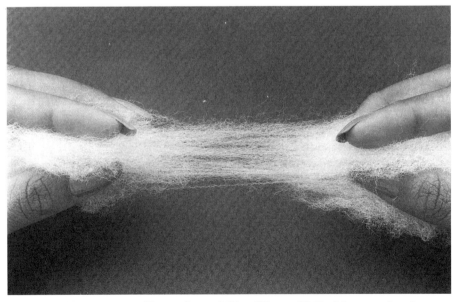

Fig. 2.7 *When you pull apart good fiberfill, you'll find long polyester fibers and few broken fragments. A superior fiberfill will make your stuffing job a breeze.*

Fig. 2.8 Types of threads for toymaking (left to right): all-purpose polyester for conventional machine, extra-fine cotton-covered polyester for machine appliqué, rayon for machine embroidery, fine monofilament nylon for invisible machine stitching, two cone threads for serger, and quilting thread for handwork.

General Techniques

Once you've assembled all the supplies, you're ready to begin toymaking. We'll cover a few key techniques that will make things easier. Your first task is to duplicate the book's patterns on your fabric.

Pattern Transfer

You can trace this book's full-sized patterns on either tracing paper or quilter's template plastic. But the easiest way to clone the patterns is to photocopy them. After copying one page, cut out a pattern piece and compare it to the book's page. Does the copy distort the original? If it does, find another copy machine. Otherwise, your toys won't look like mine.

After cutting the fabric (as described below), you'll need to transfer the pattern markings. Mark all notches and dots. When I transfer a machine-appliqué motif, I usually pin the fabric over the photocopied pattern and tape both to a makeshift light table (a window during the day or a lit television screen at night). On all but the darkest, thickest fabrics, the back light allows me to trace the design directly to the fabric's rightside with a water-soluble fabric marking pen.

When you're faced with a thick, textured, challenging fabric, try this fail-safe method: Cut out the photocopy and use the paper as a stencil. Outline the design directly on the fabric. See Fig. 2.9.

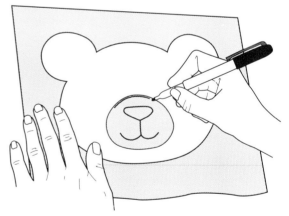

Fig. 2.9 For transferring designs to difficult fabrics, use a photocopied stencil. Snip the paper on the central design lines first. Trace them to the material. Complete the design by working from the center out, gradually cutting away more and more of the paper.

Cutting

Lay out all the traced or photocopied patterns on your fabric to check that they fit—before you start cutting. Cut notches outward or mark them (after cutting) with a fabric marker. Do not snip the notches into the seam allowances, as you do in garment sewing, because the seam allowances are usually only 1/4".

When a pattern piece specifies "cut two," fold the fabric rightsides together and cut two at once. When working on a single layer, as for fur fabric, cut one piece with the pattern rightside up and one with the pattern flipped (a mirror image of the shape). Watch the grainline direction when reversing pieces.

Sometimes you won't need pattern pieces. Projects like the quilt are assembled from rectangles and squares. A rotary cutter, ruler, and mat will simplify the cutting for these projects.

Although I do little else ambidextrously, I have learned to use my rotary cutter with either hand. This bypasses all those awkward transfers of the ruler and cutter.

When cutting sewn strips into blocks, match the ruler in two places (Fig. 2.10). Align a seam along one of the ruler's horizontal lines and a previously cut edge along a vertical line. This produces proper 90° angles.

Clipping and Trimming

Suppose you flawlessly cut out the pieces, mark them precisely, and sew them expertly. Is that enough to guarantee a perfect finished product? By now, you've probably figured out the answer. If I were to choose the two details most often neglected by sewers, they'd be trimming and clipping. Pressing runs a close third; we'll review that in a minute.

Those three culprits cause more than their share of disappointments. Often all the other steps on an inferior project were fine—someone just botched the clipping. Your job isn't completed when the seam is sewn—it's just begun.

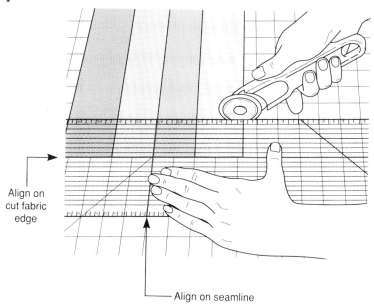

Align on cut fabric edge

Align on seamline

Fig. 2.10 To cut seamed strips into blocks, match both crosswise and lengthwise lines on the ruler.

Many of this book's patterns have 1/4" seam allowances, which often eliminates the need for trimming. When the directions specifically mention grading the seam allowances, trim the layers separately as in Fig. 2.11.

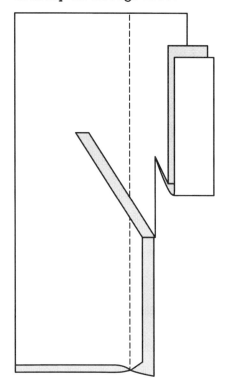

Fig. 2.11 To reduce bulk, trim each seam allowance a different width. The trimmed seam allowances generally measure between 1/8" to 1/4". Make the seam allowance closest to the front (or outside) the widest.

You should not overlook clipping any curved seam. In this text, the term clipping applies both to clipping concave (inner) curves and to notching convex (outer) curves. Gradual curves need only a few clips; sharp curves need many closely spaced clips. Follow Fig. 2.12.

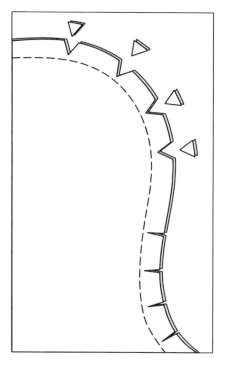

Fig. 2.12 Clip seam allowances for inside curves perpendicular to the stitching line. Notch outside curves, removing tiny triangular pieces from the seam allowances. You can also use pinking shears for the same effect.

Pressing

Once the seams are trimmed and clipped, it's time to press. You can mold and shape a three-dimensional piece with proper pressing techniques.

When "pressing" fabrics, move the iron by lifting and repositioning, as opposed to the term "ironing," which implies sliding.

When the directions instruct you to press fabrics during construction, first press the stitching flat (as sewn) from the wrongside to set the stitches. Then press the seam allowances open. If you have a point presser, it makes the job easier.

For seams pressed to the side, first press the stitching flat (as sewn) from the wrongside; lift one side; then, working from the rightside, slide the iron across the seam to open the top fabric. The directions won't always spell out the first step, so plan ahead.

Child-safe Eyes and Noses

Safety eyes and noses install in a snap. Working from the wrongside with an awl, carefully poke a hole at the location indicated on the pattern piece. Only separate the fabric threads; try not to break them. For safety considerations, keep the hole as small as possible. From the rightside, push the shaft of the eye or nose through the hole. Set the eye or nose with the material rightside down on a padded surface.

Place the lock washer on the shaft with its teeth up. Push the washer partially down the shaft. Slip a wooden spool on the shaft and, with the palm of your hand, force the washer down as tightly as possible (Fig. 2.13). After installation, it should be hard to force your thumbnail under the eye and nose edges.

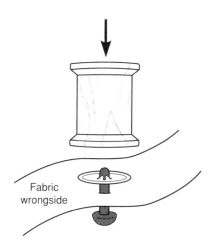

Fig. 2.13 Install the lock washer with its teeth pointing up, toward the tip of the shaft. Tighten the washer with the help of a wooden spool.

Safety Issues

Throughout every phase of toymaking, you must consider safety. Start by prewashing all fabrics and notions. For garment sewing, this is done for preshrinking and setting dyes. For toymaking, prewashing also removes sizing and chemicals (such as formaldehyde)—things a baby shouldn't teethe on. And if, during construction, you add anything (like a water-soluble glue) that isn't specifically labeled as nontoxic, wash the item before giving it to a child.

A second safety consideration is durability. Machine stitching with all-purpose thread usually produces seams that withstand vigorous play. At stress points, the text will direct you to stitch again over first stitching for reinforcement.

For hand stitching, use strong thread such as hand-quilting thread. This is especially important when closing stuffing openings, and for keeping sound makers (bells, rattles, and squeakers) away from tiny fingers. It also helps to knot your hand stitching several times along the way.

Whenever substituting items in a project's supply list, be aware of the safety implications. For example, do not substitute buttons for plastic eyes with locking washers. The buttons could pose a choking hazard. You could embroider the eyes, however, and that would be safe.

No doubt you will check any toy before giving it to your child. But remember to check all toys later, from time to time, and mend or repair worn toys. Safety eyes with locking washers are only as permanent as the material they're attached to. If the fabric in an older toy has been gnawed through, an eye can pop off. And chewing on a fused rather than sewn appliqué might, in time, lift the edges and allow it to be pulled off.

Once you have considered these safety issues, and those in Chapter 3, you are free to concentrate on the fine points. We'll cover two techniques in detail: machine appliqué and counted cross stitch embroidery.

Machine Appliqué

Many children's toys use machine appliqué for embellishment because it's durable and safe. It doesn't add foreign objects, so there's nothing to pull off or swallow.

If you have shied away from appliqué because you thought you couldn't do it, think again. Any zigzag sewing machine provides quick, durable alternatives.

Choosing an appropriate, up-to-date method will make machine appliqué simpler than you might expect. Practice the following techniques on remnants of your specific fabrics, or check your sewing machine's instruction manual for directions geared to your model. Decide which techniques give the best results. You can use any combination of methods on the same project.

If your machine has a needle-down feature, now is the time to use it. For Bernina owners, the knee lift for the presser foot also comes in handy.

In preparation for most of these methods, thread the needle with rayon, cotton, or cotton-wrapped polyester extra-fine machine-embroidery thread; wind extra-fine cotton on the bobbin. Loosen the top tension slightly, allowing that thread to pull to the underside. (Instead of

Fig. 2.14 An open-toed appliqué foot allows an unobstructed view of the appliqué's edge.

upper tension adjustment, some machines provide a special finger on the bobbin case; threading it tightens the lower tension.)

To set the machine for a perfect satin stitch, practice on scraps of the actual fabric used in your project. If you've decided to fuse your appliqué, fuse the practice pieces, too. Start with a zig-zag (stitch width of 2mm or wider). Gradually shorten the stitch length until the stitches lie right next to, but not on top of, each other. The satin stitching should form a smooth, solid line, completely covering the edge of the appliqué fabric.

Match the appliqué's grain to the background fabric's grain. Regardless of fabric type, add a layer of typing-weight paper or tear-away stabilizer (Stitch-n-Tear) beneath the background fabric to improve the feed.

To revive crushed or wrin-kled tear-away stabilizer, press it before using.

Remove the stabilizer after completing the satin stitch-ing.

Lock the beginning and end-ing threads by stitching in place or pulling them to the wrongside and tying. When stitching a closed appliqué where the stitching line ends at its beginning, start with 1/2" of straight stitches (0 width). Clip the thread tails, then satin stitch (2mm or wider) around the entire shape and cover the begin-ning straight stitches. Lock ending threads.

A fat satin stitch overwhelms the design. To avoid this common error, begin with a 2mm stitch width on your practice remnants. When necessary, increase the width by slight increments until it conceals the raw edges. If you start narrow and the appliqué's initial satin stitching is imperfect, you can always widen the stitch and work around the shape a second time.

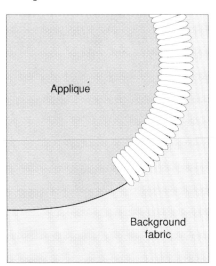

Fig. 2.15 The body of the satin stitch should lie on the appliqué fabric, not on the background. Only the point of the needle extends beyond the edge on the needle's right swing.

For layered designs, first complete the pieces under-neath. The pattern directions specify the order.

Fused Appliqué

I use this method for 80% of my machine appliqué pieces. It is so adaptable that you will probably need the other methods only for specialty fabrics.

Naturally, fused appliqué requires a fusible web. A transfer web like Wonder-Under or Trans-Web with a paper backing is the easiest. It adds body to the appliqué, often desirable in toys. However, this stiffness can be objectionable in clothing, and a smarter choice for bibs, shirts, receiving blan-kets, and other items that come in direct contact with baby's skin would be Fine Fuse. This supple webbing requires a nonstick pressing sheet, such as one from Easy Way Appliqué (see Suppliers on page 174). Follow the manufacturer's directions or one of these methods:

For Wonder-Under and Trans-Web

1. Trace the flipped appliqué pattern (a mirror image of the shape) on the paper side of the adhesive web. To keep track of the grain, also mark a vertical arrow pointing up. Cut the web with an extra border on all sides.

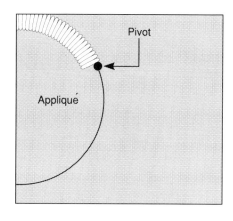

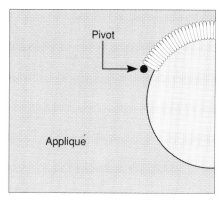

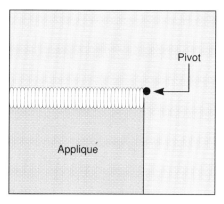

Fig. 2.16 Working clockwise, pivot with the needle down on the right swing for outer curves. Use the left needle-down position for inner curves. Turn outer corners from the right needle-down position, restitching the corner.

2. Place the Wonder-Under's rough side against the appliqué fabric's wrongside. (Match the appliqué's grain arrow to the fabric's grain.) Press for three seconds with a dry iron, "wool" setting. Let cool.

3. Cut on the traced line. Carefully peel off the paper backing.

4. Place the appliqué rightside up on the background fabric. Using an iron set for "wool" and a damp press cloth, press for 10 seconds.

5. Oversew the appliqué's raw edges with a satin stitch.

For Fine Fuse

1. Cut a piece of appliqué fabric larger than the pattern; cut a matching piece of Fine Fuse. (For some fabrics, you can cut both layers at once.)

2. Lay the Fine Fuse on the appliqué's wrongside. Sandwich both between two layers of a folded Teflon pressing sheet.

3. Press with a dry, "wool" iron for about seven seconds. Cool completely.

4. Peel the fused fabric off the sheet. Transfer the pattern and cut out the appliqué shape.

5. Complete as for Wonder-Under (above), steps 4 and 5.

Twice-stitched Appliqué

This tried-and-true method works for all fabric types and sizes.

1. Cut a piece of appliqué fabric larger than the design. (Reinforce flimsy fabrics with fusible interfacing.) Transfer the design to the rightside.

2. Pin the appliqué on the background, both with right-sides up.

3. Stitch around the entire outline first with a narrow, short zigzag (stitch width 1mm or less, length about 1.25mm or 20spi).

4. Trim the excess appliqué fabric to the stitching line.

5. Oversew the appliqué's raw edges with a satin stitch, concealing the previous stitching.

Terry Cloth Appliqué

Appliquéing terry cloth on items like bibs and towels adds a second layer of absorbency, but fusing large areas makes terry less thirsty and defeats the purpose. So instead of bonding large pieces, fuse only the edges.

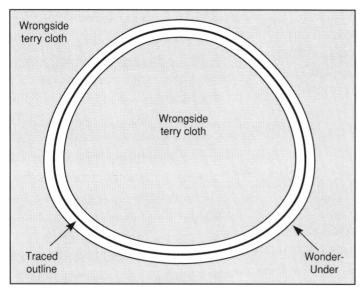

Wrongside
terry cloth

Wrongside
terry cloth

Traced
outline

Wonder-
Under

Fig. 2.17 By applying adhesive web to only the edges, terry cloth retains its absorbency.

1. Trace the flipped appliqué pattern (a mirror image of the shape) to the paper side of an adhesive web like Wonder-Under. Cut out the web outline, allowing a total of 1/2", 1/4" on both sides of the traced line (Fig. 2.17).

2. Smooth the trimmed Wonder-Under, paper side up, against the appliqué fabric's wrongside. Press for three seconds with a dry iron, "wool" setting; let cool.

3. Cut on the traced line. Peel off the paper backing.

4. Position the appliqué rightside up on the background terry and place both face down on the ironing board. Due to the terry's thickness, you will need to press longer than for thinner fabrics. Using an iron set on "cotton" and a damp press cloth, press the appliqué's edges for 10 to 15 seconds.

5. Oversew the appliqué's raw edges with a satin stitch. If some terry loops escape the stitching, clip them as short as possible and satin stitch the entire shape a second time with a slightly wider stitch.

Glued Appliqué

Water-soluble glue provides an alternate way to adhere fabric. No More Pins (a clear liquid in a squeeze bottle) bonds the appliqué easily, doesn't gum up the machine needle, and washes out. Dennison's Glue Stic (a solid, rub-on stick) also quickly bonds fabrics; it has the added advantage of being nontoxic.

If you use a product not specifically labeled "non-toxic," wash the finished article before giving it to children.

When using water-soluble glues, first cut the appliqué fabric the desired finished shape. Next, on the appliqué's wrongside, apply glue along the raw edges. Position the appliqué rightside up on the background fabric; press firmly with fingers. When dry, oversew the raw edges with a satin stitch.

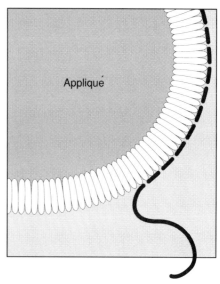

Appliqué

Fig. 2.18 For a nice finishing touch, topstitch with a contrasting thread around the outer edge of a finished appliqué. After completing the white satin stitching on Chapter 8's Panda Bib, I added a line of navy, all-purpose thread with an automatic, reinforced (triple) stitch.

Fur Fabric Appliqué

For detailed instructions on working with fur fabrics, see **Learn Bearmaking** *(check Bibliography).*

Synthetic furs can make sumptuous, highly textured appliqués. Pick a washable, good quality fur that won't shed. (When a baby chews on a fur toy, he shouldn't end up with a mouthful of fuzz.) Follow these tips when working with pile fabrics:

1. Outline the design on the fur's wrongside with a permanent marker. Cut out the fur, snipping only the backing, not the pile, with just the tips of your scissors.

2. To transfer the interior design lines to the fur's rightside, align the pattern with the fur's wrongside. Poke pins through the paper and the fur along the lines. Part the pile at the pins and draw the lines directly on the fur's backing (rightside). Try not to mark the pile. Remove the pins.

3. Optional step: To keep the fur fibers out of your way, first machine baste 3/16" to 1/4" from the raw edges, pushing all pile away from the cut edge and toward the center of the piece.

4. Affix the fur to the background fabric with a water-soluble glue (see above).

5. Make your first run around the edges with a medium zigzag, width 2mm or less, pushing all pile away from the cut edge.

6. When covering fur with another appliqué, clip the pile in the area underneath. Also see Fig. 2.19.

7. For details like mouth lines or eyebrows, part the pile along the stitching line. Satin stitch, stitching over pearl cotton if desired. After stitching, clip any pile that hides detailing.

Fig. 2.19 When layering fur fabric on top of another fur, machine baste both pieces separately to keep all pile out of the way.

Non-fraying Appliqué

Leather, imitation suede, and vinyl allow an almost invisible stitch. A Teflon embroidery foot will glide over these specialty materials. Use fine, monofilament nylon thread as the top thread, loosening that tension somewhat.

1. Fuse the appliqué to the background fabric following one of the methods described above. For vinyl, use a press cloth from the wrongside; do not allow the vinyl to touch the iron's soleplate.

2. Set the machine for a medium, short zigzag, about 2mm wide and 1.7mm (15spi) long.

3. Zigzag around the appliqué's raw edges. Pull threads to wrongside and knot.

No-sew Appliqué

A relatively new adhesive web, Heat N Bond, eliminates the need for sewing many appliqué fabrics. It is nontoxic and, when applied properly, adheres securely.

Because it adheres at a lower temperature than other adhesive webs, Heat N Bond works on delicate materials that cannot withstand high iron temperatures. However, it should not be used for appliqués that require machine stitching. (The needle's friction might produce enough heat to melt the web and gum up the needle.)

Try these directions for cottons:

1. Trace the flipped appliqué pattern (a mirror image of the shape) to the paper side of the adhesive web. Cut the web with an extra border on all sides.

2. With the Heat N Bond's rough side against the appliqué fabric's wrongside, press for four seconds with a medium temperature, dry iron. Let cool.

3. Cut on the traced line. Peel off the paper backing.

4. Place the appliqué rightside up on the background fabric. Press for seven to 10 seconds.

5. When working with thicker fabrics, like imitation suede, flip the appliqué and the background fabric over (after pressing the front in step 4) and press for an additional 10 seconds from the underside.

Counted Cross Stitch

We've seen that proper machine appliqué methods can produce winning results. The same holds true for hand embroidery. If you've never tried counted cross stitch, prepare for a pleasant surprise.

Unlike freehand embroidery, counted cross stitch is worked on special, even-weave fabrics. Aida, one of the most popular fabrics and the one used in this book, generates uniform stitches and beautiful finished projects. Choose a top quality fabric such as Zweigart.

Besides the evenweave fabric, what other supplies will you need? DMC six-strand cotton embroidery floss in colors listed on the charts in Chapter 5, and a #26 tapestry needle.

Although some stitchers use a #24 needle for Aida, I prefer size #26. The smaller size accurately splits threads for 1/4 and 3/4 stitches.

A tapestry needle has a blunt tip that separates the fabric's threads rather than piercing them. Optional supplies include masking tape or a seam sealant (Stop Fraying) and an embroidery hoop or frame (Fig. 2.20).

The thread count per inch of fabric determines the size of the finished design. Each of this book's cross-stitched projects specifies the fabric count and the working piece's measurements. Don't prewash the Aida. When cutting, avoid the fabric's center fold whenever possible. Raw edges may be serged, zigzagged, overcast, bound with masking tape, or treated with a seam sealant (Stop Fraying) to prevent raveling.

Fig. 2.20 A needlework scroll frame, like this one from E-Z Stitch, keeps the lengthwise and crosswise fabric threads perfectly aligned. This makes it easier to block the finished piece. Also, note that properly mounted fabric rolls with the rightside toward the rod. This keeps the face of the work clean.

The arrows mark the centers of the charts. Determine your starting point by counting out from the center of your fabric.

Separate a length of floss into three strands for 11 count fabric, two strands for 14 or 18 count, or one strand for 22 count. Take the first stitch from back to front, holding the tail of the thread behind the fabric. Work the first few stitches over this end to secure it. Fig. 2.21 shows an alternate method.

Make one cross stitch for each of the chart's squares. For even stitches, pass the needle from back to front, then front to back, "stabbing" rather than sewing in and out (Fig. 2.22).

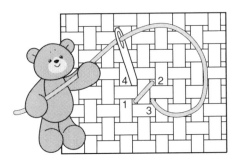

Fig. 2.22 *Each square on the chart represents one cross stitch.*

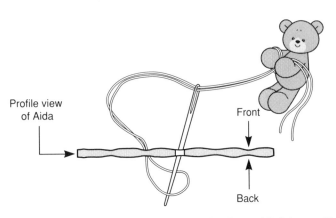

Fig. 2.21 *To start without a knot when stitching with two strands of floss, cut the floss 36" to 44" long, or roughly double your normal working length. Fold one strand in half and thread both ends through the needle's eye. Bring the needle up from back to front, leaving the midpoint's loop extending at the back of the work. Take one stitch, turn the work over, and pass your needle through the starting loop; tighten. Bring needle to front and continue stitching.*

For a row of stitches the same color, work the first half of each stitch from left to right.

Complete the cross stitches from right to left (Fig. 2.23).

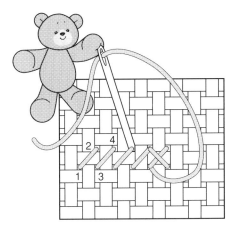

Fig. 2.23 Complete full rows of the same color by crossing all stitches in the same direction.

All the stitches' top threads should lie in the same direction. End off by running the thread under stitches on the back of the work.

Some charts split squares diagonally into two colors. Fig. 2.24 shows how to form these 1/4 and 3/4 stitches. When in doubt as to which of two colors should be the 3/4 stitch, select the color that has the least number of adjacent squares matching it.

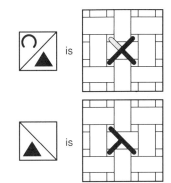

Fig. 2.24 For squares split on the diagonal, work 1/4 and 3/4 stitches.

After completing the cross stitches, backstitch the chart's heavy outlines (Fig. 2.25). Use two strands for backstitching on 11 count fabric and only one strand for other fabric sizes.

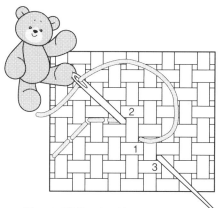

Fig. 2.25 Backstitch after completing the cross stitches.

Some animal charts show highlighted eyes. Complete the cross stitches for the eyes and then add a tiny stitch of two strands of white floss where indicated. For this detailing, a regular needle (like a Betweens #10) will easily pierce the multiple thread layers.

Even if the finished embroidery looks clean, it should be laundered to remove oils from your hands. Soak the piece in tepid water with a mild detergent. Rinse thoroughly and blot between white terry cloth. While still damp, block with a warm iron by pressing gently, face down, on a well-padded surface. Also see Block in the HelpLine (page 22).

At this point, you have a firm foundation in techniques and toymaking know-how. Undecided about which project to make first? Chapter 3 will explain how different types of toys help babies develop various skills. Its discussion should help you decide.

This glossary lists sewing terms, hand and machine stitches, and techniques. For terms not defined here, check a comprehensive sewing guide such as Reader's Digest Association's **Complete Guide to Sewing**.

Aida. An evenweave fabric for use in counted cross stitch embroidery. The most common sizes are 11, 14, or 18 squares to the inch.

Backstitch. Machine stitch forward for several stitches, backward over the same stitches, and forward again to secure beginning and end. A minimum of five stitches is recommended for toymaking. For hand stitching, *see* **Fig. 2.26.**

Bar tack. Set the stitch width at about 5mm, and the stitch length at 0 (or drop or cover the feed dogs). Take eight or nine wide stitches on top of each other. End by entering the needle in the same hole several times to lock the

threads. Most computerized machines can program this stitch sequence.

Bias. A diagonal line at a 45° angle from the lengthwise or crosswise fabric grain. Woven fabrics stretch on the bias.

Blanket stitch. Decorative machine stitch. *See also* **Fig. 2.27.**

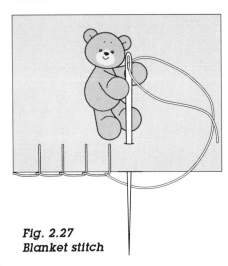

Fig. 2.27
Blanket stitch

Blind hem stitch. Practical machine stitch. Hook and loop tape (Velcro) can be applied with this stitch instead of a zigzag. *See* **Fig. 2.28.**

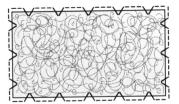

Fig. 2.28 Blind hem stitch

Block. Lay a damp embroidery piece face down on a padded surface. Smooth out any wrinkles and straighten the lengthwise and crosswise fabric threads at right angles. Press with a dry iron preheated to "wool." Place the iron down, applying gentle pressure for a few seconds; reposition the iron by lifting instead of sliding. Do not move the embroidery until it is bone-dry.

Box-lock stitch. A reinforcing stitch used at stress points on webbing, binding, and so on. *See* **Fig. 2.29.**

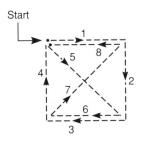

Fig. 2.29 Box-lock stitch

Box pleat. *See* **Fig. 2.30.** *See also* **Fig. 2.34.**

Fig. 2.26 Backstitch

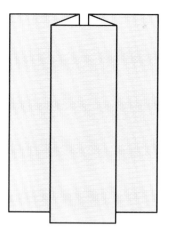

Fig. 2.30 Box pleat

Catchstitch. Also called **herringbone stitch**. *See* **Fig. 2.31.**

Clip curves. On an inside curve, make a series of straight snips through the seam allowance, perpendicular to the stitching line. For an outside curve, cut small, V-shaped notches from the seam allowance. *See also* **Fig. 2.12, page 12.**

Dart. Fold the fabric with the rightsides together, matching the dart's dots and stitching lines. For a normal dart, start stitching from the broad end, tapering at the point. For a double-pointed dart, start at one point and stitch along the broken lines to the other point.

Disappearing pen. A special pen, often purple, used for marking fabric; also called air-erasable or fade-away marking pen. The marks completely disappear within 48 hours, sometimes starting to fade in as little as 15 minutes. Not recommended for heirloom projects, like quilts.

Ditch-stitch. Machine stitching usually done on the rightside, sewing exactly on top of a previous stitching line. Same as **stitch-in-the-ditch.**

Ease. To distribute excess fabric evenly when seaming edges of different lengths.

Edgestitch. To stitch just inside the fabric's perimeter or edge. Some machines feature special edgestitching feet to help guide fabrics. *See also* **Topstitching.**

Fastener tape. *See* **Hook and loop tape.**

Finger press. Instead of using an iron to press fabric, use your finger. Usually

done with a small seam allowance, such as 1/4".

Flat-fell seam. *See* **Fig. 2.32.**

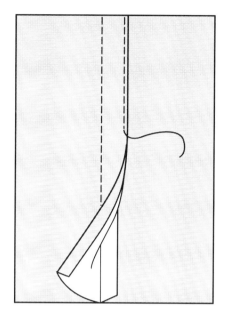

Fig. 2.32 Flat-fell seam

Free-machine quilt. Place quilt top, batting, and backing in a hoop. Remove the presser foot; cover or lower the feed dogs. Insert hoop in machine; lock threads. Stitch the design lines by moving the hoop in any direction desired. While working, keep the fabrics against the machine's throat plate.

Fuse. Using heat to bond fusible interfacing or fusible web to fabric. Follow manufacturer's directions when available, or place the interfacing's coated side against the fabric's wrongside and press for 10 seconds with a dry iron on "wool" setting. If the fusible does not adhere well, steam for 10 seconds with a damp press cloth.

Fig. 2.31 Catchstitch

Grade seam. To trim one seam allowance narrower than the other, in order to reduce bulk. *See also* **Trim seam.** *See* **Fig. 2.11, page 12.**

Grain, grainline. For a woven fabric, the direction of the threads, both lengthwise and crosswise. For a knit fabric, the direction of the rows of stitches.

Grain-perfect. Aligned with the lengthwise and crosswise fabric threads. Same as "on-grain."

Hidden ladder stitch. *See* **Fig. 2.33.**

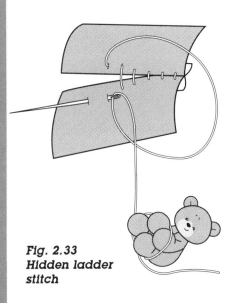

Fig. 2.33 Hidden ladder stitch

Hide-a-Rattle. A term, coined for this book, describing a flat, plastic rattle (1-1/2" diameter, 3/8" thick) designed specifically for enclosure in a child's toy. See the Suppliers on page 174 under Aardvark. *See also* **Fig. 8.2, page 111.**

Hide threads inside. *See* **Lose threads.**

Hook and loop tape. A two-part fastener tape, also called **touch fastener.** One piece has stiff little hooks on it, while the corresponding loop piece is fuzzy. Velcro is the most common brand name. Most toys use the sew-in type, although the Mobile (page 33) also uses the self-sticking kind. To apply fastener tape by machine, use either a medium zigzag or a blind hem stitch (**Fig. 2.28, page 22**).

Inverted box pleat. *See* **Fig. 2.34.** *See also* **Fig. 2.30, page 23.**

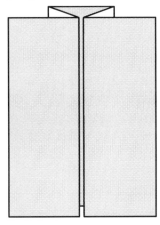

Fig. 2.34 Inverted box pleat

Lock stitches. To knot stitching at the beginning or ending of machine appliqué or embroidery, take several stitches in the same hole. With the stitch width at 0, either set the length also at 0 or drop the feed dogs.

Loop tape. *See* **Hook and loop tape.**

Lose threads. To bury the thread tails after knotting, especially inside a stuffed piece. *See also* **Fig. 2.35.**

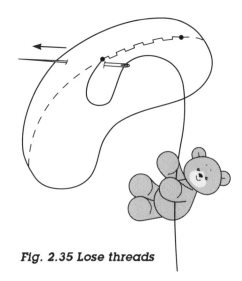

Fig. 2.35 Lose threads

Mat knife. *See* **Utility knife.**

Miter. A right angle formed by either folding or seaming fabrics at a 45° angle.

Multi-zigzag. Practical machine stitch, also called **multistitch zigzag.** Compare Serpentine stitch. *See also* **Fig. 2.36** and **Fig. 2.40, page 25.**

Fig. 2.36 Multi-zigzag

On-grain. Aligning the straight sides of a rectangle with the lengthwise or crosswise fabric weave. Same as "grain-perfect."

Overcast. *See* **Fig. 2.37.**

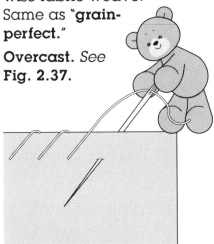

Fig. 2.37 Overcast

Overhand knot.
See **Fig. 2.38.**

Fig. 2.38
Overhand knot

Oversew. Working a decorative machine stitch or satin stitch to cover an edge (of fabric, appliqué, etc.) or previous stitching line.

Pin basting. Using safety pins to temporarily fasten the top, batting, and backing of a quilt together in preparation for hand or machine quilting.

Pivot. With the needle in the down position, lift the presser foot and turn the fabric. Lower presser foot and continue stitching.

Press. To apply downward pressure with a heated iron, either with or without steam. Reposition the iron by lifting, as opposed to the term "ironing," which implies sliding.

Quarter. To divide into fourths by folding and marking with pins. When joining two pieces of different sizes,

both can be quartered and then pins matched to distribute the ease evenly.

Quilting pins. Strong straight pins, about .60mm in diameter, with 1-3/4" or slightly longer shafts. Usually they come with glass or plastic heads, although flat flower heads are also available.

Quilt-weight. Describes shirt-weight fabrics like muslin, broadcloth, or calico.

Rotary cutter. A sharp, circular blade in a plastic handle used with a special mat for cutting fabric. Often used with a clear ruler to quickly cut quilt strips. Popular brands are Olfa and Dritz.

Satin stitch. In machine stitching, a line of zigzag stitches with a short, tight stitch length and any width (other than 0). Extra-fine machine-embroidery thread gives the smoothest results. For hand embroidery, *see* **Fig. 2.39.**

Fig. 2.39 Satin stitch

Selvedge. Literally "self edge," the finished lengthwise edges of fabric which do not ravel. Since selvedges often shrink at a different rate than the main cloth, usually they are trimmed off before cutting quilt strips, or avoided when laying out patterns.

Serpentine stitch. Practical machine stitch. *See* **Fig. 2.40.** Compare **multi-zigzag** in **Fig. 2.26.**

Fig. 2.40 Serpentine stitch

Shim. A small piece of cardboard, plastic, or similar material (about 1/8" thick or less), used under the otherwise unsupported part of the presser foot when sewing uneven thicknesses.

Slipstitch. *See* **Fig. 2.41.**

Fig. 2.41 Slipstitch

Spi. Stitches per inch. For example, a stitch length reference like 2.5 – 3mm (8 – 10spi) means a length of 2.5 to 3 millimeters, or 8 to 10 stitches per inch.

Stitch-in-the-ditch. *See* **Ditch-stitch.**

Straight stitch. *See* **Fig. 2.42.**

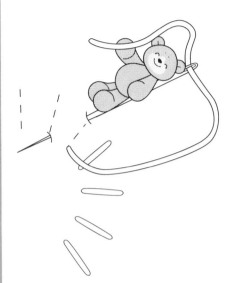

Fig. 2.42 Straight stitch

Straighten. To trim the crosswise fabric edges at a right angle to the lengthwise selvedges. Most quilt-weight cottons now have permanent press finishes that preclude straightening by pulling a crosswise thread.

Strip piece (verb), **strip piecing** (noun). A quick, assembly-line method replacing time-consuming hand piecing. Long bands of different fabrics are first stitched together and then cut apart perpendicularly or at an angle to the seamlines, forming individual strips of multiple fabrics.

Swatch card. Fabric samples taped, stapled, or glued to an index card or lightweight cardboard. Especially useful to keep track of quilt fabrics. *See also* **Fig. 11.2, page 151.**

Topstitching. Machine stitching done on the fabric's rightside, often next to a seam, edge, or some other design element. *See also* **Edgestitch.**

Trim corners. For right-angled corners, to cut off the seam allowance's excess material at a 45° angle. *See also* **Fig. 2.43.**

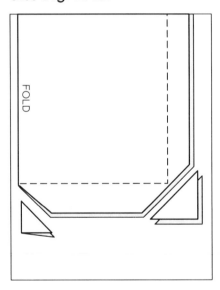

Fig. 2.43 Trim corners

Trim seam. Reducing the width of the seam allowances by cutting them. With shears parallel to the seamline, two layers may be trimmed at once, reducing them an equal amount. *See also* **Grade seam.**

Utility knife. A cutting tool with a retractable, razor-edged blade; also called a **mat knife.**

Velcro. *See* **Hook and loop tape.**

Walking foot (also called "even-feed foot"). A sewing machine attachment that feeds the top layer of fabric. Prevents uneven seams on bulky materials. Especially useful for quilting multiple layers and for napped fabrics.

Webbing. A strong, woven strip of tough fiber (often cotton, nylon, or polypropylene) as used for belts. The most common width is 1".

Zigzag. Automatic machine stitch with both width and length.

CHAPTER 3

CHILD DEVELOPMENT—
BIRTH TO 18 MONTHS

With just a few simple materials and a little know-how, you can create top-quality toys for your baby's all-important early play-times. You can sew safe, stimulating, skill-building toys—toys as unique as he is. Your handmade toys will help your child learn and grow in confidence and security.

To better understand how the toys in this book can benefit your baby, take a look at the changes a child undergoes during his first 18 months of life. What stages does he pass through? When does he develop certain skills? This chapter discusses these issues. It also presents toy safety guidelines.

Toys for All Stages

Even though babies develop specific skills according to their own schedules, all babies develop the skills in a predictable and universal sequence. The timing of each ability will differ from child to child, but the order remains the same (a baby learns to sit before he learns to walk). By being prepared, you can anticipate the sequence and introduce the right toy at the right time.

For the purposes of this discussion, typical age ranges have been assigned to each stage. However, the rate of development varies greatly from one child to the next. For that reason, the suggested age ranges should be used only as guidelines. Your child could be months off the listed range and still be perfectly normal.

With a premature baby, it is often helpful to figure developmental age by using what would have been the full-term delivery date rather than the actual birth date.

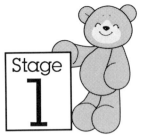

Stage 1

Birth to 2 months:

The newborn's first developmental stage is limited to what he can see and hear. He cannot shift himself and depends on you to prop him in a comfortable position and to provide something interesting to look at and listen to. His focal range is about 8" to 12" (which, not by chance, matches the distance from his face to yours while he's nursing or cradled in your arms). First-stage babies prefer looking at faces to anything else.

Since the newborn can't move toward toys, they need to be placed directly in his field of vision, ideally 8" to 12" from his eyes. To attract attention, first toys should have bright, primary colors rather than pastels. Newborns find complex geometric patterns intriguing, especially black-on-white checkerboards and bull's-eyes.

The classic toy for the first stage is the **Changeable Mobile** (page 33); additional projects include the **Alpha-Pet Quilt** (page 47), **Crib Pals** (page 86), and **Texture Pads** (page 109).

2 to 4 months:

The second stage starts when babies discover their hands as moving objects. They will often stare at their fists for minutes at a time. If you place a rattle or other object in a baby's hand, he might hold it for a few minutes before dropping it because his natural instinct is to keep his fists clenched.

As yet, he lacks the ability to voluntarily reach out and grab a toy (although he begins practicing this skill during the overlap between this stage and the next). For his first attempts at reaching, he needs stable toys suspended over him for batting and swiping.

The definitive early project for this stage is the **Chit-chat Mitt** (page 77). **Crib Pals** (page 87) and their crib support are also appropriate, in addition to the projects listed for the previous stage.

3 to 5 months:

At the beginning of the third stage, an infant opens his fists and can clasp his hands together over his tummy. During the next couple of months he will practice reaching with both hands to grasp a toy within arm's length. This action is called visually directed reaching, and it's a very important developmental step. It lays the foundation for all later eye-hand coordination.

Even as early as 3 months, you can start reading to a baby. Use picture books, short and simple.

During stage three, babies need to handle a wide variety of objects to master their grasping abilities. Soon they'll be able to reach with precision and purpose. They also learn to target and kick objects during this stage.

The **Crib Pals** (page 87) and their crib support are perfect for reaching and kicking. Additional items to suspend from the crib support include the **Teethe-n-Clutch** (page 125) and the **Puff Block** (page 163).

6 to 9 months:

The fourth stage involves accomplishments in a number of areas, most notably mobility. A child learns to sit and to crawl during this period.

Once a baby can sit unsupported, both hands are free to fiddle with toys. The first skill gained in stage four is transferring items from one hand to the other. Toys with more than one handhold encourage this ability.

From 7 to 9 months a baby creeps and eventually crawls. With his newfound mobility, his entire environment becomes accessible. Toys to crawl over, under, and through, and toys to chase make popular choices now. Usually during this time, babies also begin to understand language.

For fourth stage babies, peekaboo games reinforce an important concept called object permanence: things (including people) still exist even when the baby can't see them. This realization helps a child develop confidence and security.

Stage four toys include the **Teethe-n-Clutch** (page 125), **Puff Block** (page 163), **Texture Pads** (page 109), and **Peek-a-Pocket** (page 135).

Stage 5

10 months and over:

In the fifth developmental stage, babies pull themselves up to standing, cruise around furniture, and finally walk on their own. Children new to walking need toys they can carry easily and toys safe for them to topple onto. They like lightweight toys to refine a newly acquired throwing skill, too.

At 1 year, babies are ready for more complex object manipulation. They find hinged toys and containers fascinating. They begin to understand the concepts of inside and outside, part and counterpart. And they still enjoy peekaboo games.

Appropriate toys for stage five are the **Peek-a-Pocket** (page 135), **Teethe-n-Clutch** (page 125), and **Texture Pads** (page 109). Several of the toys from the next volume of this series (see page 182) can also be introduced at 11 to 12 months.

Since we've covered all the early developmental stages, you'll be able to anticipate your baby's next step. Watch that you *help* him toward the next stage, not that you *push* him toward it. Let your baby set the pace.

Play It Safe

Learning should also be safe. Throughout all stages of development, the paramount concern must be safety. In the past few decades, great strides have been made in child safety research. Toy manufacturers have set voluntary industry standards. Government and private groups have set tough safety regulations. The result? Commercial toys are safer than ever before. Even so, each year in the United States more than 150,000 children suffer serious toy-related injuries.

This section discusses some of the safety issues related to baby toys and playthings. For a broader discussion of child safety, many excellent pamphlets are available free of charge. (Check listings in the Bibliography, page 172.)

Adult Supervision: There is no such thing as an absolutely safe toy. It doesn't matter how many adults try to anticipate the possible ways a toy could pose a hazard—children still manage to do the unexpected. For that reason, many toys, even the ones in this book, should be used only with adult supervision.

Hand-Me-Downs: Many older toys do not meet current safety standards and should be discarded or, in the case of handmade toys, put on a high shelf as display items, not playthings.

Also keep in mind that patterns and designs in older books and publications are sometimes outmoded by more recent toy safety recommendations.

Mobiles: A mobile is intended for baby's visual entertainment only. Since it is not meant to be handled by children of any age, hang it out of reach.

Strings: To prevent entanglement, toys should not have cords, strings, or ribbons longer than 12". This includes bows tied around stuffed animals.

Crib Toys: Traditional crib gyms pose one of the most serious toy-related hazards for infants. Avoid toys strung across the crib because a child can pull up on them and become entangled. Babies have managed to hook their chins over crib gyms, cutting off their air supply. When the child is unattended, remove all toys from the crib for these reasons: **1)** The materials may not be fire resistant. **2)** A sleeping child could snuggle too close to a toy and not receive enough air. **3)** A baby could lodge a toy in his mouth and not be able to cry for help. **4)** A toddler could use the toy as a step to help him climb up and over the crib side, resulting in a serious fall.

Rattles: To prevent possible strangulation, do not tie rattles (or teethers or pacifiers) around a child's neck on a cord, string, ribbon, or elastic. Don't allow toddlers to walk or run with toys in their mouths. A fall could jam the rattle into the throat and block air passages.

Age Guidelines: Follow the manufacturer's age recommendations. For example, don't give a 20-month-old baby a toy designed for children over 3 years. Many parents tend to think their children are advanced intellectually and are ready for more stimulating toys. In truth, the age rating probably has more to do with the size of the parts than with mental prowess.

Small Parts: Do not give a child less than 3 years old any toys with parts smaller than the dimensions in Fig. 3.2. This includes all balloons, whether inflated or deflated. (When sucked on or bitten, inflated balloons can burst, sending bits of rubber down the windpipe.) Also avoid sticks or thin pieces that could poke an eye, nose, ear, or throat. See also Fig. 3.3.

Squeeze Toys: When in its most compressed state, a squeeze toy should be larger than the dimensions in Fig. 3.2. The toy should not contain a small squeaker that could be chewed off or otherwise detached.

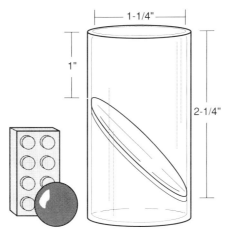

Fig. 3.2 Dimensions of No-Choke Testing Tube

Fig. 3.3 Use a small parts cylinder to find out which toys or objects are too small for children under 3 years. If a piece fits entirely inside the cylinder, it fails the test. Toys to Grow On offers this No-Choke Testing Tube for a nominal charge. (The Suppliers list has ordering information.)

Sharp Edges: Toys for children under 8 years should not have sharp points or edges. Check toys periodically to make certain they have not broken, exposing edges that could cut, poke, or pinch.

Nontoxic: All dyes, paints, stuffing, and materials used for toys should be hygienic and nontoxic.

Packing Materials: Discard all plastic bags and packing supplies from new toys. The boxes and shipping materials were not designed as toys in themselves, and some are dangerous.

Toy Chests: The lid of a toy chest should have spring-loaded supports that hold the lid in any position and keep it from closing on a child. Inspect often to confirm the springs function properly. The chest also needs ventilation holes or spaces in case a child climbs inside.

Now you have a good, solid foundation to guide your toy selections. In the next eight chapters you'll find loads of projects to make playtime a special time for both you and your baby.

RAINBOW CUBS MOBILE
PLAY GUIDE *a few suggestions to help you gain the most from this toy*

Age Range

Birth to 5 months, especially from 3 to 9 weeks. Once a baby can reach out and grasp objects (3 to 6 months), you've missed the optimum time.

Mounting Instructions

Most babies prefer to look toward one particular side. Watch your baby to see which he prefers, and mount the mobile on that side. (When on their backs, young babies don't have the ability to hold their heads in midline to look straight up. However, you may not observe a marked preference until the second month.) In the ceiling, install a plant or lamp hook with a toggle bolt rated for at least a 15-lb. load.

You have two height adjustments: the buttonholes in the dowel casing and the height of the crib mattress. Adjust until the objects hang 8" to 12" from the baby's eyes, but not so close that he can touch the mobile.

A bright light on the mobile will make it more exciting, especially at night. Something as simple as a fixed flashlight beam will spark interest.

Skills Development

Complex, dynamic, intricate patterns attract the newborn's attention. The mobile's geometric disks, particularly the black-and-white checkerboard and bull's-eye, interest even the youngest babies. Infants also adore looking at faces, and the Rainbow Cubs provide four bright faces to study.

Also by 2 months, a baby should *track* an object with his eyes. The mobile's movement from side to side across the field of vision is easier for a young baby to follow than up and down, or in and out. The slow, predictable movement and bright primary colors help a child to focus and follow the mobile's mesmerizing action.

The music box will encourage a child to search for the source of the sound. Newborns like soft, rhythmic, repetitious sounds.

The music box provides cause-and-effect feedback: *Mom winds the music box and the music and motion starts up again.* An older baby will quickly catch on to the next game: *If I fuss when the mobile stops, Mom comes and winds it up again.*

Play Suggestions

To prevent boredom, exchange items often. You can change all four objects at once, or just opposite pairs. Try greeting cards, magazine pictures, aluminum foil, or bright, colorful bows from gifts, and fasten them with sticky-backed fastener tape (Velcro) to the ruffled bases. Even the bases alone serve as a change of pace.

After the child has outgrown the mobile, the Rainbow Cubs can be converted to sock puppets. Using quilting thread, hand stitch a 2-1/4" piece of hook fastener tape (Velcro) to the rightside of a child's tube sock. Place the hook tape vertically, toward the toe. Stick the sock on a youngster's hand, and change Rainbow Cubs as desired. The puppets will supply creative, role-playing, imaginative play.

Safety Considerations

A mobile is intended for baby's visual entertainment only. It is meant to be handled by adults. None of the attachments, like mylar or laminated disks, are childsafe. Hang everything out of reach.

When attaching objects by fastener tape, first align the full length of the tapes. Press firmly, then tug to assure that the items will not detach and drop into the crib.

The dowel prevents the long casing from becoming a strangulation hazard. Do not remove the dowel at any time.

Once children begin to push up on hands and knees (at about 5 months) remove the mobile. It would become an entanglement problem if pulled or knocked into the crib.

Once a child is old enough to handle the Rainbow Cubs, inspect the toys periodically to confirm the eyes and noses still attach firmly. Make sure the fabrics have not worn through, exposing the lock washers.

Care Instructions

Hand wash the Rainbow Cubs in lukewarm water with mild soap. Rinse thoroughly, blot between terry towels, and air dry. The music box cover and the ruffle bases are surface washable.

*This toy is from the book **Soft Toys for Babies** in Judi Maddigan's **Stitch & Enrich** series.*

CHAPTER 4

RAINBOW CUBS MOBILE

From birth to 5 months, your baby needs:

- Slow, interesting motion
- Bright colors and bold patterns
- Soft, rhythmic sounds

This toy provides:

- Fascinating movement (the frame turns and pauses, then the individual objects spin)
- Rainbow Cub faces that can interchange with mylar, cellophane, and geometrics
- A soothing music box

Staring at your face is what a newborn baby enjoys most, and you could spend hours gazing, dreaming, and marveling at him. But when you're occupied elsewhere, bring on some teddy bear faces.

This mobile with its four Rainbow Cubs will delight your baby. It was designed from his point of view. Motion. Color. Shape. Sound. Warmth and friendly smiles. These are what your baby will experience.

Imagine lying in one position for hours at a time. Pretty boring stuff, being a newborn, right? Not necessarily. Because everything—even the smallest detail we take for granted, like a sunbeam spilling through the curtains—is entirely new to him.

Of course, things don't stay new for long. That's where this mobile differs from the store-bought variety. Thanks to fastener tape on its ruffled bases, you can change the suspended items often.

Alternatives to the Rainbow Cubs are mylar and cellophane crinkles, stunning with reflected light. Other options are bold, black-and-white patterns. Photocopy them from the book (page 45), laminate them, stick on fastener tape, and you're all set.

Materials

See color pages. The directions assume you have read Chapters 1 and 2. Also check the HelpLine on page 22 when needed.

For Mobile:

A mobile is not a toy. Check this chapter's Play Guide for important safety information.

- 8 removable metal lids (2-3/4" diameter) from 12 oz. frozen-juice cans. Use only the type that opens by pulling a plastic strip.
- The inner ring from a 9" wooden embroidery hoop
- 30" of 3/8"-wide grosgrain ribbon
- White glue (Sobo)
- Polyester fiberfill
- All-purpose, woven, fusible interfacing (Stacy Shape-Flex)
- Screwdriver or other stuffing tool
- 48" of 1"-wide ecru eyelet
- 3 yd fine polyester Gosling cord (as used for stringing Roman shades)
- Upholstery needle large enough to thread Gosling cord
- Awl

For Music Box Cover:

The music box cover is optional. To suspend this mobile from an armature you might already have purchased with another mobile, see Fig. 4.12 on page 40.

- 2 flexible plastic 8 oz. margarine tub lids (4-1/4" diameter)
- 1 music box 2-1/2" x 2" x 1-1/4" with safety key (Fig. 4.2)

Fig. 4.2 Craft shops sell music boxes with either regular keys (left and center) or safety keys. Purchase a special, spring-loaded safety key (right) that cannot be removed once installed.

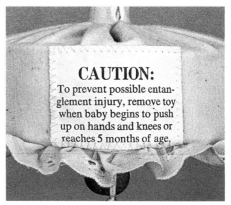

Fig. 4.3 An inexpensive caution label is available by mail (see Suppliers listing under Judi Maddigan).

- 1/4 yd muslin
- Caution label (Fig. 4.3)
- 30" of hardwood doweling, 7/16" diameter

The mobile's overall length is based on an 8-foot ceiling. If your ceiling differs, adjust the dowel length.

For Ruffle Bases:

- 1/8 yd each of four fabrics, 100% cotton or blends, broadcloth weight

- 12-lb test fish line (optional, Fig. 4.4)

- For conventional machine edging: extra-fine machine-embroidery thread. (Or, for serger rolled hem: two or three spools of fine monofilament nylon thread.)

- 9" of 3/4"-wide hook and loop fastener tape (Velcro)

For Rainbow Cub Faces:

- 1/8 yd of four different 100% polyester (no cotton or acetate content) knit robe velours

- Four pair 7.5mm black plastic eyes with safety washers

- Four 15mm D-type triangular noses with metal lock washers

- 1-1/3 yd of 5/8"-wide grosgrain ribbon

- Topstitching or heavy-duty thread to match velour colors

- 3-1/2" soft sculpture doll-making needle

- Needle-nosed pliers

Fig. 4.4 Fish line adds body to a ruffle's edge. Small spools of clear nylon line, labeled "leader material," are sold with sporting goods.

Cutting Directions

Music Box Cover:

Fuse interfacing to wrongside of muslin. From the interfaced muslin, cut one Music Box Cover Base circular pattern; cut one on-grain rectangle to measure 13-7/8" x 3-3/4" for the cover's top and sides; cut one on-grain strip 37" x 2-1/2" for the dowel casing.

Ruffle Bases:

From each of the four ruffle fabrics, cut two round Ruffle Bases and a 30" x 1-5/8" on-grain strip. Cut four Interfacing Guide pattern pieces in fusible interfacing.

Rainbow Cubs:

Note that the patterns' arrows align with the fabric's *stretch* (the crosswise grain). From each of the four robe velours, cut one Rainbow Cub Face, one Head Back, and two Ears.

It's easier to cut velour folded wrongsides together.

Transfer all pattern markings, except for those on the Ruffle Bases.

Sewing Directions

Music Box Cover:

1. Make a 3/4" buttonhole in the circular Music Box Cover Base where indicated on pattern.

2. Gather an 18"-length of eyelet along the bound edge. Pull up gathers to measure 14-1/2". Pin eyelet to the edge of the circular cover piece, overlapping ends 1/2". The eyelet's bound edge should match the circle's raw edge, with the ruffled eyelet toward the center of the circle. Baste.

3. If you are using a Caution label (Fig. 4.3), zigzag it to the rightside of the 13-7/8" x 3-3/4" rectangle's lower right corner, allowing for seam allowances. Turn under 1/4" on each short end of the muslin rectangle; press. Run two gathering threads along one long side (the top) of the rectangle, 1/4" and 1/8" from the raw edge.

4. With rightsides together, pin the rectangle's other long side (the bottom) to the circular base, sandwiching the eyelet between the muslin. Butt the short, pressed edges together. Stitch the pinned long side, following the eyelet basting line as a guide. Trim eyelet seam allowance; clip curves.

5. Pull up the top gathers to measure 2-1/2". (Gathers will be tightly packed.) With rightsides together and raw edges even, pin the gathers to a short end of the dowel casing, leaving the casing's 1/4" side seam allowances free. Sew the 2" seam.

6. Fold the dowel casing in half lengthwise with rightsides together. Seam the casing along the short, free end; pivot and seam the long edges. End your stitching 1" before you reach the gathers. Trim top corners.

7. Turn the dowel casing and music box cover to the rightside through the bottom opening. Press the casing flat to make a 1"-wide strip, creasing along the fold.

8. Mark three 3/4" buttonholes positioned lengthwise on the strip, centered. Place the first buttonhole 1/2" from the free end, the second buttonhole 2-1/2" from the end, and the third 4-1/2" from the end. Work buttonholes. The mobile will be hung by a buttonhole from the hook you install (see page 32).

9. With the tips of sharp scissors, carefully poke through and snip a 1/4" hole in the center of one plastic lid. Slit the lid 1/4" on both sides of the hole so there is a 3/4" gash. Poke the key through the hole and check that it turns freely. If necessary, enlarge the hole. Place this lid and music box inside the muslin cover with the key extending out the bottom through the buttonhole.

10. Insert the other plastic lid on top of the music box. Stuff the area between the two lids firmly, working around the sides of the music box. Do not put any stuffing between the music box and either lid.

11. Insert the 30" dowel into the casing. Slipstitch the opening closed.

Ruffle Bases:

Repeat the following for each of the four fabric colors.

1. Center and fuse an interfacing circle to the wrong-side of one Ruffle Base. Transfer all pattern markings to the fabric's rightside.

2. Zigzag a 2-1/4" piece of hook fastener tape to the rightside of the other Ruffle Base along the pattern's placement lines (or see the HelpLine under Blind hem).

3. Finish the raw edge of the 30" ruffle using one of the following methods:

Conventional sewing machine: Press under 3/8" along one long edge. From the rightside, zigzag on the fold with extra-fine machine-embroidery thread. Set stitch width about 2mm and length about 20spi. If desired, zigzag over fish line, feeding the line under the presser foot like cording (Fig. 4.5). After stitching, use sharp scissors to trim the excess hem allowance close to the zigzag.

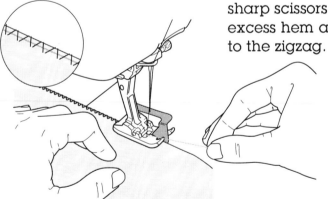

Fig. 4.5 A conventional machine can mimic the look of a serged rolled hem. An edgestitch foot makes this easier. When using fish line, feed it over the front of the foot and under the back, keeping the line just to the left of the foot's guide. Hold the beginning tails of the fish line, needle thread, and bobbin thread to start. Zigzag over the fish line alone for an inch or two, then begin to feed the folded fabric under the foot.

Serger: Set machine for a narrow 2- or 3-thread rolled edge using monofilament nylon thread in needle and looper(s). Adjust stitch length to about 1.9mm (13spi). If using fish line, serge over the line for a few inches before inserting fabric under foot. Finish one long edge of fabric with a rolled hem, trimming 1/4" with knives.

After completing the narrow hem by either method, smooth the fabric over the fish line before cutting it.

4. Seam the strip's short ends using a flat-fell seam.

5. Gather the ruffle with two rows of machine basting stitches, 1/4" and 1/8" from the raw edge. Pull up gathers.

6. With rightsides together, pin the ruffle to the Ruffle Base that has the hook tape. Place the flat-fell seam at the triangular mark. The ruffle's raw edge should match the circle's raw edge, with the ruffle extending toward the circle's center. Stitch a 1/4" seam around the entire circle. Refer to Fig. 4.6 to reduce the bulk of the gathers.

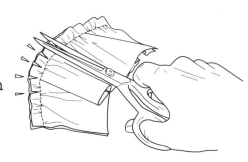

Fig. 4.6 To reduce bulk, hold scissors flat against the gathers. Snip from the seamline toward the raw edges, clipping small V-shaped pieces from the seam allowance only.

7. Pin interfaced Ruffle Base over the ruffle, rightsides together, sandwiching the gathers between the two circles. Stitch seam, leaving open between dots. Use care not to make the seam wider than 1/4" because then the lid will not fit inside. Clip seam and turn to rightside.

8. Insert a metal lid. Slip-stitch the opening closed, turning the raw edges to the inside. The fabric should fit tightly around the lid.

Rainbow Cubs:

Repeat the following for each of the four velours.

1. With rightsides together, fold each Ear in half on the solid line. Stitch around the raw edges; trim seam. Slit each Ear along the fold line from stitching line to stitching line. Turn rightside out.

2. Put a small amount of stuffing into each Ear, keeping the bottom 1/4" empty. Beginning in the center of each Ear, machine stitch a straight, 5/8" line to the cut edges, backstitching at both ends (Fig. 4.7). Set Ears aside.

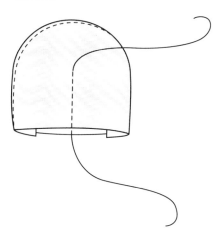

Fig. 4.7 Topstitching line on Ears

3. With rightsides together, fold the Face horizontally, matching the pairs of small dots beside the eyes. Stitch from dot to dot along the lines indicated on the pattern, back-stitching at both ends. This forms a tuck at the bridge of the nose.

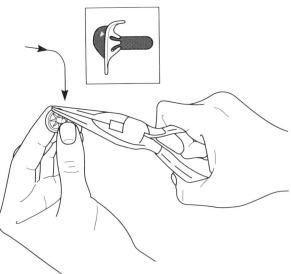

4. Pin the Face's center front dart, matching the raw edges. Stitch from the nose to the neck edge.

5. Run a gathering thread around the Face's outer edge from dot to dot.

6. Install the eyes and nose at the marked locations according to the directions in Chapter 2 on page 12. For safety, make the holes for the eyes and nose as small as possible. With a pair of needle-nosed pliers, bend the top of the nose's metal washer away from the fabric and toward the nose's shank (Fig. 4.8). This improves the expression of the bear. Bend only the edge of the washer, not the central prongs, so that it remains permanently installed.

Fig. 4.8 Bending nose lock washer with needle-nosed pliers (fabric not shown for clarity)

7. On the rightside of the Head Back, zigzag a 2-1/4" piece of the loop tape (or see the HelpLine under Blind hem). Follow the pattern's placement lines.

8. Fold the center of a 12" length of 5/8"-wide ribbon in half, *lengthwise*. With the top of the Head Back up, place the center of the ribbon vertically on the rightside at the square mark. Notice that the square is slightly above, rather than on, the bottom 1/4" seamline. Zigzag a horizontal row of tight, narrow stitches at the square, working through three layers (one of backing, two of ribbon).

9. With the tops of the Ears extending toward the center, and the slit ends of the Ears even with the Head Back's raw edges, pin the Ears to the rightside of the Head Back. The pattern shows the proper location. Baste Ears along seamline.

10. Pin the Face to the Head Back, matching dots and notches, sandwiching the ears between the two layers. Pull up gathers to fit, distributing most of the fullness below the Ears, in the cheek areas. Seam from dot to dot, with Face toward feed dogs, leaving the bottom open for turning.

11. Trim the Ears' bottom seam allowances to reduce bulk. Turn the head rightside out and insert a metal lid into it. Stuff the head firmly, keeping the lid against the Head Back. Pack extra fiber-fill into the muzzle area, checking the profile view often to assure that the nose juts forward (Fig. 4.9). Stuff the cheeks so they round out nicely. The overall shape of the face is wider at the bottom and

Fig. 4.9 Profile view of a Rainbow Cub

somewhat triangular. The ribbon will pull forward as you stuff the cheeks. (Don't panic—the bear isn't cute at this stage. Soft sculpting creates his expression.) When you are pleased with the shape of the head, close the opening with a doubled length of heavy-duty thread. Use the hidden ladder stitch shown in Fig. 2.33.

Sculpting the Face

For additional soft sculpting techniques, consult Learn Bearmaking.

12. You will mark the mouth with a pin at each side. Using a tape measure, find the location for the first pin by measuring 5/8" down from the bottom of the nose and 3/8" to the left of the center dart. Place the second pin 3/8" to the right of the dart (Fig. 4.10). The pins should be 3/4"

Fig. 4.10 Placement for mouth pins

apart, and correspond to points 3 and 4 in Fig. 4.11.

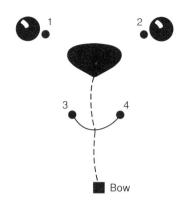

Fig. 4.11 Rainbow Cub's soft sculpture: B - 1 - B - 2 - B - 1 - (3 - 4) - 2 - 4 - 2 - 4 - 1 - 3 - 1 - 3 - 2 - 1 - 2 - B

13. Thread the 3-1/2" needle with a 48" length of heavy-duty thread (single thickness). Form a large knot 6" from the end of your thread.

14. Insert the needle beside the ribbon's zigzag. Take a long stitch through the stuffing, bringing the needle out at the inside corner of the eye (point 1 in Fig. 4.11).

15. Insert the needle close to the eye, taking a stitch about 1/8" long. Bring the needle back to the zigzag.

To begin shaping, push down on the eye with your thumb as you pull on the thread.

16. Take a 1/8" stitch and bring the needle through the head to the inside corner of the other eye (point 2). Take a stitch as before, and return to the zigzag. Push down on both eyes as you tighten the thread. Continue to shape the face by pushing down on the eyes throughout the next steps.

The directions give complete soft sculpting details, but after you have made one Rainbow Cub, you will probably be able to sculpt additional ones by simply following the stitch shorthand in Fig. 4.11.

(The shorthand representation for the stitches you've taken so far is:
B - 1 - B - 2 - B.
This stands for "from the bow, to point 1, to the bow, to point 2, to the bow.")

17. Take a 1/8" stitch at the ribbon and emerge at point 1. Take a 1/8" stitch, bringing the needle out at point 3. Make a 3/4" stitch, inserting the needle at point 4 and bringing it out at point 2. Remove pins.

18. Continuing to take a 1/8" stitch at each point, proceed to point 4, then point 2, then point 4 again. Tighten the thread, pushing up on the corner of the mouth and down on the eye. Stitch the other side of the smile by going to point 1, point 3, point 1, and point 3 again; tighten. Coax the eyes closer together: take stitches from point 2, to point 1, to point 2.

19. Finish by bringing your thread up next to your starting 6" tail. Knot the threads together and lose the ends of the working thread inside the head. (See Fig. 2.35 on page 24.) Then thread the 6" tail on your needle and hide it inside, too.

20. Tie the grosgrain ribbon in a bow. Trim the ribbon ends at an angle. Squeeze a dot of glue inside the bow's knot to keep it tied.

Mobile Assembly

1. Center and glue the 3/8"-wide grosgrain ribbon to the outside of the wooden embroidery hoop.

2. Cut two 1-1/2 yd pieces of Gosling cord. Thread both pieces through the slot in the music box's key (or see Fig. 4.12). Bring the four ends

Fig. 4.12 Did your baby receive a mobile for a shower gift? To hang this mobile from the hook of a purchased mobile's musical winder, knot the cords to a small plastic curtain ring.

together and form an overhand knot in the middle of the cords; tighten the knot against the key. Mark each of the cords 6" from the knot.

3. Tie the cords evenly spaced around the hoop as follows: Measure the hoop's circumference and divide it into fourths. At each location, leave the previously marked 6" of cord free between the music box key and the hoop. Bring the cord down through the center of the hoop, around the outside, and back down the inside, looping it in an overhand knot on the inside of the hoop (Fig. 4.13).

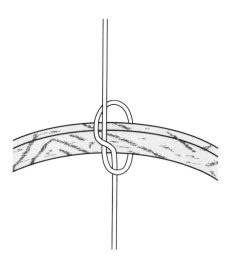

Fig. 4.13 Knotting cords to embroidery hoop

4. Suspend the mobile and check that the hoop hangs correctly. Adjust the cords as necessary. Once the hoop is level, dot the four knots with glue to prevent slipping.

5. Glue the eyelet's bound edge around the inside of the hoop. Overlap and glue the short ends.

6. For each of the four ruffle bases, thread an upholstery needle with a free end of cord. Poke the needle in at the mark on the back of the ruffle base.

Note that the dot is slightly above the center of the circle so that the base will hang at an angle. If you have difficulty tugging the cord through, use an awl to separate the fabric threads and enlarge the holes.

Bring the needle out at the pattern's triangle, close to the flat-fell seam. Adjust the length of the cord so that the ruffle base dangles 6" or so below the hoop; the cords can be different lengths. Knot the cord at the flat-fell seamline. Secure the knot with a dot of glue. Cut and discard the excess cord.

7. Attach the finished Rainbow Cubs, or keep reading for other ideas.

Geometric Disks

For a quick change from the Rainbow Cubs, photocopy page 45's four geometric patterns onto white card stock (also called coverweight paper). Cut out the circles. Either have your printing company laminate them (5 mil sheets) or cover both sides with clear, self-adhesive plastic such as Con-Tact (Fig. 4.14).

Fig. 4.14 Completely transform the mobile with this easy, no-sew option: photocopied and laminated black-on-white patterns. Switch all four Rainbow Cubs at once, or introduce only one geometric at a time.

Cut the laminated circles about 1/8" larger than the original paper. On the back of each geometric, affix a 2-1/4" piece of self-sticking loop fastener tape (the type by Velcro that comes with a pressure-sensitive, sticky backing).

Do not allow infants or young children to play with or handle the geometric disks, mylar, or cellophane. They could present a choking hazard. Check this chapter's Play Guide for additional safety information.

Attach the geometric disk to a ruffle base. When detaching the disk, preserve the loop tape by sliding your thumb between the corners of the hook and loop tapes and gently lifting them apart. Pull on the tape itself instead of yanking only on the disk.

Mylar and Cellophane Crinkles

For each Crinkle, cut three 3" x 7" rectangles of mylar or cellophane.

A rotary cutter and mat cut both mylar and cellophane well.

(You may mix or match the colors and layers. For example, use a bottom layer of mylar topped with two layers of cellophane.)

On the back of the bottom rectangle, affix a 2-1/4" piece of self-sticking loop fastener tape (the type by Velcro that comes with a sticky backing). See Fig. 4.15.

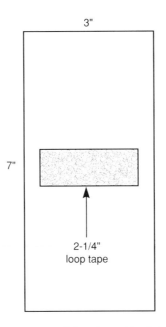

Fig. 4.15 Apply self-sticking loop tape to mylar rectangle.

Stack the three rectangles and pleat them in the middle along the entire 7" length. Using a 12" piece of Gosling cord, tie the rectangles tightly in the middle (Fig. 4.16).

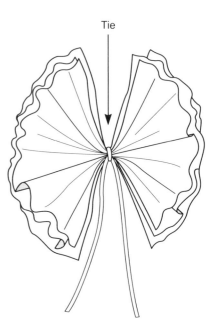

Fig. 4.16 Pleating and tying each Crinkle

If you need help holding the pleats while tying, clamp them with a clothespin.

Knot on the back, snip cord ends, and dot the knot with glue. Open the layers. To attach and remove from the ruffle bases, check the directions for the Geometric Disks (above).

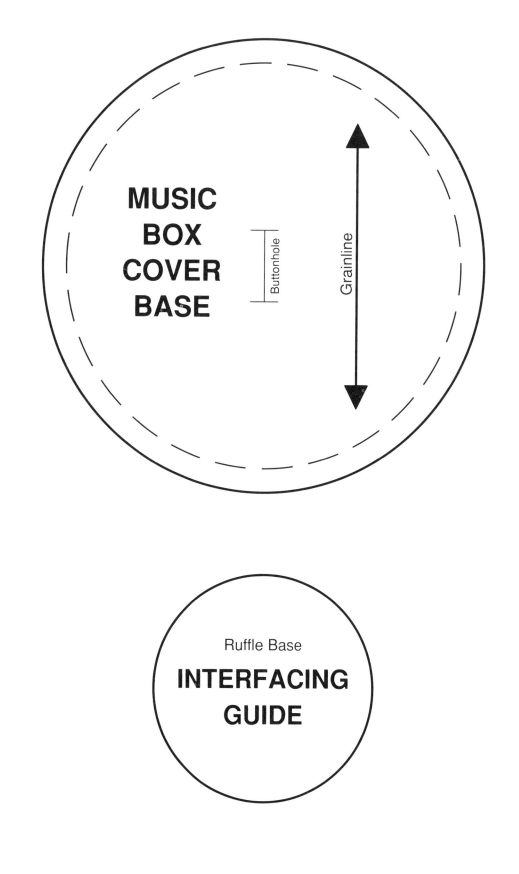

MUSIC
BOX
COVER
BASE

Buttonhole

Grainline

Ruffle Base

INTERFACING
GUIDE

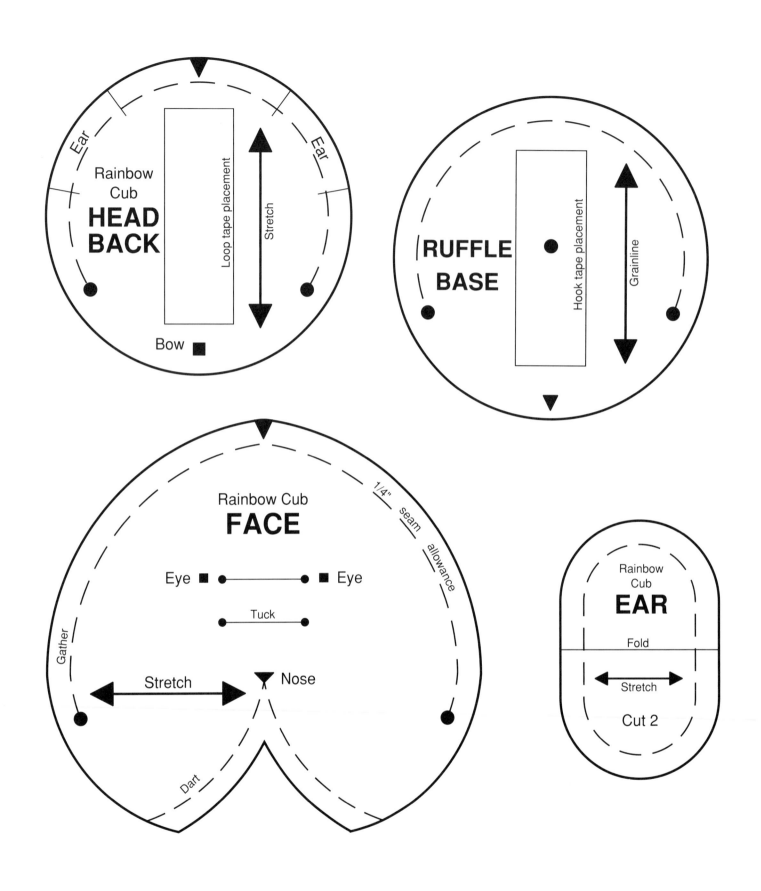

Rainbow Cub
**HEAD
BACK**

Ear

Ear

Loop tape placement

Stretch

Bow

**RUFFLE
BASE**

Hook tape placement

Grainline

Rainbow Cub
FACE

1/4" seam allowance

Eye ■ • — • ■ Eye

Tuck

Gather

Stretch

Nose

Dart

Rainbow
Cub
EAR

Fold

Stretch

Cut 2

ALPHAPET QUILT PLAY GUIDE
a few suggestions to help you gain the most from this toy

Age Range

From birth on.

Security Blankets

At some point between 4 and 18 months, a baby may form an attachment to a special object like a stuffed animal, quilt, or blanket. This "cuddly" will become his dearest possession, and it serves a very real purpose. It comforts him when a parent isn't available, helps him cope with stressful situations, and calms separation anxiety. Many children, for example, find the transition into day care traumatic. A security object can ease the way by providing a piece of home away from home.

Not all children form attachments to comfort objects, but those who do, benefit from them. Naturally, you can't force a child to adopt the AlphaPet Quilt as his security blanket, but you can *encourage* him to do so by always having it available. When you rock your baby on your lap, or read him a story, snuggle together under his quilt. Take it with you on car trips and tuck it into his stroller. If you make the quilt part of your cozy times together, it will soon represent those happy memories to your child. (But if he should bond to another item, don't press the issue.)

Play Suggestions

For a newborn, drape the quilt over the crib's bumper pads or over the bassinet side. Prop the baby on his side, 8" to 12" away from the quilt. The bright colors and pattern will attract his attention. After the baby has become accustomed to the quilt, hang it so the pattern runs diagonally.

As early as 10 months, a baby can understand the names of the animals even though he won't be able to say them. Your baby will especially like you to imitate animal sounds. By 18 months, he'll mimic the sounds, too.

Once your toddler is talking, ask which is his favorite animal and why. Make up tales about the animals together. Listen to your child's stories—they give you a fascinating glimpse at how his mind works.

When he's older, the AlphaPet Quilt makes educational games fun. For the following preschool games, you'll need alphabet cards. You can photocopy a set or make your own by printing the 26 letters on 3" x 5" cards.

1. Introduce only two or three alphabet cards at a time. Say the letter and match it to the appropriate animal on the quilt. Then have the child match them. Add more cards as needed. Once the child has learned upper case letters, switch to lower case. You can also substitute other alphabet sets you might have, like magnetic letters. (The quilt blocks make great counting practice, too.)

2. For an excellent memory game, cover two animals with cards. Say, "Find the cat . . . ." Start by hiding only a few animals, and increase gradually.

3. An advanced game uses lowercase letters to spell the names of the animals. Of course, some blocks are easier than others. Start with cat and dog; save unicorn and elephant for later.

Safety Considerations

Note that untreated cotton fabrics are flammable.

Care Instructions

Wash by hand. Use a bleach-free, pH-balanced detergent like Orvus Quilt Soap or Ensure Quilt Wash. Soak for about 20 minutes in tepid water with a minimum amount of soap; rinse thoroughly. Drain without wringing or twisting. Blot between terry towels. Lay the quilt flat on fresh towels and smooth out wrinkles. After an hour, remove the towels.

Reshape the Aida squares as much as possible while still damp. Dry flat. If you must touch up the Aida (only a last resort), press *lightly* using a damp press cloth on the rightside. Use the tip of the iron to lightly press only the background fabric, not the embroidery. Do not flatten the batting.

This toy is from the book **Soft Toys for Babies** *in Judi Maddigan's* **Stitch & Enrich** *series.*

CHAPTER 5

ALPHAPET QUILT

From birth on, your child needs:

- Visual stimulation
- Comforting objects
- Games that teach letters and numbers

This toy provides:

- A full color spectrum
- An heirloom-quality security blanket
- Twenty-six animals for counting or matching to alphabet cards

My baby brother had a security cat—a mangy stuffed thing, made from rabbit's fur. He would grab that threadbare kitty by the tail, rub it gently across his nose, and suck his thumb. With the wisdom of my six years, I looked askance at the situation. How could he adore something that scruffy?

Now I understand what my brother saw in that tattered toy. A comfort object can give a child great consolation. If your baby should adopt one, be happy and supportive. He has taken the first step toward independence and self-sufficiency.

If you make an AlphaPet Quilt for your baby, it just might become his special security object. He couldn't do better. (But don't build your hopes up—he might still bond to that "scruffy little cat." That's okay, too.)

A quilt is soft, warm, snug, and inviting. No wonder we call a thick quilt a *comforter*. This quilt, with its 26 blocks of engaging cross-stitched animals, flaunts rich textures and colorful details. It brings new elegance to the word "blankie."

Granted, if your child drags his quilt about, it will not look brand-spanking new for long. You have to choose: either you want a picture-perfect display piece, or you want a quilt for your child to snuggle under, to cuddle up with, to stroke along a tear-stained cheek. Any number of objects could serve the former purpose. Only one special item will satisfy the latter.

So what if it gets dirty? It's washable. So what if it gets torn? It's mendable. Then again, you could always quilt two.

Every baby should be lucky enough to form an attachment to his original quilt. And every quilter should be lucky enough to know the satisfaction of having made it possible.

Materials

See color pages. The directions assume you have read Chapters 1 and 2. Also check the HelpLine on page 22 when needed.

- 1/2 yd ivory 14 count Aida, 58" wide

- 4" embroidery hoop or 6" scroll frame (optional)

- DMC 6-strand cotton embroidery floss in the colors listed on page 60

- #26 tapestry needle

- 1/4 yd each of 12 solid-colored quilt fabrics, 44" wide, 100% cotton recommended. (See page 50 for my color choices or choose whatever colors please you; see the Suppliers list on page 174 for a kit of my colors available from Keepsake Quilting.)

- 1/2 yd unbleached cotton muslin, 44" wide

- Navy pin dot fabric, 44" wide, 100% cotton recommended, for piecing and binding: 1 yd for bias binding, or 1/2 yd for on-grain binding

- 1-3/8 yd backing material, 44" wide, such as a coordinating navy calico, 100% cotton recommended
- 3/8 yd batiste or other 100% cotton, lightweight, closely woven lining to match Aida
- No More Pins (optional)
- Seam ripper
- 38" x 45" bonded 100% polyester batting, low loft
- About fifty 1-1/2" rust-proof safety pins (optional, for pin basting)
- Quilting frame or masking tape
- Neutral color (like beige) all-purpose sewing thread to seam the quilt strips
- Fine monofilament nylon thread
- Cotton sewing thread to match the backing fabric
- Fabric marking pencil, silver (Berol) suggested

Counted Cross Stitch

To work without a hoop, cut 26 squares of Aida, each measuring 5-1/2". This size will also suit a 4" hoop, if desired.

Alternately, the quilt's motifs will nicely fit a 6" needlework scroll frame, such as one from E-Z Stitch (See Suppliers on page 174 or Fig. 2.20 on page 19). In this case, cut the 1/2 yd Aida into three 6"-wide crosswise strips. Mount one full strip on the frame, winding the excess fabric on one of the rods. After completing each animal, scroll the fabric up 6". Work eight or nine motifs on the 58" strip before removing it from the frame.

Following the directions for cross stitch in Chapter 2 (page 19), complete the 26 animal charts on pages 61 to 73. The charts' numbers refer to the DMC embroidery floss colors listed on page 60.

Hand launder the completed squares with gentle soap to remove any traces of oil from your hands. Block according to the directions in the HelpLine (page 22).

Trim the finished blocks to measure 4" square, centering the designs carefully.

To cut squares, try a wide acrylic ruler and rotary cutter. Referring to the center arrows marked on each chart, align the 2" mark on the ruler with first the vertical and then the horizontal center of each design.

Back each square with a 4" square of prewashed batiste. Either baste together within the seam allowances, or dot with No More Pins in each corner to bond. For assembly, treat both layers as one.

Colors

See the color photography. If you have selected different colors, plan how you want them arranged. To help visualize placement, I laid my folded fabrics on top of each other with about 1" of each exposed, alternating lighter and darker shades. I chose the order red, orange, plum, pink, purple, lavender, blue, turquoise, dark green, light green, gold, yellow.

The fabrics seamed directly to the central Aida squares (pink, lavender, turquoise, light green, yellow, and orange in the color photo) are called "frame" fabrics. The darker colors that make up the horizontal and vertical rows between the blocks (red, plum, purple, blue, dark green, and gold) are the "lattice" fabrics.

Once you have determined the order, glue a swatch of each fabric to a piece of heavy paper and label it with the name of my color that you intend to replace with it. Refer to this swatch card throughout the cutting and piecing directions, substituting your fabric whenever I mention a specific color.

Cutting Directions

Machine wash the fabrics in warm water with mild detergent, separating lights and darks, and tumble dry. Particularly vivid colors may require additional washings. In fact, the turquoise for my quilt needed three washings before it stopped bleeding.

If you launder a scrap of white cotton fabric with your colors, you will find out which, if any, bleed.

For each fabric, remove selvedges and straighten one cut edge. Cut all strips (other than the bias binding) on grain. A rotary cutter, wide acrylic ruler, and cutting mat (Fig. 2.5 on page 8) will streamline cutting.

For each of the six lattice colors: Cut one full crosswise strip 1-1/2" wide by 44" long.

Additional lattice pieces will be cut after stitching the frame colors.

For each of the six frame colors: Cut three strips measuring 1-1/2" x 44".

Muslin: Cut four strips measuring 1-3/4" x 44". Cut four 7" squares.

Navy Pin Dot: Cut a total of 4-3/4 yd of bias strips, 3-1/4" wide. (Strips may be cut on grain, if you prefer.) Seam the short ends together (Fig. 5.2) to form one long strip. Fold binding in half lengthwise, wrongsides together; press. From the same fabric, cut six 1-1/2" x 12" strips *on the straight of the grain* (not on the bias).

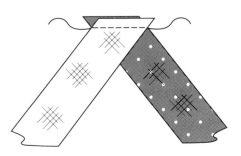

Fig. 5.2 Seaming bias strips

Piecing the Quilt Top

All seam allowances are 1/4". For piecing the quilt strips and the lattice cylinder, shorten your stitch length to 1.6 – 1.8mm (14 – 16spi).

The direction you press seams is a matter of personal preference. These instructions often specify pressing the seams open, but you may choose to press the seams away from the center squares, or toward the darker fabrics. Use whatever method gives you the best match on your cross-seams.

For additional help with seam matching, as well as alternate cutting, piecing, and binding methods, consult **The Complete Book of Machine Quilting** *by Robbie & Tony Fanning (see Bibliography).*

Frame Colors:

These directions refer to the cross-stitched squares by the first letter of the animal's name (A for ape, B for bear, C for cat, and so on). The term "square" refers only to the cross-stitched Aida. After fabric strips have been stitched to the squares, they become "blocks." Thus, the term "block B" means the bear square with its attached strips.

1. Using a 1/4" seam allowance, stitch the left edge of square A to a pink strip with the strip rightside up and square A face down on it. Without removing the fabric from the machine, continue to join the left edges of squares F, L, and R to the same pink strip (Fig. 5.3). Butt the top of each new square to the bottom of the previous square, without backstitching.

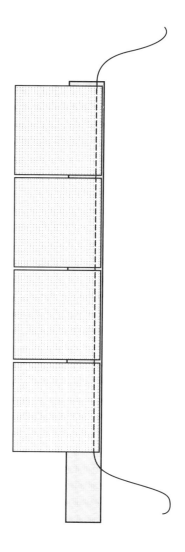

Fig. 5.3 Seaming Aida squares to frame strip, first step

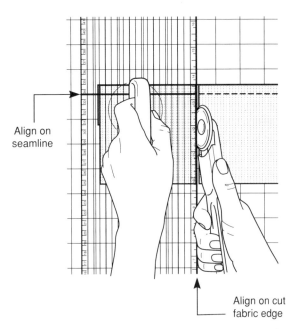

Align on seamline

Align on cut fabric edge

Fig. 5.4 When cutting blocks apart with a rotary cutter, align your ruler in two places. For example, match the edge of the square with the cutting edge of the ruler, and the block's seamline with one of the ruler's shorter, perpendicular lines. This assures accurate right angles.

2. Press the seam away from the Aida squares. (Always press embroidery from the wrongside on a well-padded surface.) Cut apart between the blocks, at a right angle to the seamline (Fig. 5.4). Cut only the fabric strip, not the Aida. Stack these blocks and set aside. Throughout the directions, keep each group of blocks together in a stack.

3. Following the techniques in steps 1 and 2, join the left edges of squares B, G, M, S, and X to a lavender strip. Seam squares C, H, N, T, and Y to a turquoise strip. Seam squares I, O, U, and Z to a light green strip. Seam squares D, J, P, and V to a yellow strip. Seam squares E, K, Q, and W to an orange strip.

For clarity, the following directions explain one color at a time. Alternately, you could sew as much as possible on all colors and then cut all at once.

4. Complete the pink frames as follows: Stitch the right edges of blocks A, F, L, and R to a pink strip (Fig. 5.5). Press seam away from Aida; cut apart between blocks. Join the top edges of these blocks to a pink strip. Press and cut apart. Join the blocks' bottom edges to a pink strip. Press and cut apart.

5. Following the procedure in step 4, complete the frames for each of the remaining groups of blocks in the other five frame colors.

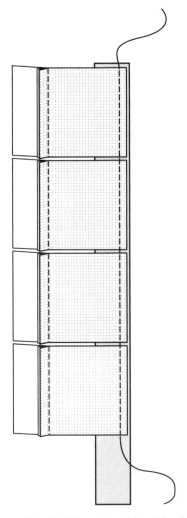

Fig. 5.5 Seaming Aida blocks to frame strip, second step

Horizontal Lattice Strips

6. For each of the six lattice colors, cut one rectangle 12" long and about 6" wide. Find the rectangle's precise width by measuring the tops and bottoms of several frame pieces. Mathematically, they should measure 6", but yours may vary. For instance, my frames were just under 6" wide, so I cut my six lattice rectangles 12" x 5-15/16" for a perfect match.

To simplify piecing, first construct a cylinder alternating the six 6" x 12" rectangles with the six 1-1/2" x 12" navy pin dot strips as directed below. Then slice the cylinder perpendicular to the seamlines to make the horizontal strips. For all cylinder seams, match a long edge of a navy strip to a 12" side of a solid rectangle, rightsides together. Do not backstitch or knot your seams.

7. Seam the first navy strip to the red rectangle. Seam the second navy strip to the red rectangle's opposite side. Join the plum rectangle to the second navy strip. Seam the third navy strip to the plum rectangle's other edge. Following the same technique, join the remaining pieces in the following order: purple, blue, dark green, and gold rectangles, each separated by a navy strip. Your pieced fabric should measure about 12" x 39-1/2". Seam the gold rectangle to the raw edge of the first navy strip, forming a cylinder or tube (Fig. 5.6). Press the seams open.

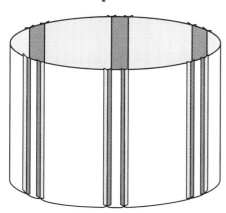

Fig. 5.6 Constructing the cylinder

8. Flatten the tube, matching the raw edges. Straighten the raw edges, if necessary, trimming them at a right angle to the stitching lines. Slice the cylinder into seven 1-1/2" sections, or rings (Fig. 5.7). Set aside.

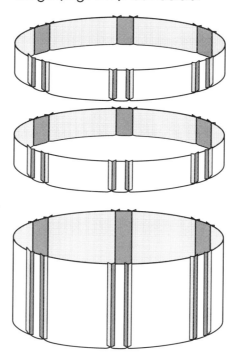

Fig. 5.7 Cutting cylinder into rings

Vertical Lattice Strips

9. Join the left edges of blocks E, K, Q, and W to the red strip (Fig. 5.8). Press the seam *open*; cut blocks apart.

10. Join the left edges of blocks A, F, L, and R to the plum strip, and join the *right* edge of block W to the same plum strip. Press seam open; cut apart.

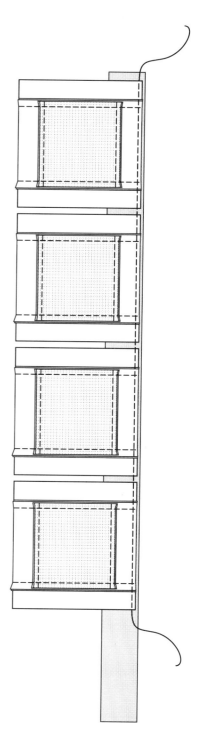

Fig. 5.8 Seaming Aida blocks to lattice strip

11. Join the left edges of blocks B, G, M, S, and X to the purple strip, and join the *right* edge of block R to the same purple strip. Press seam open; cut apart.

12. Join the left edges of blocks C, H, N, T, and Y to the blue strip, and join the *right* edge of block M to the same blue strip. Press seam open; cut apart.

13. Join the left edges of blocks I, O, U, and Z to the dark green strip, and join the *right* edges of blocks C and H to the same dark green strip. Press seam open; cut apart.

14. Join the left edges of blocks D, J, P, and V to the gold strip, and join the *right* edge of block Z to the same gold strip. Press seam open; cut apart.

15. Arrange your blocks in the layout shown in Fig. 5.14 on page 59. Seam the right edge of block D to the left edge of block E. Without removing the fabric from the machine, join I to J, N to O, and S to T. The blocks will be chained together on the same threads. Always check which side of the blocks you should seam, so when you open the blocks, the letters appear in alphabetical order.

16. With one continuous line of stitching, join B to C, F to G, K to L, P to Q, U to V, and Y to Z.

17. With continuous threads, join G to H, L to M, Q to R, and V to W.

18. With continuous threads, join A to B, E to F, J to K, O to P, T to U, and X to Y.

19. After completing the stitching, snip all the threads to separate the rows.

Assembling Horizontal Rows

20. Refer to the diagram of the quilt top and the color photo. Notice that each horizontal lattice row begins and ends with a navy square. The top and bottom row have only three additional colors. The remaining five rows each omit one color. For each of the 1-1/2" rings cut in step 8, remove the unnecessary piece(s) by ripping two stitching lines.

21. Check the placement for the lattice strips by laying out the entire quilt top. Notice that the lattice colors zigzag through the quilt from the upper left toward the lower right. Once you have confirmed the order, label the lattice strips. Number 1 is at the top, number 7 at the bottom.

22. Pin strip 1 to the top edge of blocks A, B, and C, matching all cross-seams (Fig. 5.9). Pin strip 7 to the bottom edge of blocks X, Y, and Z. Stitch seams, checking that each cross-seam aligns perfectly as it reaches the presser foot. You may want to use a walking or

even-feed foot to prevent the top fabric from creeping. Check the seam matches on the rightside. Rip stitching and redo any mismatched areas. Press seams open.

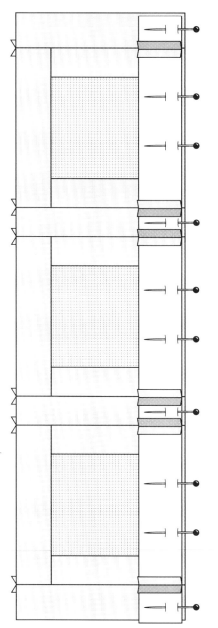

Fig. 5.9 Attaching horizontal lattice to top row

Corner Squares

23. With a fabric marking pencil, transfer the outlines of the letter motifs on pages 74 to 75 to the rightside of the muslin squares.

To personalize a quilt you can embroider a child's name, birth weight, length, and birth date in the four muslin corner squares rather than stitching the four block letters.

24. Seam the right edge of the muslin square with the letter A to the left edge of block A. Seam the left edge of the B muslin square to the right edge of block C.

25. Join the right edge of muslin square C to the left edge of block X. Join the left edge of muslin square D to the right edge of block Z.

26. Press the seams open, being careful not to touch your iron to the pencil lines. (Heat sets most markers.)

Completing the Lattice Strips

27. Pin strip 2 to the top edge of blocks D through H, matching all cross-seams. Stitch seam, checking that each cross-seam aligns perfectly as it reaches the presser foot. Check the seam matches on the rightside. Remove stitching and redo any mismatched areas. Press seam open. Pin the raw edge of strip 2 to the bottom edge of the quilt's top row (blocks A, B, and C with the attached muslin squares). Seam and press.

28. In the same manner, join the remaining lattice strips between the appropriate rows of blocks. Press the seams open.

Border Strips

29. Seam two of the 1-3/4" muslin border strips to the left and right edges of the quilt top.

30. Press seams open, remembering to keep the iron away from the pencil lines on the corner squares. Trim the strips even with the quilt top.

31. Seam muslin strips to the top and bottom of the quilt. Press and trim strips.

Basting

32. Straighten one crosswise edge of the backing fabric, and remove one selvedge. Trim both the quilt batting and the fabric backing's other two edges to the size of the quilt top, allowing at least a 1/2" margin on all sides. Attach the three layers to a quilt frame, if you have one. If not, tape the backing wrongside up on a large worktable or clean floor, keeping the lengthwise and crosswise grains square. Spread with the batt, then center the pieced top right-side up, matching grainlines with the backing.

33. Working from the center out, baste the three layers together. Either hand stitch with contrasting thread, or use safety pins placed about 6" apart.

34. Remove the quilt sandwich from the frame, or untape from your work surface. *For conventional machine:* Sew around the raw edges of the quilt top using a wide, long zigzag; trim the excess batting and backing. *For serger:* Serge the edges of the quilt top with a wide, long, balanced 3-thread overlock, trimming only the batting and backing with the knives.

Machine Quilting

35. Thread the machine with a fine monofilament nylon in the needle and a bobbin of cotton thread that matches the backing fabric. Leave thread tails at the beginning and ending of each stitching line. After stitching, pull all thread tails to the quilt back; knot. Thread the ends on a needle and lose them inside the quilt sandwich (Fig. 5.10).

36. Ditch-stitch along the vertical lattice strips, starting with the middle rows and working toward the edges. Always stitch from top to bottom to prevent shifting. On the outside rows, extend your stitching lines to include the seam between the corner muslin squares and the border strips.

Fig. 5.10 Pull all quilting thread tails to the back of the quilt. After making a square knot, thread the ends on a long, thin needle. Insert the needle next to the knot, taking a stitch through the batting. Emerge a few inches away; tug on the threads and snip them close to the backing.

37. Complete the lattice quilting on the horizontal rows.

38. Ditch-stitch around each Aida square to define it from its frame fabric.

39. Switch to monofilament nylon thread in the bobbin as well as in the needle. Using a darning foot, and dropping or covering the feed dogs, free-machine quilt (see page 23 in the HelpLine) the outlines of the four letters in the corner muslin squares.

If free-machine quilting is new to you, practice on remnants first. Hold the quilt sandwich taut while working, or use a hoop. Experiment and find what works best for your machine. If your trial runs do not measure up to your standards, Lauri Realini (who machine quilted the book's sample) suggests using a walking foot instead of stitching free motion.

Binding

40. Pin the prepared binding to the bottom edge of the quilt top, rightsides together and raw edges even, starting in the center rather than at a corner. (Follow Fig. 5.11 for folding the ends of the binding.) Plan ahead so that your binding seams will not land on a corner.

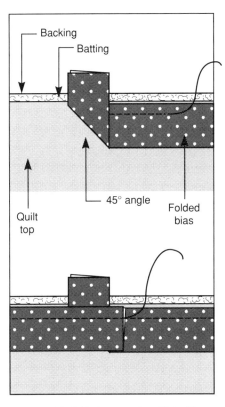

Fig. 5.11 Splicing ends of binding

41. Stitch to within 3" of the first corner. Align the binding with the next side, pleating the binding at a 45° angle (Fig. 5.12). Stitch to within 1/2" of the edge; lock stitches.

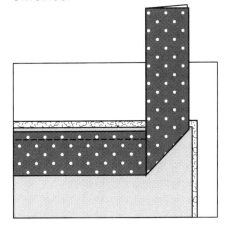

Fig. 5.12 Mitering the binding, first step

42. Pivot the quilt 90°. Holding the quilt in position, raise the needle and pull about 1" extra needle thread. Lift the binding's pleat and flip it behind the presser foot to clear the stitching (Fig. 5.13). Lower

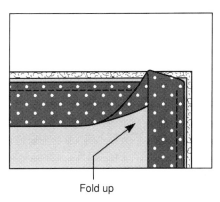

Fold up

Fig. 5.13 Mitering the binding, second step

the needle 1/2" from the corner (where you ended stitching previously). Lock stitches. Finish binding the remaining sides and corners in the same way.

43. Turn the binding to the back of the quilt, encasing the raw edges. Pin the binding's folded edge to the seam on the quilt backing, mitering the corners. Slipstitch the binding's folded edge to the quilt back. Also hand stitch the corner folds and the ending splice. Remove any basting threads.

Error Correction

If you make a mistake, approach the solution creatively. In making one of the quilts for this book, we accidently reversed the top horizontal lattice row so that the colors went green, blue, purple instead of purple, blue, green. We were so eager to see the finished quilt, we didn't notice the error until after completing the machine quilting. (You know that sinking feeling?) Here's how we fixed it without ripping:

I cut a strip of purple to cover the green fabric, and a strip of green to cover the purple, including 1/4" seam allowances. I pressed under the 1/4" on all sides and checked it against the quilt, making adjustments until the folded piece was a perfect match for the wrong color. By hand, I appliquéd the new piece on top of the old. Working between the layers, I used the equivalent of a tiny backstitch. On the finished quilt, you can't see the corrections.

Although the backstitch variation worked admirably, it was a little awkward. The needle took the longer stitch from right to left through the quilt, but the shorter stitch went from left to right through the fold of the applied piece. My editor, Robbie Fanning, suggests a small slipstitch would work as well and would keep the direction of the stitches consistent.

Alphabet Cards

For children over 4 years old, make a set of alphabet cards to use with the quilt. These cards are not safe for younger children, regardless of their reading ability. Photocopy the alphabet pages at the front and back of the book onto white card stock (also called cover-weight paper). Cut out the cards just inside the solid lines. Either have your printing company laminate them (5 mil sheets) or cover both sides with clear, self-adhesive plastic such as Con-Tact. Cut the laminated card stock apart, leaving about 1/8" margin of clear plastic around each card. See this chapter's Play Guide for suggested games.

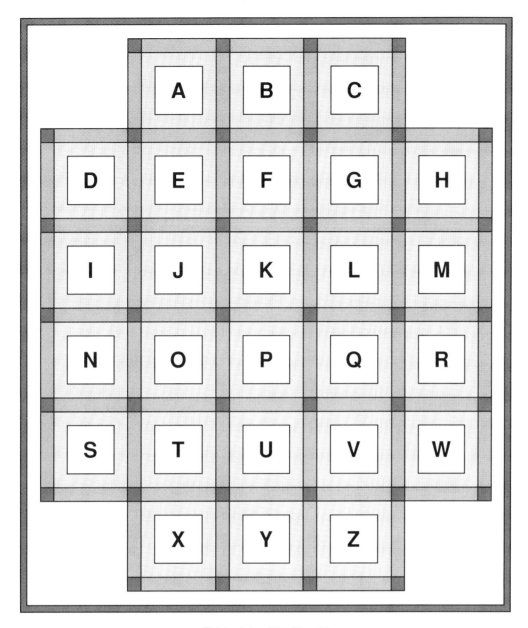

Finished size: 36-1/2" x 43"

Fig. 5.14 Quilt top

AlphaPet Quilt DMC color numbers:

White	**704** Apple Green	**905** Parrot Green
301 Mahogany	**720** Rust	**911** Emerald Green
310 Black	**722** Pale Rust	**913** Lt. Emerald Green
318 Steel Gray	**725** Gold	**919** Dk. Copper
341 Pale Blue Violet	**726** Lt. Gold	**920** Copper
353 Lt. Coral	**727** Yellow	**921** Lt. Copper
402 Camel	**729** Honey Gold	**922** Pale Copper
407 Dk. Rosy Tan	**738** Lt. Tan	**928** Silver Blue
413 Charcoal	**739** Pale Tan	**936** Bottle Green
415 Silver	**745** Pale Yellow	**938** Dark Walnut
422 Tan	**754** Peach	**939** Blue Black
433 Med. Brown	**761** Lt. Salmon	**948** Pale Peach
434 Lt. Brown	**762** Lt. Silver	**950** Rosy Tan
435 Dk. Honey	**775** Baby Blue	**951** Lt. Apricot
437 Honey	**776** Pink	**955** Mint Green
451 Dk. Dove Gray	**780** Dk. Topaz	**976** Golden Brown
452 Dove Gray	**781** Topaz	**977** Lt. Golden Brown
469 Moss Green	**783** Lt. Topaz	**3021** Dk. Brown Gray
471 Lt. Moss Green	**792** Dk. Cornflower Blue	**3022** Pewter
535 Charcoal Gray	**793** Cornflower Blue	**3023** Lt. Pewter
543 Lt. Beige	**801** Lt. Walnut	**3024** Pale Pewter
603 Bright Pink	**823** Navy Blue	**3031** Dk. Mocha
611 Drab Brown	**834** Antique Gold	**3032** Mocha
645 Dk. Slate Gray	**838** Dk. Pecan Brown	**3033** Pale Mocha
646 Slate Gray	**839** Pecan Brown	**3045** Dk. Sand
648 Lt. Slate Gray	**840** Beige Brown	**3064** Suntan
676 Old Gold	**841** Lt. Beige Brown	**3072** Pearl Gray
677 Lt. Old Gold	**844** Black Gray	**3345** Hunter Green
680 Dk. Old Gold	**869** Cherrywood	**3371** Black Brown
699 Dk. Kelly Green	**898** Walnut	

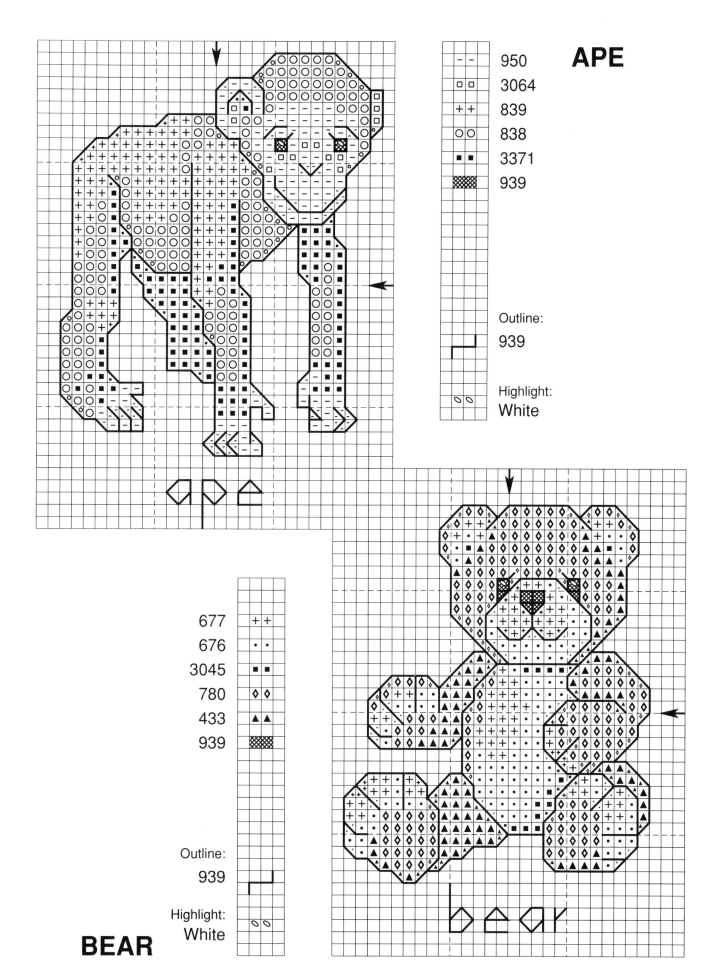

APE

- -	950	
□ □	3064	
+ +	839	
○ ○	838	
■ ■	3371	
▓	939	

Outline:

939

Highlight:

White

BEAR

677	+ +	
676	· ·	
3045	■ ■	
780	◇ ◇	
433	▲ ▲	
939	▓	

Outline:

939

Highlight:

White

CAT

Color	Symbol
White	- -
762	△ △
402	○ ○
922	✕ ✕
844	▲ ▲
761	• •

Outline:
939

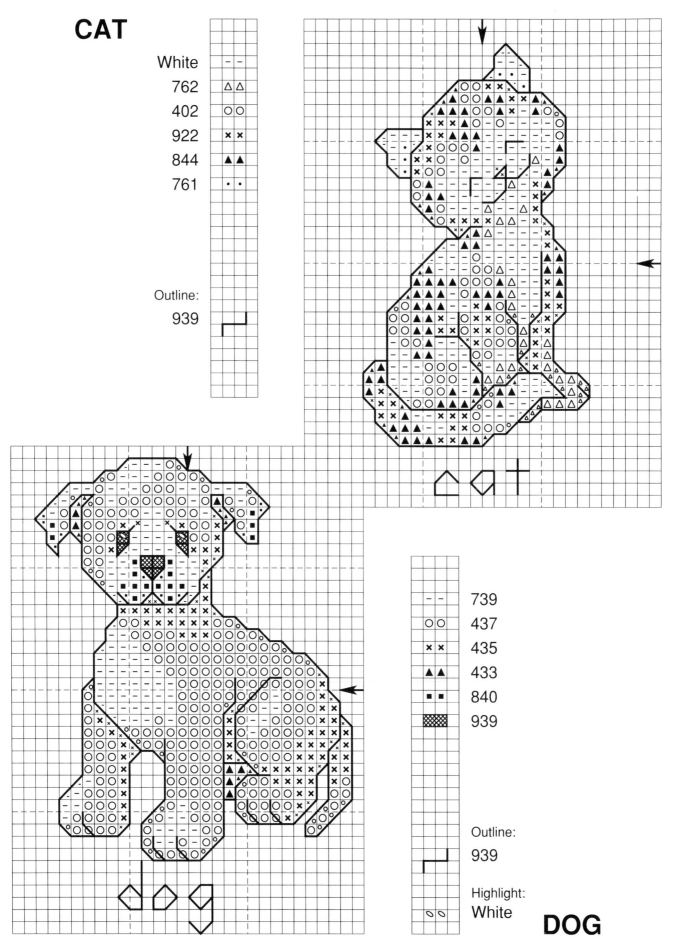

DOG

Symbol	Color
- -	739
○ ○	437
✕ ✕	435
▲ ▲	433
▪ ▪	840
▨	939

Outline:
939

Highlight:
White

ELEPHANT

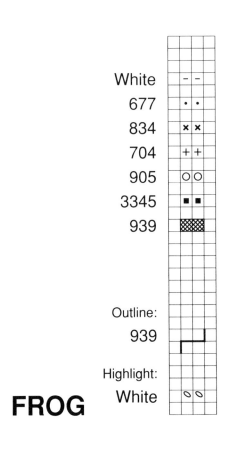

· ·	White	
– –	762	
△ △	452	
+ +	950	
∨ ∨	451	
■ ■	413	
▨	939	

Outline:

939

Highlight:

White ⌀ ⌀

FROG

White	– –
677	· ·
834	× ×
704	+ +
905	○ ○
3345	■ ■
939	▨

Outline:

939

Highlight:

White ⌀ ⌀

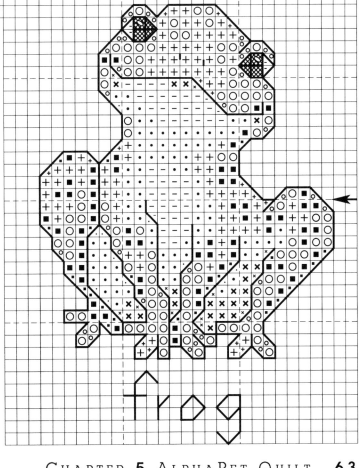

GOAT

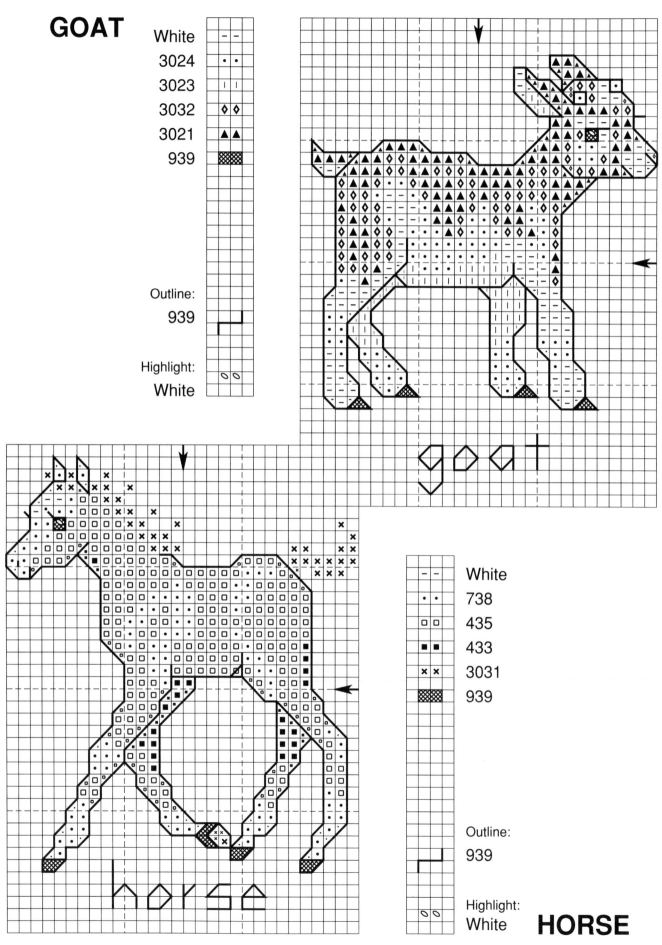

	White
- -	White
• •	3024
I I	3023
◊ ◊	3032
▲ ▲	3021
▨	939

Outline:
939

Highlight:
White

goat

- -	White
• •	738
▢ ▢	435
■ ■	433
× ×	3031
▨	939

Outline:
939

Highlight:
White

horse

HORSE

INSECT

- -		955
□ □		913
○ ○		911
■ ■		699
I I		422
▨ ▨		939
▲ ▲		869

Outline:

939

Highlight:
White

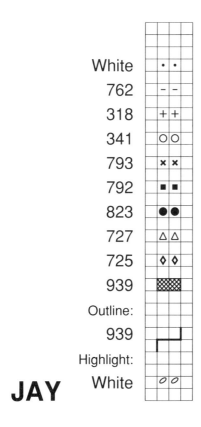

White	• •	
762	- -	
318	+ +	
341	○ ○	
793	× ×	
792	■ ■	
823	● ●	
727	△ △	
725	◊ ◊	
939	▨ ▨	
Outline:		
939		
Highlight:		
White	⌀ ⌀	

JAY

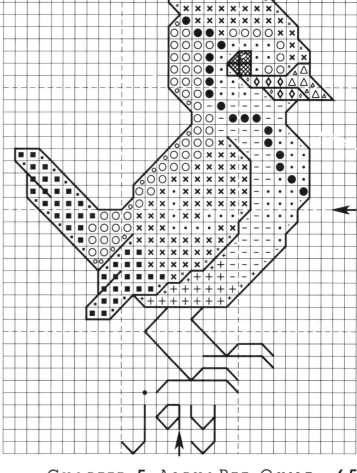

KOALA

White	- -
677	○ ○
783	× ×
780	■ ■
869	▲ ▲
939	▨ ▨

Outline:
939

Highlight:
White ◡ ◡

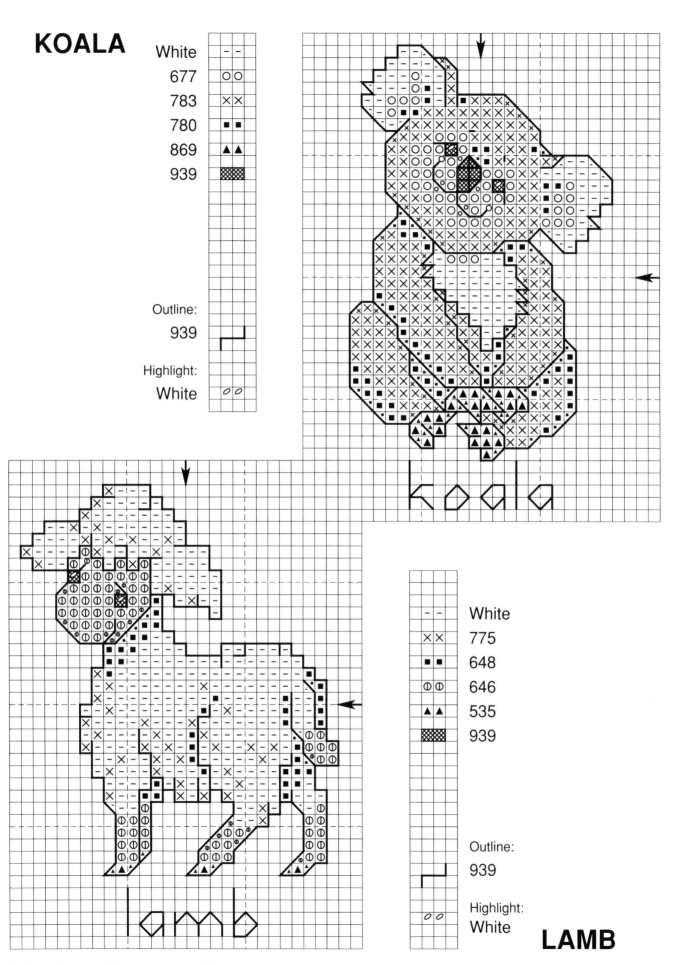

White	- -
775	× ×
648	■ ■
646	⏀ ⏀
535	▲ ▲
939	▨ ▨

Outline:
939

Highlight:
White ◡ ◡

LAMB

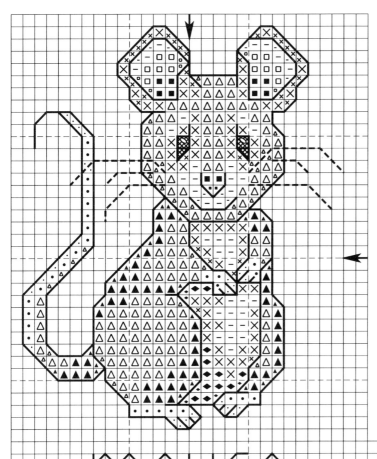

MOUSE

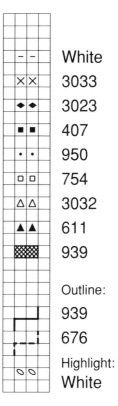

−	−	White
×	×	3033
◆	◆	3023
■	■	407
·	·	950
□	□	754
△	△	3032
▲	▲	611
▦	▦	939

Outline:

939

676

Highlight:

White

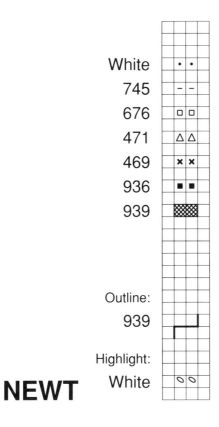

White	·	·
745	−	−
676	□	□
471	△	△
469	×	×
936	■	■
939	▦	▦

Outline:

939

Highlight:

White

NEWT

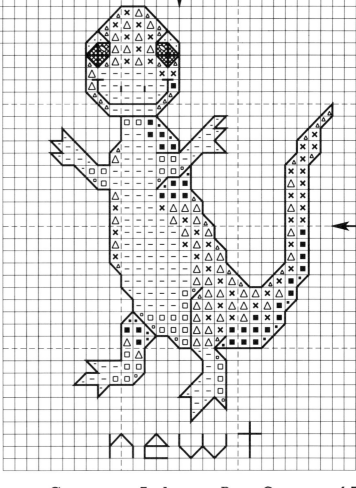

OWL

White	– –
677	· ·
676	+ +
783	□ □
433	× ×
939	▨
780	▲ ▲
3024	△ △
781	v v
838	■ ■

Outline:

939

Highlight:

White

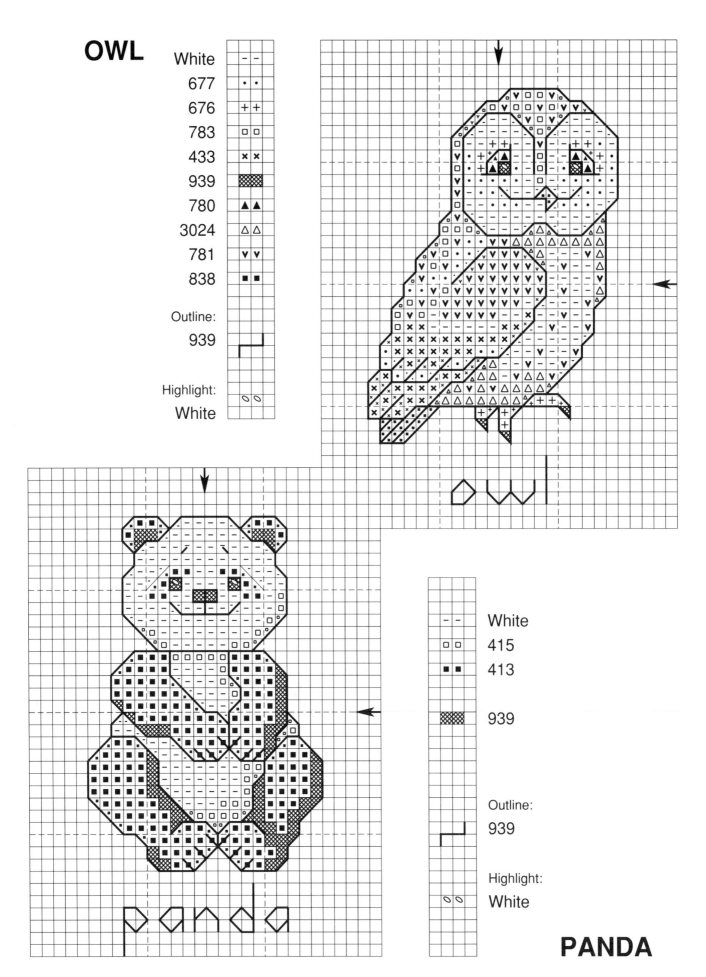

White	– –
415	□ □
413	■ ■
939	▨

Outline:

939

Highlight:

White

PANDA

QUAIL

– –	White
· ·	3033
+ +	754
v v	976
◆ ◆	725
▲ ▲	920
□ □	977
× ×	780
o o	801
▨	939
Outline:	939
French knots:	
● ●	939

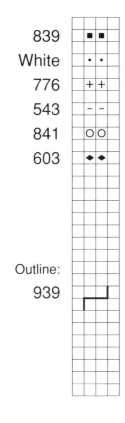

839	■ ■
White	· ·
776	+ +
543	– –
841	o o
603	◆ ◆
Outline:	
939	

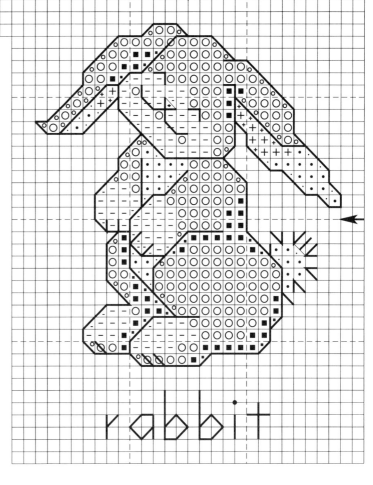

RABBIT

SEAL

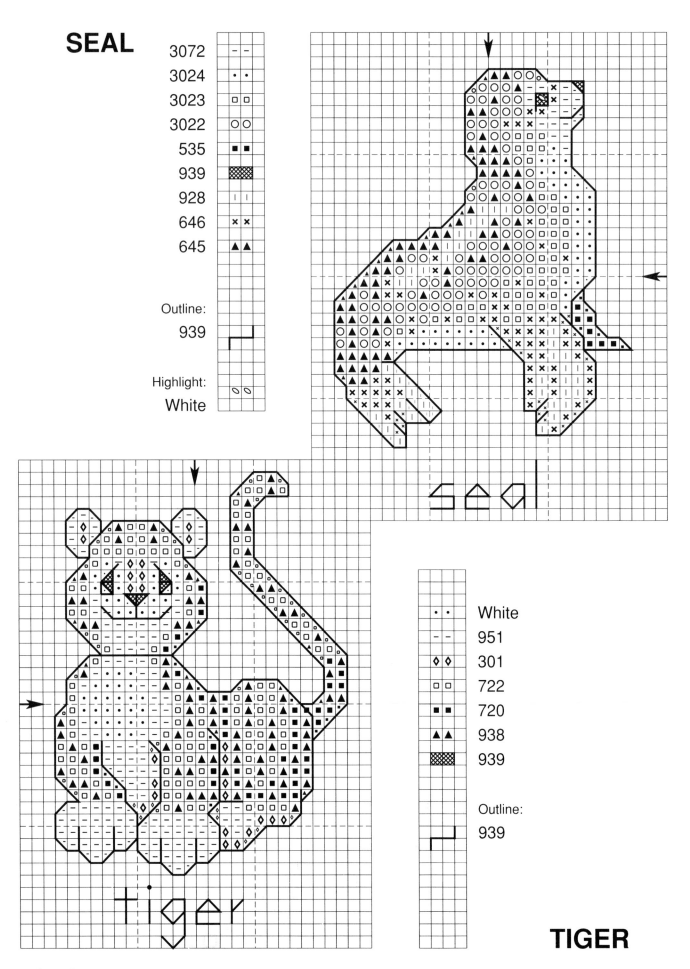

3072	- -	
3024	• •	
3023	□ □	
3022	○ ○	
535	■ ■	
939	▨	
928	I I	
646	× ×	
645	▲ ▲	

Outline:
939

Highlight:
White

White
951
301
722
720
938
939

Outline:
939

TIGER

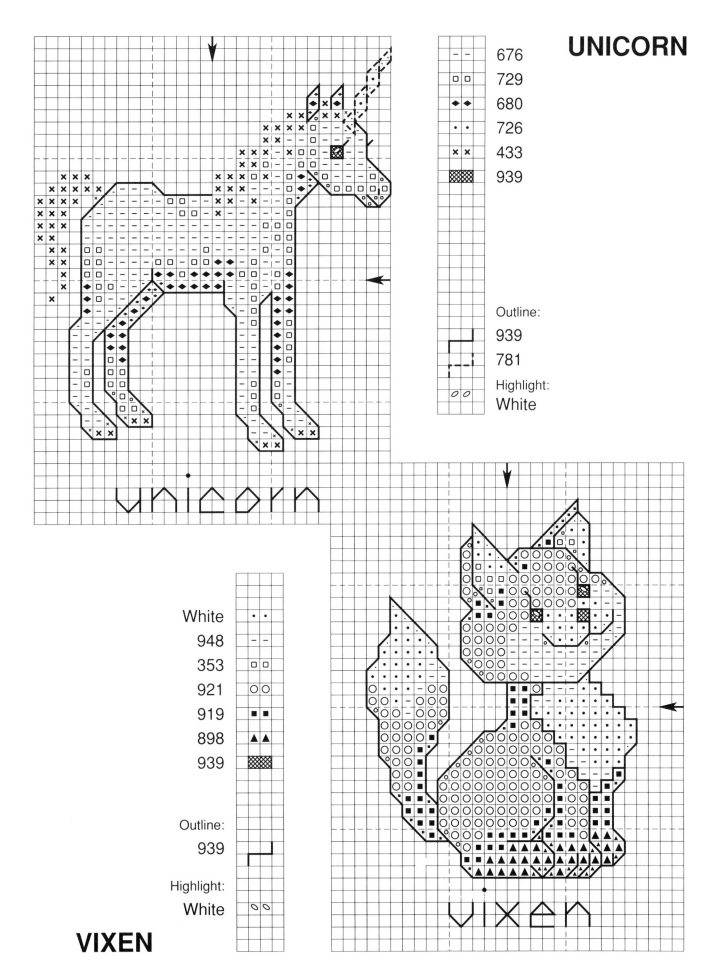

UNICORN

-	-	676
□	□	729
◆	◆	680
.	.	726
×	×	433
▦		939

Outline:

939

781

Highlight:

White

White

948

353

921

919

898

939

Outline:

939

Highlight:

White

VIXEN

WHALE

White	- -
318	o o
762	▢ ▢
413	✗ ✗
310	▲ ▲
939	▦ ▦

Outline:
939

Highlight:
White

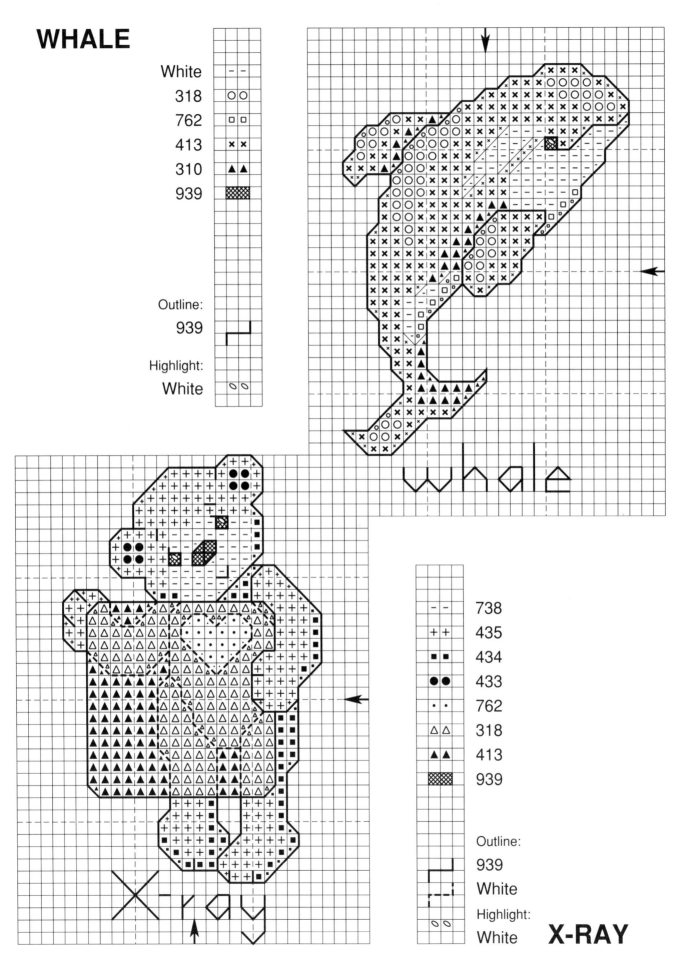

- -	738
+ +	435
■ ■	434
● ●	433
· ·	762
△ △	318
▲ ▲	413
▦ ▦	939

Outline:
939
White

Highlight:
White

X-RAY

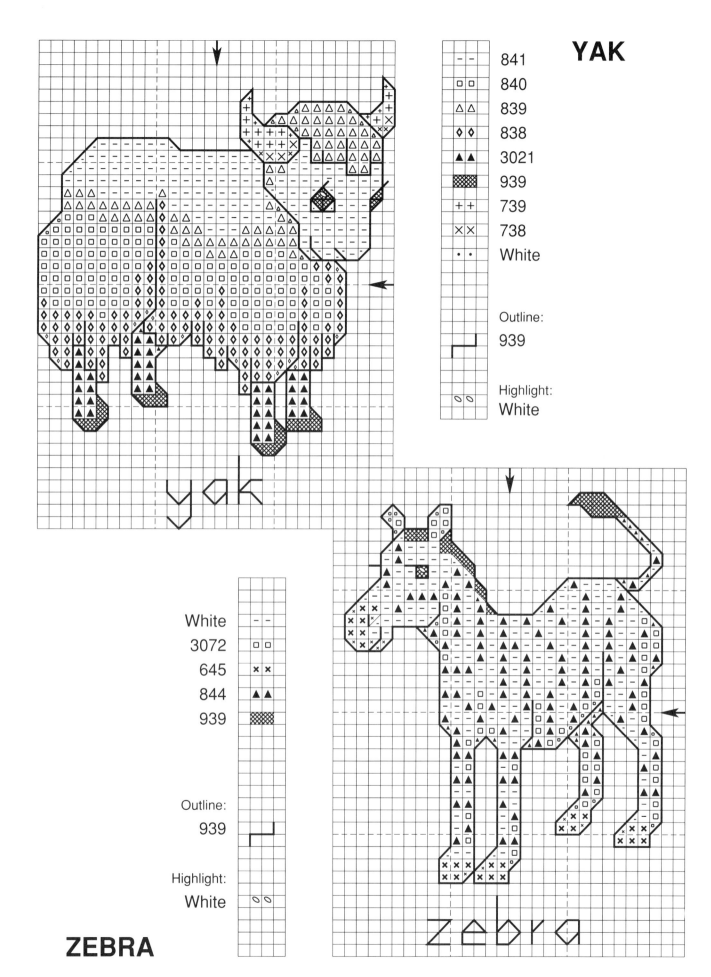

YAK

-	-	841
□	□	840
△	△	839
◇	◇	838
▲	▲	3021
▨		939
+	+	739
×	×	738
·	·	White

Outline:

939

Highlight:

White

ZEBRA

White	-	-
3072	□	□
645	×	×
844	▲	▲
939	▨	

Outline:

939

Highlight:

White

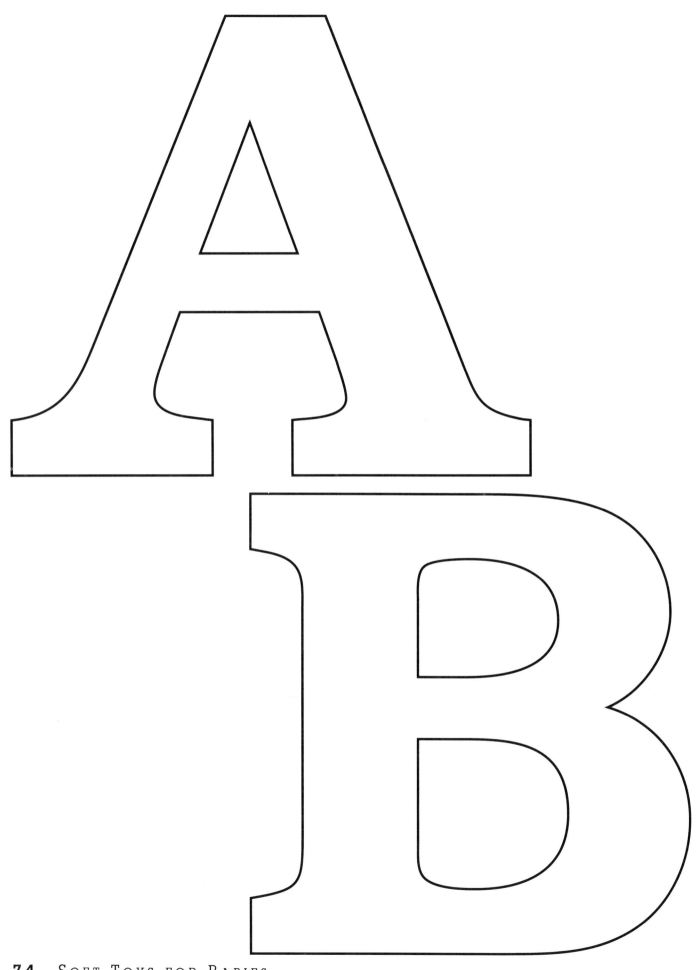

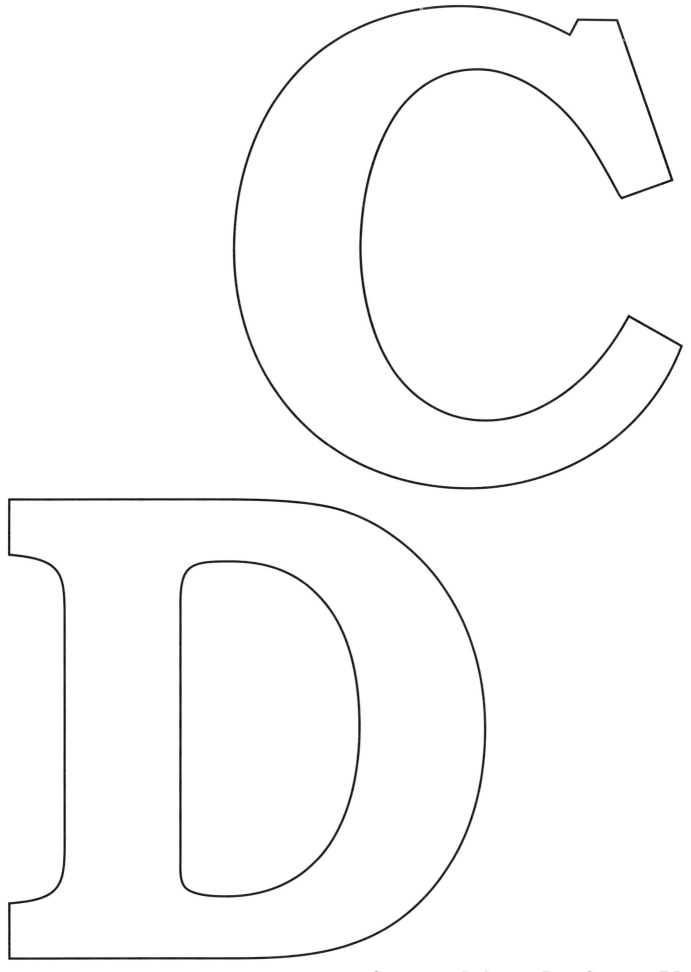

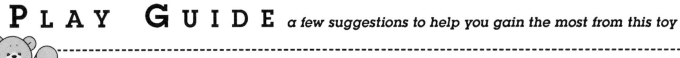

CHIT-CHAT MITT
PLAY GUIDE *a few suggestions to help you gain the most from this toy*

Age Range

2 to 4 months.

Skills Development

Babies discover their hands at about 2 months. The Chit-chat Mitt assists this process because it's easier to locate a noisy hand than a quiet one. And, since the mitten doesn't need to be held, it's appropriate for babies who have not yet opened their fists. (A baby doesn't grasp objects well until the third month or later.)

This mitt starts the early phases of *cause-and-effect* reasoning. The baby learns that when he moves his hands, things happen. When he sounds the rattle initially, it's by chance. But soon enough the movement becomes deliberate. Even though he doesn't have complete control yet, it's a big step. For the first time, he is causing something to occur in his environment rather than simply responding to it.

Eye-hand coordination comes next. The rattling sound encourages the baby to search for the source. To find it, the baby must move both his hand and his head. Once he does find it, the vivid primary colors and engaging design hold his attention. This interdependence between eyes and hands lays the groundwork for the later development of fine motor skills like sewing.

Play Suggestions

By 2 months, a baby usually prefers looking

to a particular side. Observe your baby to see his favorite side, and start with the Chit-chat Mitt on that hand.

Once you've fastened the mitt to your baby's wrist, resist the temptation to shake his arm and rattle the mitt. Let him discover it on his own.

A young baby tends to respond to stimulation with his entire body. It will take him a while to fine-tune the movement and wave only the hand with the mitt. Even though it may not seem that a 2-month-old is aware of the rattle, in time you will notice that the arm with the rattle moves more wildly than the one without.

While flailing his arms, the baby will probably slam his fist onto the mattress or the floor, right beside his head (if he's lying on his back). The rattle will make a loud, sharp noise, especially close to his ear, and it will no doubt startle him. While he will eventually avoid this, he will startle less in the meantime if you first pad the area under his arm with a wadded receiving blanket.

Use the mitten on the same hand until the baby can predictably wave that arm, find the mitten with his eyes, and focus on it. Then switch to the other hand.

If you have two mittens, introduce only one at a time. After the baby has refined his responses, you can combine mitts on both hands.

Once your baby is accustomed to a mitt on his hands, fasten it on his foot instead. (It fits around the instep, not the ankle, and covers

the toes.) This presents yet another set of sensations to ponder and solve.

You can also use the mitt when the baby is on his stomach. Wait until he can hold his head up and support this weight on his forearms (around the third month).

Safety Considerations

Always supervise a baby wearing the Chit-chat Mitt. Remove it as soon as he fusses, since there is no way for him to escape it on his own. (You can always reintroduce it later.)

Since all the Chit-chat Mitt's fabrics have been prewashed, it is safe for a baby to mouth or chew this toy. However, don't leave the mitten on a baby for extended periods. Remove it before putting him down to sleep.

Fasten the elasticized mitt loosely around the baby's wrist. It should not mark the skin.

Occasionally check the mitt's fabric and stitching, and repair if necessary.

Care Instructions

Hand wash the Chit-chat Mitt in lukewarm water with mild soap. Rinse thoroughly, blot between terry towels, and dry flat.

This toy is from the book Soft Toys for Babies in Judi Maddigan's Stitch & Enrich series.

CHAPTER 6

CHIT-CHAT MITT

From 2 to 4 months, your baby enjoys:

- Soft, appealing toys
- Toys that don't need to be held
- Noisemakers to draw attention

This toy provides:

- An engaging face and vivid colors
- An adjustable cuff for either wrist or foot
- A hidden rattle that sounds when baby moves

Try this experiment: Hold your arms, almost straight, in front of you and about three feet apart. Point your index fingers at each other. Close your eyes and try to bring the tips of your fingers slowly together. Did you miss? Now do the same thing with your eyes open.

The reason you can meet your fingers automatically with your eyes open is because you have eye-hand coordination. We take it for granted, but it's not something we're born with. It's learned. And since it is vital for many other skills, it's learned early.

Your baby starts to link his eyes and his hands at about 2 months. Even before he can reach out and grasp objects, the Chit-chat Mitt can help him discover his hands. It covers his fist with a padded noisemaker that he doesn't need to hold.

Almost since birth, he has known how to locate a sound. Now, each time he moves, the rattle prompts him to look for the source.

You can make a mitten with either a panda face or a teddy bear face. Use the same pattern, but substitute appropriate colors, like a yellow teddy on a royal blue mitt. For the teddy, omit eye patches. Maybe you'll want to make two different mittens—one for each hand.

The book's sample shows a black-and-white panda on a red background, a real eye-grabbing combination. When choosing your colors, stick with bright, vivid primaries. For instance, if you want to make a pink mitten for your little girl, go with a hot pink rather than a soft pastel.

Materials

See color pages. The directions assume you have read Chapters 1 and 2. Also check the HelpLine on page 22 when needed.

- 1/4 yd cotton or cotton blend interlock knit
- Remnants of both white and black interlock knits for appliqué
- 12" of 3/8"-wide grosgrain ribbon
- 1-1/2" of hook and loop fastener tape (Velcro) at least 1/2" wide
- 1/8 yd of 3/8"-wide clear polyurethane elastic
- 1 Hide-a-Rattle (3/8"-thick flat plastic rattle, 1-1/2" diameter) available from Aardvark Adventures (see Suppliers list on page 174)
- Black and white 6-strand cotton embroidery floss
- Stabilizer (Stitch-n-Tear)
- Disappearing or water-soluble fabric marking pen
- Fine, *permanent* black marking pen (Sharpie or Pilot)
- Nontoxic fabric glue like Sobo (optional)

Cutting Directions

Cut one Mitt from main color interlock knit, placing it on a crosswise fold. Cut two Mitt appliqués in white interlock knit, one placed crosswise and one placed lengthwise.

To cut both a crosswise and lengthwise piece at the same time, fold fabric on the bias. Align grain arrow with one straight edge.

Cut two Mitt Ears in black. Transfer all pattern markings, including the fold line on the Mitt.

Appliqué Directions

1. Trace or photocopy the face on page 85 and tape it to a window during the day (or a light table or TV screen at night). Center the appliqué (use the crosswise one) over the copy. Trace the face on the fabric with a temporary fabric marker.

Do not touch a heated iron to the fabric marker lines because you will want to remove the lines later.

2. Practice on a scrap. Fill in only the eye patches (not the eyes) with the permanent black marker. Because the ink spreads, stay inside your previously traced lines. You can always make the areas larger, but you cannot erase.

3. Fold each ear in half, rightsides together, along solid line. Stitch curved edges together (Fig. 6.2). Grade seams and clip curves; slit the fold line from dot to dot. Turn to rightside and press.

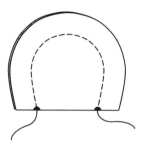

Fig. 6.2 Sewing ears

4. With raw edges toward the outside and ears extending toward the eyes, baste the ears to one appliqué following the pattern placement (Fig. 6.3).

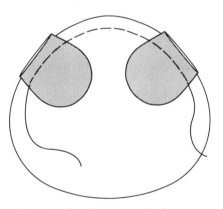

Fig. 6.3 Basting ears to face

5. Pin the two appliqués with rightsides together, sandwiching the ears. Stitch, leaving open between dots (Fig. 6.4). Press stitching line only. Grade seam, clip

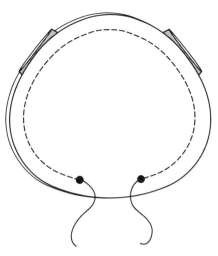

Fig. 6.4 Stitching face

curves. Turn to rightside and press the edges, turning under the opening's raw edges. Baste the opening closed.

6. Using a satin stitch (Fig. 2.39 on page 25) and one strand of black floss, hand embroider the eyes and nose. If the embroidery's edges turn out uneven, backstitch (Fig. 2.26 on page 22) the outlines of each shape. Backstitch the mouth.

Using a single strand of white floss, embroider the eye highlights and the whites of the eyes.

7. Remove the temporary pen lines with water; let dry. To set the black marker, cover the appliqué with a press cloth and press for five seconds with an iron set to "cotton."

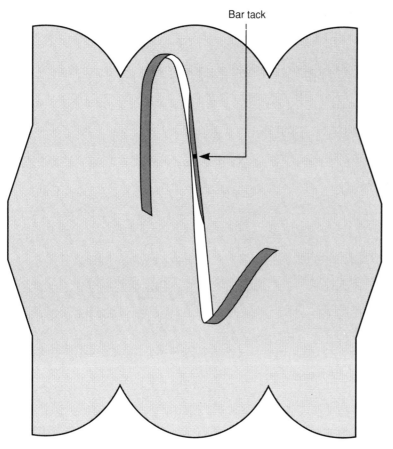

Fig. 6.5 Bar tacking ribbon

8. Fold the middle section of the grosgrain ribbon in half lengthwise and bar tack its center to the Mitt at the square mark (single thickness). See Fig. 6.5.

9. Pin the appliqué to a single thickness of the Mitt following the pattern placement. The appliqué should cover the ribbon's bar tack, with both ribbon ends extending at the bear's neck (Fig. 6.6). Back with a stabilizer and apply by machine with either straight edgestitching or

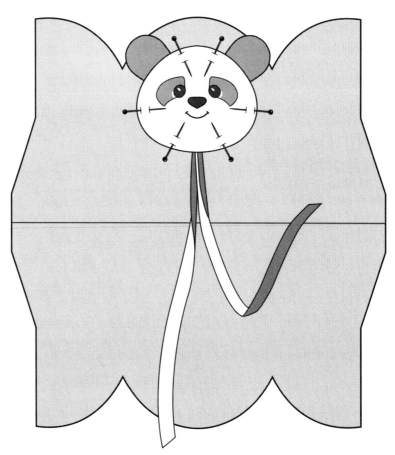

Fig. 6.6 Appliquéing face to mitten

one of your machine's decorative stitches (like a blanket stitch, Fig. 6.7). Stitch over the base of the ears, but leave the rest of the ears free. Remove stabilizer.

Fig. 6.7 In addition to trying various decorative stitches like the blanket stitch shown here, experiment with specialized presser feet. I found my bulky overlock foot best controlled the thick appliqué because the bottom of the foot is designed for uneven layers.

10. Tie the ribbon in a bow. Trim the excess ribbon at an angle. Bar tack the bow on both sides of its knot to prevent untying (Fig. 6.8).

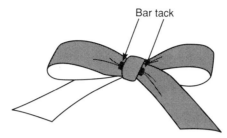

Fig. 6.8 Bar tacking bow's knot

Sewing Directions

11. Cut a piece of clear elastic 3-1/2" long. Apply the elastic to the Mitt's wrongside, just below the fold line. Start the first end of the elastic 1" from the fabric's edge (Fig. 6.9). Using a wide serpentine or multi-zigzag, stitch for 1/2" without stretching the elastic. Stop with the needle down. Next, stretch the elastic until the other end is 1/2" inside the opposite edge. Keeping the elastic taut, stitch to the elastic's end. (The presser foot will prevent the final 1/2" of elastic from stretching.)

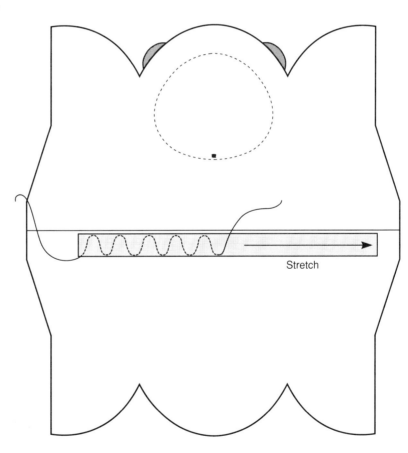

Fig. 6.9 Applying elastic with a serpentine stitch

12. Trim the loop fastener tape to measure 1-1/2" x 1/2". Working on the fabric's rightside, zigzag the loop tape, overlapping one of the elastic ends (choose the one with the least gathers). Have one long edge aligned below the fold line and 3/8" inside the Mitt's raw edge (Fig. 6.10).

13. Trim the hook fastener tape to measure 1" x 1/2". Zigzag the hook tape to the fabric's rightside with one long edge placed above the fold line and 3/8" inside the raw edge, opposite the end with the loop tape.

14. Fold the Mitt along the fold line, rightsides together. Stitch each center back below its dot (Fig. 6.11). Clip the seam allowances to the dots. Trim seams and corners. Turn to rightside and press. Topstitch 1/2" from the fold line, stretching the elastic (Fig. 6.12).

The distance between the two fastener tapes should measure about 2-1/2". If your elastic is longer, and you need to tighten it for a baby with a tiny wrist, simply run a couple of strands of elastic thread through the casing.

15. Working from the wrongside, carefully snip a 1-1/4" vertical slit in the Mitt fabric (one layer) underneath the appliqué

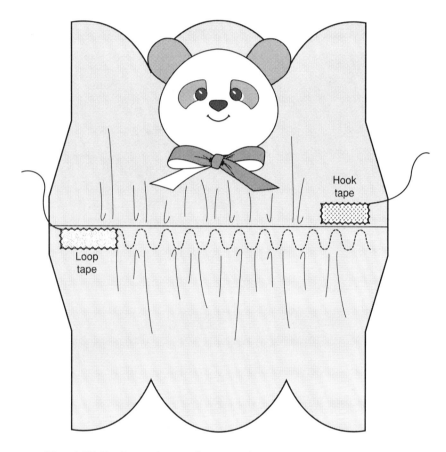

Fig. 6.10 Fastener tape placements

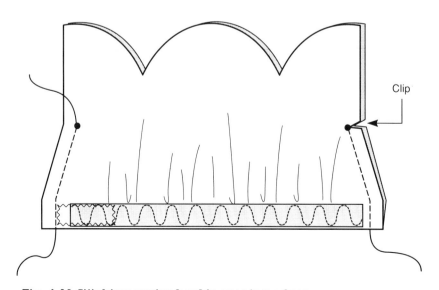

Fig. 6.11 Stitching center back's opening edges

Fig. 6.12 Stitching elastic casing

(Fig. 6.13). Nudge the rattle through the slash. Draw the cut fabric edges together and close by hand with a catchstitch (Fig. 2.31 on page 23).

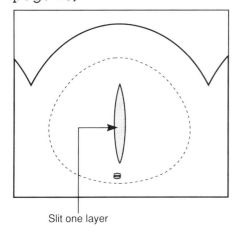

Slit one layer

Fig. 6.13 Vertical slit for rattle

16. To keep the ears out of the way, fold them over the face and hand baste (Fig. 6.14).

17. With rightsides together, pin the center back seam; stitch above the dot through four thicknesses (Fig. 6.15). To reduce bulk, trim the middle two fabric layers next to the stitching. Finish the seam allowances by zigzagging the remaining raw edges together, trapping the trimmed ones inside.

Fig. 6.14 Basting ears down over face

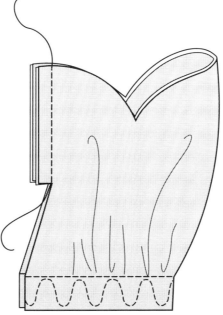

Fig. 6.15 Seaming before trimming and zigzagging center back seam

18. With rightsides together, match the center back seam to the center front notch. Using a zipper foot, seam from one dot, around the top curve, to the other dot (Fig. 6.16). Trim and zigzag the seam allowances.

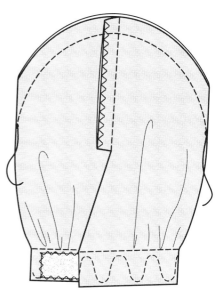

Fig. 6.16 Seaming top of mitten

19. Turn to rightside. Remove basting threads. If desired, coat the ribbon's ends with a nontoxic glue to prevent raveling.

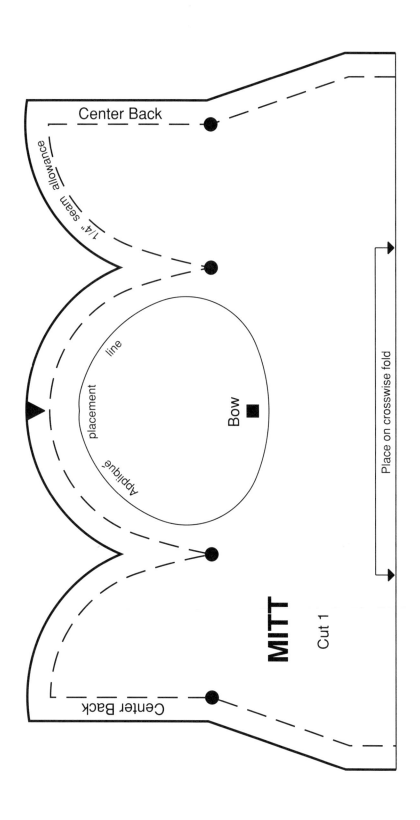

Center Back

1/4" seam allowance

placement line

Appliqué

Bow ■

MITT

Cut 1

Place on crosswise fold

Center Back

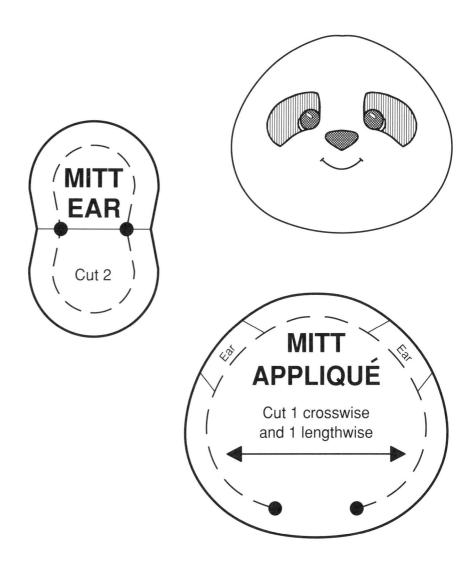

MITT
EAR

Cut 2

MITT
APPLIQUÉ

Ear

Ear

Cut 1 crosswise
and 1 lengthwise

CRIB PALS
PLAY GUIDE *a few suggestions to help you gain the most from this toy*

Age Range

All ages, especially 3 to 7 months, for the rattles. Birth to 5 months for the crib support. Ideal range for batting and kicking is 3 to 5 months.

Skills Development

The newborn will enjoy looking at the Crib Pals as a change of pace from his mobile. Many items can be dangled for his visual entertainment. But by 3 months, he can do more than just watch.

The Crib Pals aid in the development of *eye-hand coordination*, the connection between seeing an object and the ability to reach for it and pick it up. This seemingly simple skill involves complex processes and much trial and error. Batting and swiping at suspended objects helps refine the movement. Sound and motion reward a successful hit and create excitement.

By the fourth month, most babies can reach for and *grasp* an object. At that point they will start to manipulate Squiggles, Wiggles, and Giggles (the bear rattles) and will pay close attention to tiny details like the eyes, noses, and ears.

By age 7 to 9 months, a baby can practice passing a single bear rattle from one hand to the other. At 10 months, he's ready to hold a bear in each hand.

Play Suggestions

To help a 2-month-old focus on a moving object, use one bear rattle at a time.

With the baby on his back, move the rattle slowly, keeping it about 12" from his eyes. Start with small, steady movements, allowing the baby to easily follow the bear by moving just his eyes. Gradually increase the movement, which will require him to move his head (but keep the speed slow). Eventually, he will *track* the bear from one side to the other.

Also at 8 to 10 weeks, many different rattles, teethers, and lightweight toys can be dangled from the foam crib support. Wrap the support's extensions around the slats and fasten them outside the crib. Snap on a toy without rattling it so that your baby can cause the first sounds himself.

To start, place the items just a few inches above the baby's fists so that he'll bat the toys easily. (To change the height, you can change the location of the support, adjust the height of the mattress, or add plastic toy links between the toys and the support's snap tape.)

Switch items often to avoid boredom. Safe household gadgets like napkin rings, one-piece bracelets, or a set of measuring spoons will also attract attention. Attach items with inexpensive plastic toy links or shower-curtain rings (which are toys in themselves). Babies in this stage especially like mirrors, and a suspended, unbreakable toy mirror (4" to 5") will captivate him.

Once the baby is used to the crib support, move the support so that he can kick the rattles with his feet. This introduces an entirely new learning process for a different set of muscles—and it's great exercise.

The individual bears can also be attached to car seats, walkers, etc., using plastic toy links.

Safety Considerations

Five months is the top age for the crib support. You should remove it *before* the child can push up on hands and knees. Do not use the crib support for a baby over 5 months because he could use it as a step to climb out of the crib.

Many materials, including untreated cotton, are not fire-retardant. Therefore, remove crib toys when the baby sleeps.

When substituting household items on the crib support, make certain they are unbreakable and can't separate into small parts. For example, some measuring spoons come on a detachable ring that would pose a choking threat.

Check the stuffed bear rattles periodically to assure that the eyes and noses are still firmly attached and the fabric has not worn through, exposing the lock washers.

Care Instructions

Remove the foam before washing the crib support. Hand wash the crib support and the bears in lukewarm water with mild soap. Rinse thoroughly, blot between terry towels, and air dry.

This toy is from the book **Soft Toys for Babies** *in Judi Maddigan's* **Stitch & Enrich** *series.*

CHAPTER 7

CRIB PALS

Up to 5 months, your baby needs:

- Targets for batting and kicking
- Stable, not mobile, toys
- Practice in grasping

This toy provides:

- Rattles that reward a successful hit with delightful sounds
- A foam crib support with interchangeable toys
- Three easy-to-hold bears

What happens when you dangle the Crib Pals within your baby's reach? At first, he squirms and knocks it by accident. *Oops, what's this?* He gets excited, and in his wiggling he swats it again. It bounces and dances, with merry, jingling sounds. *Oh boy!* The more he moves, the more noise it makes, and the more excited he gets, the more it moves . . . *What fun!*

Your baby gains control over something in his environment, something apart from himself. Up to now, when you propped something in front of him, he reacted. Now, he alone *causes* something to happen.

Three friendly bears, Squiggles, Wiggles, and Giggles, help him along. They're perfect for a baby's first reaching and touching because they're soft, safe, adorable, and wonderfully noisy. The panda, teddy, and koala have floppy paws with jingle bells inside ping-pong balls to create almost musical clatter.

To attach the bears to your baby's crib, use the foam supporting arm. It grabs the slats with special gripper fabric that will not mar furniture. The support detaches quickly.

Old-style crib gyms posed the hazard of a baby pulling himself up and hooking his chin over a cord, bar, or ribbon strung across the crib. This could cut off his air supply. The foam crib support is a safe alternative because it does not suspend anything across the crib.

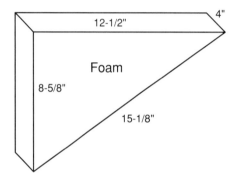

Fig. 7.2 Dimensions for cutting foam triangle

Foam Crib Support Materials

See color pages. The directions assume you have read Chapters 1 and 2. Also check the HelpLine on page 22 when needed.

- 4"-thick, high-density foam cut to the dimensions shown in Fig. 7.2
- 5/8 yd prequilted fabric
- 11" x 14" non-slip fabric (Jiffy Grip) as used in children's pajama feet (see Suppliers on page 174)
- 6" x 12" robe velour for appliqué
- 18" zipper
- 9" of 100% cotton snap tape with plastic snaps (Dritz)
- Two 3/4" "D" rings
- 1/4 yd hook and loop fastener tape (Velcro), 3/4" wide
- Caution label (Fig. 4.3 on page 34)
- Extra-fine machine-embroidery thread
- Black embroidery floss
- 2 pair 4.5mm black safety eyes (optional) with locking washers
- 1/2 yd ribbon, 1/4" wide
- Stabilizer (Stitch-n-Tear)
- Fusible web (Wonder-Under), optional
- Double-sided transparent tape (Wash-A-Way Wonder Tape)

Cutting Directions

From the gripper fabric, cut one rectangle and four straps following Fig. 7.3.

From the prequilted fabric, cut two triangles and three rectangles following the dimensions in Fig. 7.4. Cut the triangles mirror images of each other.

Mark the points of the triangles as shown in Fig. 7.5. Also mark dots 5/8" inside the corners of all rectangles (other than the straps).

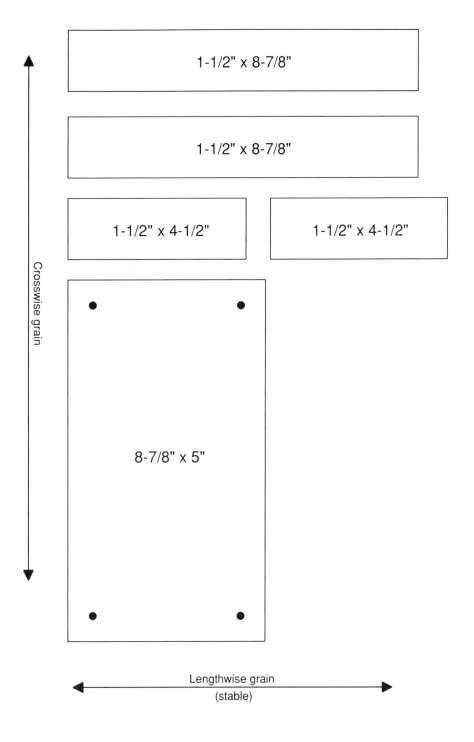

Fig. 7.3 Dimensions for cutting gripper fabric

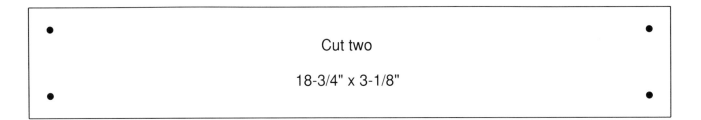

Cut two

18-3/4" x 3-1/8"

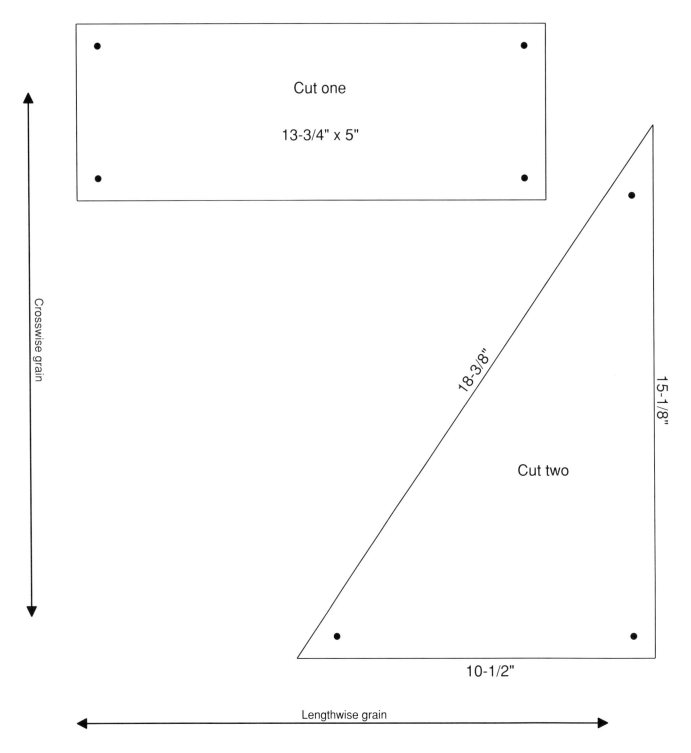

Cut one

13-3/4" x 5"

Crosswise grain

18-3/8"

15-1/8"

Cut two

10-1/2"

Lengthwise grain

Fig. 7.4 Dimensions for cutting prequilted fabric

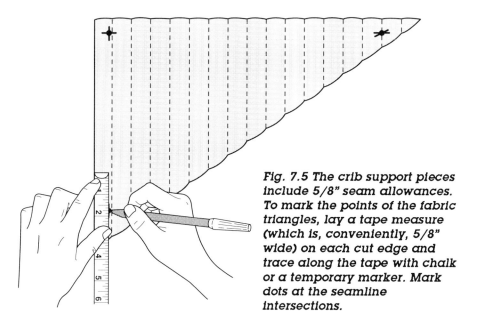

Fig. 7.5 The crib support pieces include 5/8" seam allowances. To mark the points of the fabric triangles, lay a tape measure (which is, conveniently, 5/8" wide) on each cut edge and trace along the tape with chalk or a temporary marker. Mark dots at the seamline intersections.

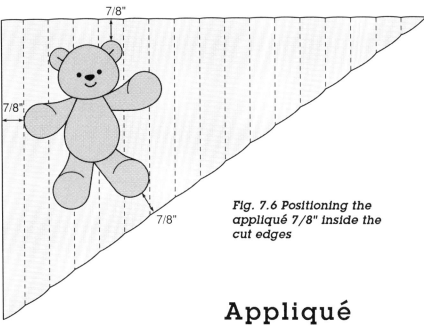

7/8"

7/8"

7/8"

Fig. 7.6 Positioning the appliqué 7/8" inside the cut edges

Appliqué

Cut two bears from robe velour (see page 103). Make one a mirror image. Machine appliqué a bear on each triangle using Wonder-Under or one of the other techniques in Chapter 2, page 13. Position an appliqué on the rightside of each triangle, 7/8" inside the cut edges (Fig. 7.6). The two bears will be mirror images of each other. Each bear's raised arm should point toward the triangle's tip.

I fused my appliqué first, then drew the inner lines with a fabric marker. If I had drawn the details first, the iron would have set the marker.

Satin stitch in the following order: inner ear lines, outer ears, arms, legs, body, and head.

Optional: Remove the quilting lines covered by the appliqué, making it puffier. Working from the wrongside, rip the quilting stitches inside the bear's satin-stitched outline.

Hand embroider the mouths with a backstitch and the noses with a satin stitch.

Check the HelpLine on page 22 for embroidery stitches.

Install the safety eyes following Chapter 2's instructions on page 12, or embroider the eyes.

Cut the ribbon in half. Tie two bows and trim the ends at an angle. Secure a ribbon just below each bear's neck with a bar tack on both sides of the bow's knot (see Fig. 6.8 on page 81).

Sewing Directions

Straps

1. For each strap, center a strip of double-sided tape lengthwise on the gripper fabric's wrongside. Fold the cut lengthwise edges to the middle, sticking them to the tape (Fig. 7.7).

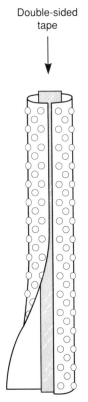

Double-sided tape

Fig. 7.7 Folding straps with double-sided tape

2. Thread a short strap through the curved side of a "D" ring. Fold the strap in half, with the taped edges toward the inside. Using a zipper foot, topstitch as shown in Fig. 7.8. Repeat for the other short strap.

When sewing non-slip fabric by machine, place stabilizer against the fabric's right-side. To stitch two fabric layers wrongsides together, use stabilizer both on top and underneath. Otherwise, the fabric will grab the presser foot and the sole plate.

3. For the longer strap, match a 4"-length of hook

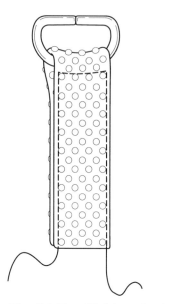

Fig. 7.8 Topstitching short strap with "D" ring

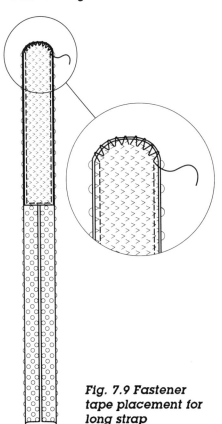

Fig. 7.9 Fastener tape placement for long strap

tape to one end of the gripper fabric, with the wrongside of the tape toward the inside of the strap. Round the corners by trimming as in Fig. 7.9.

Topstitch along three sides; zigzag around the curved end.

4. Position a 4-1/4" length of loop tape next to the hook tape, leaving the strap's last 5/8" free. Topstitch along four sides.

5. Repeat steps 3 and 4 for the second long strap.

6. With rightsides together, center the Caution label on the bottom end of the gripper rectangle, 3/8" inside the cut edge. Zigzag along the label's top edge (Fig. 7.10).

Fig. 7.10 Zigzagging label to gripper rectangle

Fig. 7.11 Snap tape's flat-fell seam and narrow hem

Snap Tape and Zipper

8. Separate the snap tape. Leaving the maximum amount of tape possible at each end, cut a piece of the male tape with two snaps and a piece of the female tape with four snaps. With the non-working sides facing each other, join a male and female tape with a flat-fell seam (using a 1/2" seam allowance). See Fig. 7.11. Hem the free end of the male tape by turning up 1/4" twice and topstitching.

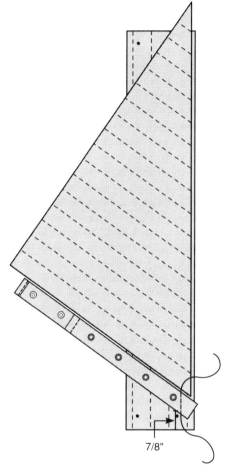

7/8"

Fig. 7.12 Positioning the snap tape by using the triangle's angle

7. Fold the bottom end of the rectangle under 5/8". Topstitch 1/4" from the fold, keeping the label free.

9. Pin the other end of the snap tape to the rightside of a 3-1/8"-wide fabric rectangle, 7/8" from a short end. To allow the tape to hang vertically, sew it at an angle. Use the lowest point of the large triangle to gauge the correct angle (Fig. 7.12), then stitch the tape just inside the seamline.

10. Pin the other 3-1/8"-wide rectangle to the first, right-sides together, sandwiching the snap tape. Stitch in a 5/8" seam for 1-3/4". After backstitching, machine baste the remainder of the seam for the zipper.

11. Press seam allowances open. To strengthen the snap tape, topstitch from the rightside, catching one seam allowance and the tape extension, but leaving the tape itself free (Fig. 7.13).

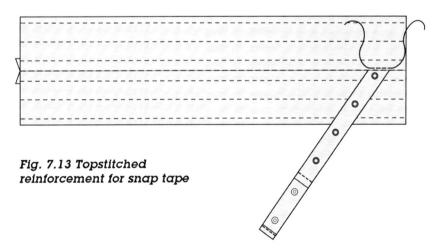

Fig. 7.13 Topstitched reinforcement for snap tape

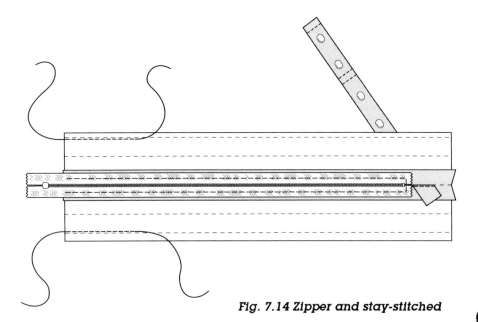

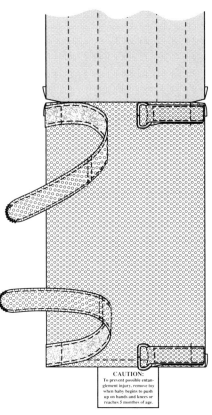

Fig. 7.14 Zipper and stay-stitched

12. Apply the zipper using a centered application. Let the excess zipper tape extend at the top. Reinforce near the top of the zipper with several inches of stay stitching just inside the outer seamlines (Fig. 7.14).

Gusset

13. With rightsides together, seam the short, raw end of the gripper fabric to the 13-3/4"-long quilted rectangle, from dot to dot.

Seam the opposite end of the quilted rectangle to the snap tape's end of the zippered section, stitching from dot to dot (Fig. 7.15). Trim seams; finger press open.

14. Place the straps against the gripper fabric's rightside as shown in Fig. 7.16. Stitch across each strap's end, inside the seamline. Pin the gusset to one triangle, rightsides together. Start with the gripper fabric section.

Fig. 7.16 Positioning straps on gripper fabric

Match the two gusset seams to the top two dots on the triangle. Pin the zippered section up to the third dot. Snip the gusset's seam allowance to the stay

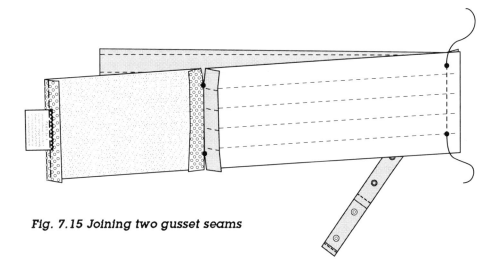

Fig. 7.15 Joining two gusset seams

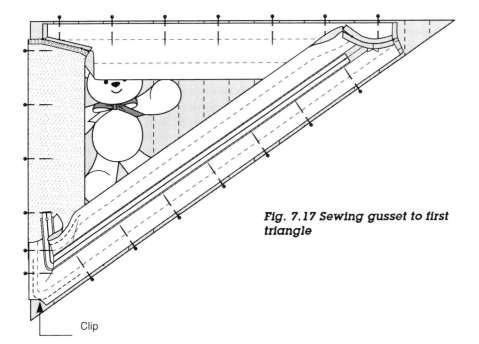

Fig. 7.17 Sewing gusset to first triangle

Clip

stitching at the dot (Fig. 7.17). Overlap the top of the zipper onto the gripper fabric by about 1-5/8". Stitch all around in a 5/8" seam.

15. Unzip the zipper halfway. Seam the second triangle to the other side of the gusset in the same manner as the previous step. Stitch again over the first stitching at each strap. Trim seams and corners. Turn to rightside.

16. Reinforce each strap by topstitching the triangle from the rightside, next to the seamline. Catch the triangle's seam allowance and the strap extension (Fig. 7.18).

17. Insert the triangular foam piece; zip. Poke the appliqué's eye shanks into the foam.

Attach to a crib by threading the long straps through the "D" rings and pressing the fastener tapes together securely. To change the height, lower the mattress, adjust the snap tape, or move the foam support on the bars.

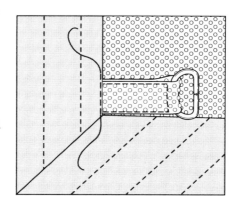

Fig. 7.18 Reinforcing straps with topstitching

Wiggles the Koala Materials

- 1/3 yd 100% polyester (no cotton or acetate content) knit robe velour
- Both normal sewing thread and heavy-duty thread (nylon upholstery, button and carpet, or topstitching thread) to match velour
- White rayon thread No. 40 (Sulky) for optional ear wisps
- Polyester fiberfill
- Four 12mm jingle bells
- 4 table tennis (pingpong) balls
- One 21mm koala nose with safety washer (see Carver's Eye in the Supplier listing on page 174)
- 1 pair 6mm black eyes with safety washers
- 3-1/2" and 5" soft sculpture dollmaking needles; curved needle optional
- Hot glue gun (suggested) or Tacky glue
- Utility knife (a razor-edged blade with a handle; same as a mat knife)
- One of the following tools: vise, C-clamp, vise-grip pliers, or groove-joint pliers (Fig. 7.19)
- Bunka brush (optional; Fig. 7.23 on page 98)

Making the Rattles

1. Find the seam in each pingpong ball. Keeping the seam horizontal, hold the ball steady with pliers.

When the directions refer to "pliers," substitute whatever tool you have chosen from those listed in Materials.

2. Using a mat knife, carefully slice the ball almost halfway open by making an incision perpendicular to the seam (Fig. 7.19). Do not cut through the seam.

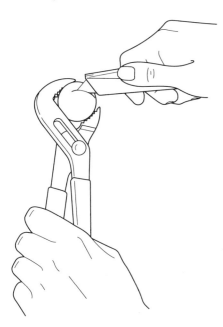

Fig. 7.19 Cutting a pingpong ball resting on a flat surface

3. Squeeze the ball between your thumb and fingers at both ends of the cut. The edges will separate so that you can pop a jingle bell inside.

4. Squeeze the ball with pliers to keep the incision partially open, and run a bead of glue along both cut edges. Press the cut edges together.

For hot glue: Flatten the ridge of glue along the incision using the *side* of the glue gun's heated nozzle. (Do not apply additional glue.)

For Tacky glue: Spread the glue with a tissue or your fingertip so that the glue forms a thin seal along the cut. Clamp edges together two or three hours until the glue sets.

Cutting Directions

Robe velour has a nap, just like corduroy, so orient the patterns' lengthwise grain arrows consistently. When cutting two layers of velour, place wrongsides together.

From the velour, cut two Koala Backs and four Legs. Cut one Koala Front placed on a lengthwise fold. Cut two Arms, each placed on a *crosswise* fold.

Transfer all pattern markings.

Sewing Directions

1. Make the dart in each Leg piece. Trim dart seam allowances and finger press open. Pin two Leg pieces together. Stitch, leaving open between the dots and along the notched edge. Trim seam allowances only where stitched; don't trim the opening's edges. Repeat for second leg. Turn legs to rightside.

2. Stitch and trim the darts in the Arms as for the Legs. Pin the Arms rightsides together. Stitch, leaving openings between the dots on each side. Trim seams where stitched; turn to rightside. The outer arms will turn easily. To turn the center section, insert the blunt end of a pen inside one arm and push it through the middle. Slip a prepared rattle inside each arm and close the openings by hand with heavy-duty thread.

3. For the Front, pin and stitch the center seam from the dart under the nose to the lower edge, pivoting at the neck dot. Stitch again over first stitching for 1/2" above and below the neck. Trim seam; clip to neck dot. Following the instructions in Chapter 2 on page 12, install the eyes and nose. For safety, make the holes for the eyes and nose as small as possible.

4. For the Back, pin and stitch the center back seam, leaving open between large dots. Stitch again over first stitching at the neck. Trim seam allowances only where stitched; clip to neck dot.

5. With rightsides together, pin the back of the head to the face. Stitch from 1/2" below one neck dot, around the head, to 1/2" beyond the other neck dot; pivot around the ears.

6. Pin the Legs to the Front, raw edges even and notches matching. With rightsides together, pin the Back to the Front matching seams and notches and sandwiching Legs. With the Front toward the feed dogs, stitch the side seams from 1/2" above one neck dot around the lower body to 1/2" above the other neck dot (yes, you stitch over previous stitching at beginning and end). Trim entire seam; clip ear curves. Clip seam allowances to the neck dots and ear dots; turn to rightside.

7. Push a small amount of fiberfill into each ear, packing it well up into the ear curves and away from the face. With the front of the head up, topstitch each ear from dot to dot to delineate it from the head.

As a guide, you can mark topstitching lines with a disappearing pen.

Topstitch from the center of each ear for 3/8", ending

perpendicular to the previous stitching line (Fig. 7.20).

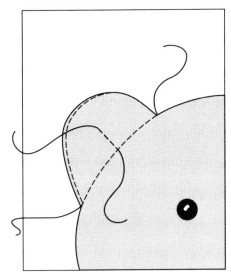

Fig. 7.20 Topstitching for ears

8. Stuff the head and body, referring to the book's photos for both front and profile views. Fill the muzzle and cheek areas firmly, but the overall animal should be soft and squishable. Gently round out the forms, making the lower body pear-shaped. Pack the stuffing evenly and massage the fabric's surface to smooth lumps. Close the body's back opening with a hidden ladder stitch (Fig. 2.33 on page 24). Knot and lose thread ends inside (Fig. 2.35 on page 24).

Fig. 7.21 Profile view of Wiggles the Koala

9. Insert a prepared rattle into each leg. Turn the seam allowances under 1/4". Using heavy-duty thread, slipstitch the leg openings closed.

Ear Wisps

10. Thread the 3-1/2" needle with six 30" strands of rayon thread; double the threads so that your needle has a 15"-length of 12 strands. Form one knotted stitch (Fig. 7.22) in the center of each ear where the topstitching lines intersect. Snip the threads the desired length and fray them (Fig. 7.23). Thin the ends by snipping with just the tips of your scissors, keeping the scissors pointing toward the knot.

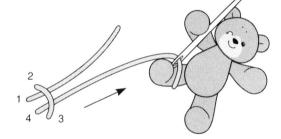

Fig. 7.22 Knot stitch for ear wisps

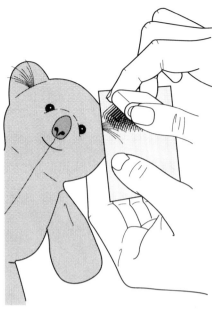

Fig. 7.23 Fray the rayon threads (remove the twists in the thread) by brushing from the knot outward with a wire Bunka brush or by repeatedly stroking with the tip of your 3" needle. Place thin cardboard between the threads and the ear to protect the velour.

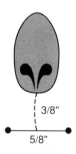

3/8"

5/8"

Fig. 7.24 Placement of the koala's mouth pins

Sculpting the Face

For additional soft sculpting techniques, consult **Learn Bearmaking.**

11. Mark the mouth with a pin at each side. Using a tape measure, find the locations by measuring down from the bottom of the nose and to the left and right of the center dart as in Fig. 7.24. The pins represent points 2 and 3 in Fig. 7.25.

12. Thread the 5" needle with a 48" length of heavy-duty thread (single thickness). Form a large knot 6" from the end.

13. Referring to Fig. 7.25, enter the needle behind the top of the ear at point 1. Take a long stitch through the stuffing and bring the needle out at point 2. Insert the needle at point 3 and come out behind the second ear at point 4. Pull on the thread to begin the mouth sculpting. Insert your needle about 1/8" away from where you emerged, bringing it out at point 3. The shorthand representation for the stitches you've taken so far is: 1 - (2 - 3) - 4 - 3. This

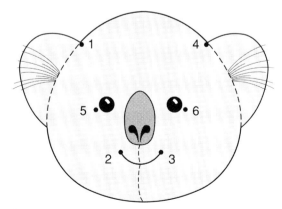

Fig. 7.25 Koala soft sculpture:
1 - (2 - 3) - 4 - 3 - 6 - 3 - 6 - 2 - 5 - 2 - 5 - 2 - 1

stands for "from point 1, to point 2, over to point 3, to point 4, to point 3." (The stitch between points 2 and 3 was long and on the right-side; all other stitches are through the stuffing with only a 1/8" stitch on the surface.)

14. Continue the soft sculpting, following the stitch order listed in Fig. 7.25. (The next step is to take a 1/8" stitch beside your thread at point 3 and emerge at point 6, then take a short stitch and return to point 3.) Mold and shape the fiberfill each time you tighten your thread. As you stitch beside each eye, push that eye down toward the

mouth. The corners of the mouth will turn up automatically in a smile.

15. After completing the sculpting, emerge next to the beginning thread tail. Knot your working thread to the tail and hide both ends inside the head (Fig. 2.35 on page 24).

Attaching the Arms

16. Pin the arms to the body, matching the side seams' square marks. With heavy-duty thread, stitch each arm to the body by hand. Since the koala is flexible, you can bend his head to the opposite side to improve access.

I use a 3-1/2" needle to attach the arms, but if you find that clumsy, switch to a curved needle.

Starting at the top square, stitch through the body and through the arm several times, making loops in the same spot; knot. Flop the arm toward the back and work between the pieces. That way you won't need to stitch through four layers at once. Take a longer stitch (downward) through the body; return with a shorter stitch (upward) through both layers of the arm. When you reach the middle, knot the thread. Progress to the bottom of the arm, anchoring that square the same way as the top one. Knot and lose thread ends inside.

Squiggles the Bear Materials

Squiggles requires the materials listed previously for Wiggles the Koala on page 95 except for the following:

- Substitute a 15mm D-type triangular nose for the koala nose.
- Omit the white rayon thread and Bunka brush.

Make four rattles as for the koala.

Cutting Directions

Follow the cutting directions for Wiggles the Koala, substituting the Bear Front and Bear Back pattern pieces.

Fig. 7.26 Profile view of Squiggles the Bear

1/2"

5/8"

Fig. 7.27 Placement of the bear's and panda's mouth pins

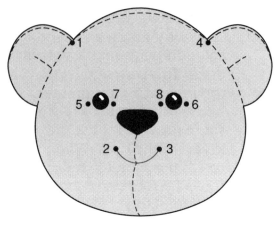

Fig. 7.28 Bear soft sculpture:
1 - (2 - 3) - 4 - 3 - 6 - 3 - 6 - 2 - 5 - 2 - 7 - 8 - 7 - 1

Fig. 7.29 Profile view of Giggles the Panda

Sewing Directions

Assemble Squiggles according to the koala's sewing directions. Omit the ear wisps.

Sculpting the Face

Follow the koala sculpting directions, substituting Figs. 7.27 and 7.28. The bear has extra stitches to draw the eyes closer together.

Finish Squiggles by attaching his arms as for the koala.

Giggles the Panda Materials

Giggles uses most of the materials listed previously for Wiggles the Koala on page 95 with the following exceptions:

- The panda requires 1/4 yd white or cream robe velour and 1/3 yd black velour.

- Exclude the white rayon thread and Bunka brush.

- Instead of the koala nose, substitute one 12mm D-type triangular nose. Choose the type with an 18mm (11/16") metal safety washer because the size of this washer defines the muzzle and affects the expression.

- Add white, 6-strand cotton embroidery floss and a black, *permanent*, felt-tipped marking pen (Sanford's Sharpie).

Make four rattles as for the koala.

Cutting Directions

From the white or cream velour, cut one Panda Front placed on a lengthwise fold. Cut two Panda Backs.

From the black velour, cut four Legs and two Panda Ears. Cut two Arms, each placed on a *crosswise* fold.

Transfer all pattern markings.

Eye Patches

Transfer the nose and eye marks to the fabric's right-side. With the tip of an awl, carefully separate the fabric threads to make holes for the eyes. For safety, keep these holes as small as possible. Place the fabric rightside up on top of scratch paper. Make a paper Eye Patch Template (page 106), snipping out the areas indicated.

Match the template to the fabric, checking the location of all the pattern markings. Using a permanent marker in an up-and-down motion, blacken the eye patches (Fig. 7.30). Fill in the shapes with a series of overlapping dots rather than stroking the pen on the nap. To heat-set the marker, cover the fabric with a press cloth and press for 10 seconds with an iron on "synthetics."

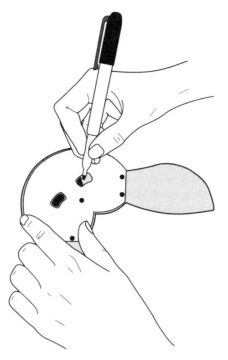

Fig. 7.30 Inking panda eye patches with paper template

Sewing Directions

Work with all the black pieces first to avoid rethreading the machine.

1. Sew the panda's arms and legs as for Wiggles the Koala, steps 1 and 2.

2. With rightsides together, fold each Ear in half on the solid line. Stitch around the raw edges; trim seam and clip curves. Slit each Ear along the fold line from stitching line to stitching line. Turn rightside out.

3. Put a small amount of stuffing into each Ear, keeping the bottom 1/4" empty. Beginning in the center of each Ear, machine

stitch a straight, 5/8" line to the cut edges, backstitching at both ends (Fig. 7.31). Set Ears aside.

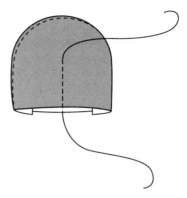

Fig. 7.31 Topstitching lines for the panda's ears

4. Proceed as for the Koala Front and Back, steps 3 and 4. After installing each eye, take two 1/8" straight stitches with two strands of white embroidery floss on each side of the eye where indicated in Fig. 7.32. From the wrongside, guide the needle between the fabric and the washer.

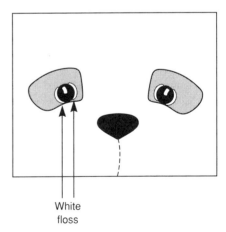

White floss

Fig. 7.32 White straight stitches for eye embroidery

5. Pin the Ears to the right-side of the face where indicated, with raw edges even and tops of Ears extending toward eyes. With rightsides together, pin the back of the head to the face, sandwiching the ears. Stitch from 1/2" below one neck dot, around the head, to 1/2" beyond the other neck dot.

6. Pin the legs to the Front, raw edges even and notches matching. With rightsides together, pin the Back to the Front, matching seams and notches and sandwiching

legs. With the Front toward the feed dogs, stitch the side seams from 1/2" above one neck dot around the lower body to 1/2" above the other neck dot (yes, you stitch over previous stitching at beginning and end). Trim entire seam. Clip seam allowances to the neck dots; turn to rightside.

7. Finish the body and legs as for koala steps 8 and 9.

Sculpting the Face

8. Follow the koala sculpting directions using Fig. 7.27 for the mouth placement. Fig. 7.33 gives the panda's soft-sculpting points and stitching shorthand.

9. Finish Giggles by attaching his arms, as for the koala.

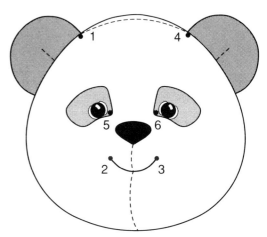

Fig. 7.33 Panda soft sculpture:
1 - (2 - 3) - 4 - 3 - 6 - 3 - 6 - 2 - 5 -
2 - 5 - 6 - 5 - 1

Bow

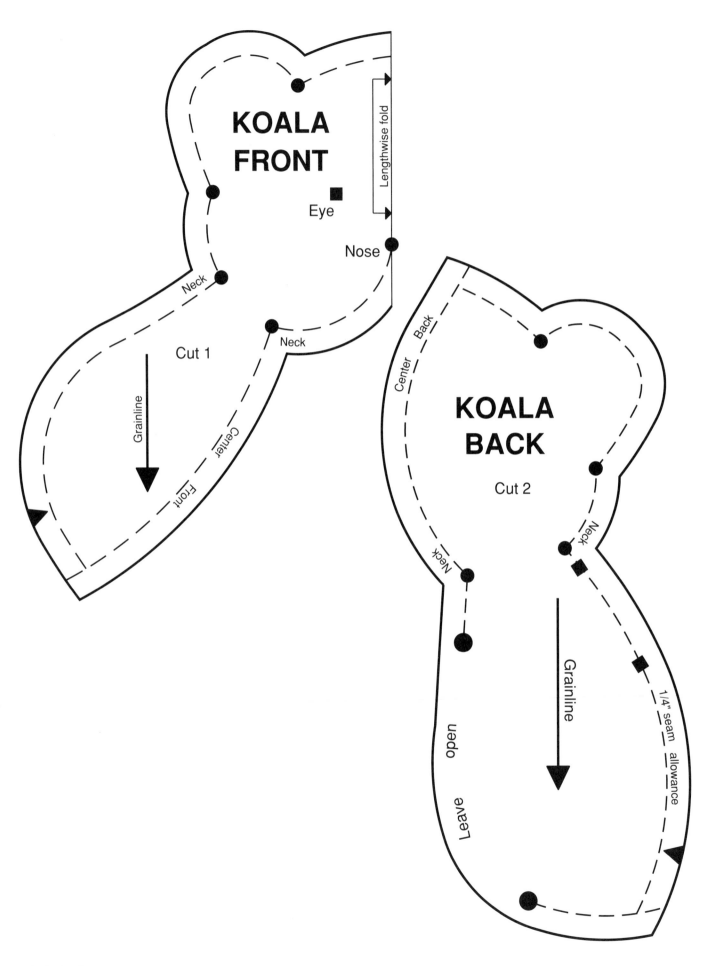

KOALA FRONT

Eye

Nose

Lengthwise fold

Neck

Neck

Cut 1

Grainline

Center Front

KOALA BACK

Center Back

Neck

Cut 2

Neck

Grainline

Leave open

1/4" seam allowance

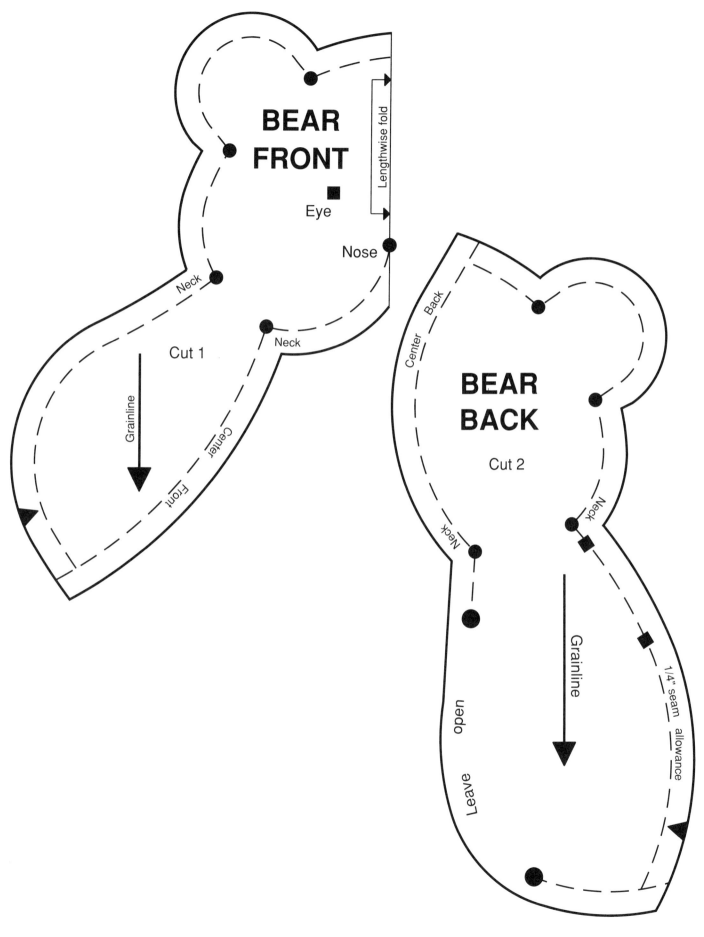

BEAR
FRONT

Eye

Lengthwise fold

Nose

Neck

Cut 1

Neck

Grainline

Center Front

BEAR
BACK

Center Back

Cut 2

Neck

Neck

Grainline

Leave
open

1/4" seam allowance

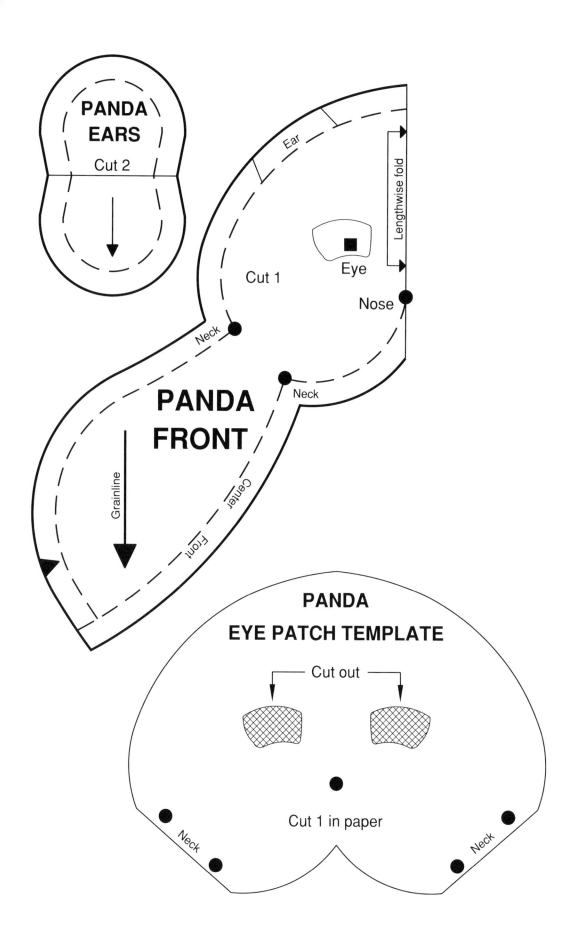

PANDA EARS

Cut 2

Ear

Lengthwise fold

Eye

Nose

Cut 1

Neck

Neck

PANDA FRONT

Grainline

Center Front

PANDA EYE PATCH TEMPLATE

Cut out

Neck

Cut 1 in paper

Neck

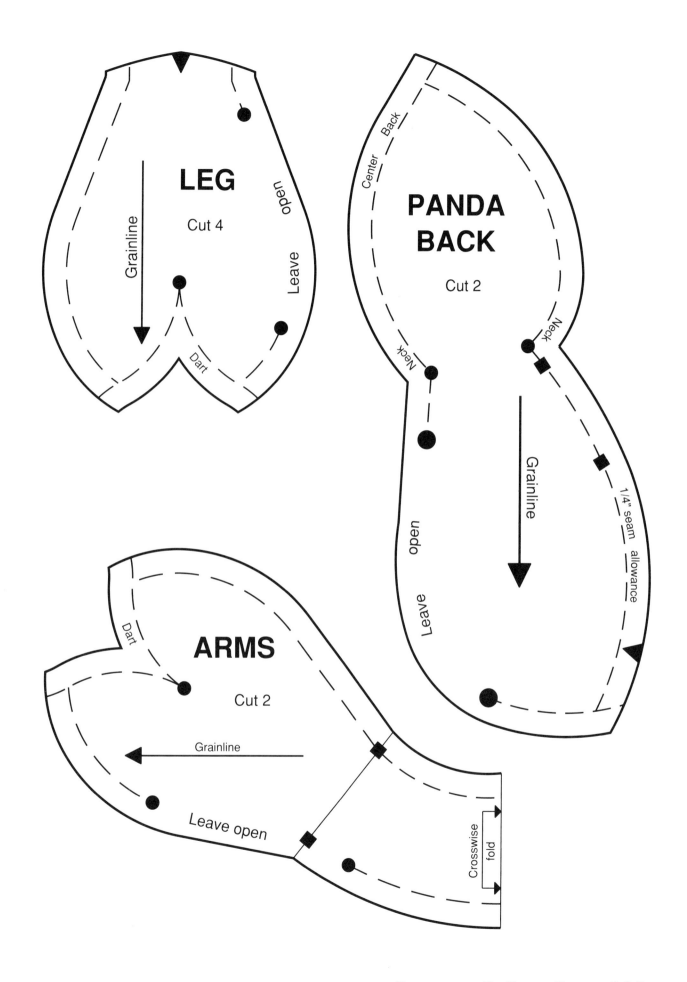

LEG

Cut 4

Grainline

Leave open

Dart

PANDA BACK

Cut 2

Center Back

Neck

Neck

Grainline

1/4" seam allowance

Leave open

ARMS

Cut 2

Dart

Grainline

Leave open

Crosswise fold

TEXTURE PADS
PLAY GUIDE *a few suggestions to help you gain the most from this toy*

Age Range

Birth to 3 years.

Skills Development

Even newborns can pay attention to a particular item in their environment. A Texture Pad offers a visually stimulating choice. By 2 months, a baby would rather look at a face than at anything else. Newborns also like black-and-white patterns, so the panda face wins on both accounts. Looking at the pads aids the newborn's *visual perception*. The colors and details grab his attention. He needs to practice focusing often, especially up to 6 weeks.

Before babies crawl, scoot, or walk, they see more than they can reach. This creates *touch hunger*. The diverse textures in this toy satisfy this craving. With rattles and squeakers in the ears, the pads provide both *auditory and tactile feedback.*

Later, playing peekaboo with the pads teaches *object permanence:* things (and people) still exist even though the child can't see them. By around 10 months, a child learns that the bear faces don't cease to exist when they're hidden. This developmental milestone helps a child gain confidence and security.

For ages 7 to 9 months, the pads fasten together in an open cube, forming a mini tunnel. If you support the tunnel, it's great fun for crawling babies and develops *large motor skills.*

Play Suggestions

For a newborn, place one texture pad inside the crib or cradle, poking the side extensions through the bars. Use a second texture pad on the outside and fasten them together (back-to-back) through the bars. Repeat for the other pair of pads. Place the newborn on the mattress, 8" to 12" away. You can switch the pads often.

Once a baby supports his head (during the third month), place him on his stomach. Put a Texture Pad in front of him so that he can prop himself up on his forearms and study it at close range.

For a baby playing on the floor, the pads will stand on their own. They'll form a cube shape if all four pads are used, or a triangle with three pads. At first, position the bears facing out. After the child sits steadily, he will be able to peek inside and find the bears if they face the interior.

If you store the Texture Pads from age 6 to 9 months, you can reintroduce them as brand new toys (wait until after the initial urge to put everything into the mouth has subsided). Since the 9-month-old is still ready for only one toy at a time, present just one pad a day. Textures fascinate children up to 3 years. Explore the different naps and weaves with your child, and talk about each one (silky, bumpy, fuzzy, prickly, and so on).

Peekaboo games are also important for this age range. Fasten two pads together along one side. Close the pads with rightsides facing each other, and open them to "Peekaboo!"

For toddlers, the freestanding pads make an open container. Encourage the child to fill the entire interior with other toys (or plastic bowls and measuring cups) and then lift the pads. The toys will come tumbling out.

Safety Considerations

When freestanding, the pads will not support the weight of a baby trying to pull himself up to standing. The pads alone are safe for a baby to fall on, but relying on them might knock him into something that isn't (like a piece of furniture). For this reason, don't leave the pads assembled in their freestanding modes during this phase.

Remove the pads from the crib when a baby is unattended. Note that the materials are not fire resistant. In addition, a child could use pads mounted on the crib as a step to climb out.

Check the appliqué stitching periodically and repair if needed. Also check that the ears attach securely and that they completely shield the noisemakers.

Care Instructions

Hand wash the Texture Pads in lukewarm water with mild soap. Rinse thoroughly, blot between terry towels, and dry flat.

*This toy is from the book **Soft Toys for Babies** in Judi Maddigan's **Stitch & Enrich** series.*

CHAPTER 8

T E X T U R E   P A D S

From birth to 3 years, your child needs:

- Stimulating textures
- Learning games
- Multi-purpose toys

This toy provides:

- Varied fabrics appealing to touch
- Fill-and-empty and peekaboo games
- Freestanding shapes, such as a cube, triangle, or tunnel

How does a 9-month-old explore the world? He uses all his senses, as he did before, but he uses them differently. For weeks after birth, his sight prevailed; at 6 months, mouthing and taste. Now the sense of touch takes on new significance.

If you show a 9-month-old a Texture Pad, he becomes quiet and intent. *Hmmm, I don't think I've seen this before.* He stares at the fabrics, peering into the fur or following a satin-stitched line. He doesn't stand back, as someone might view a painting in a museum, to take in the whole picture. He concentrates on minute details. *Nope, I know I've never seen this.*

Almost as fast as he sees, he touches. *Oo-oo-ooh. It's fuzzy!* He compares the feeling to those he has felt previously. *It's new!* He runs his finger-tips through the nap, flexing his fingers, patting and poking.

When he flicks an ear and it makes a noise, he repeats it and then tries the second one. This cause-and-effect overpowers touching, for the moment. If you should hand him a second Texture Pad now, he would head straight for the ears. Over the weeks ahead, though, he'll return again and again to finger-ing the fabrics, building his repertoire of textures.

From birth to 3 years, this toy has numerous uses. Go ahead and introduce the pads to a newborn and use them for the first 6 months, then save them for several months. Reintroduce them at 9 months and start the dis-covery process over again.

Materials

See color pages. The directions assume you have read Chapters 1 and 2. Also check the HelpLine on page 22 when needed.

- 3/8 yd of four different background fabrics. Suggestions: upholstery fabrics, texturized polyester, wool or acrylic tweeds, polished cotton, metallics, vinyl, waterproof nylon, piqué, seersucker, or flocked dot fabrics. Also dotted swiss, nylon net, or eyelet, which require a lining.
- Fusible, all-purpose, woven interfacing (Stacy Shape-Flex) to back flimsy or stretchy fabrics
- 1/4 yd of three appliqué fabrics for bears' faces. Suggestions: no-wale corduroy, robe velour, upholstery velvet, waffle weave cotton (dishcloth), imitation suede, knit suede cloth, woven (not stretch) terry cloth, cotton velve-teen, outerwear fleece, or sweatshirt fleece (wrong-side out).

The Appendix lists suppliers for appropriate furs and upholstery fabrics.

- For the bear face, 1/4 yd short-napped fur; 1/8 yd lighter fur with a slightly shorter nap than the main pile. Look for furs that do not shed.
- 1/8 yd black appliqué fabric for panda
- Small piece of white imitation fur, 1" pile, for koala's ear tufts
- Small pieces of black or dark brown vinyl, leather, imitation suede, velour, or coat wool for noses
- Black glossy vinyl for eyes
- Stabilizer (Stitch-n-Tear)
- Fusible web (Wonder-Under), optional
- 5/8 yd fleece (Pellon Fleece)
- 12" each of four different colors of hook and loop fastener tape (Velcro), 3/4" wide
- Extra-fine cotton machine-embroidery thread in black and colors to match appliqué fabrics
- White fine rayon machine-embroidery thread (Sulky) for eye highlights
- Black pearl cotton No. 3, optional
- 40" of 12" wide x 125 mil thick clear vinyl stripping (Koro Klear) as used for industrial strip doors. Look in the Yellow Pages under Doors or Plastics. You can substitute foam-backed plastic kitchen place mats

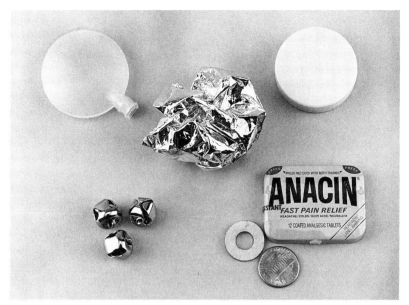

Fig. 8.2 Flat noisemakers, clockwise: 12mm jingle bells, flat squeaker, crumpled mylar, Hide-a-Rattle (available from Aardvark Adventures), aspirin tin with pennies

or two layers of plastic canvas, 7 squares per inch (sold with needlework supplies). Pads made with place mats or plastic canvas will not stand as well on their own.

- Utility knife or heavy scissors to cut vinyl stripping
- Choose four noisemakers (Fig. 8.2): six 12mm jingle bells; crumpled mylar; 2 flat squeakers, 1-5/8" or smaller diameter; 2 Hide-a-Rattles (flat plastic rattles, 3/8" thick, 1-1/2" diameter—see page 174); 2 aspirin tins with pennies or 1/4" washers inside.

Check that your noisemaker fits inside the ear pattern with at least 1/2" extra material on all sides (1/4" seam allowance and 1/4" presser foot clearance). If necessary, enlarge the ear pattern to accommodate your noisemaker.

Directions

Prewash all fabrics except interfacing.

Reinforce flimsy or stretch fabrics with fusible interfacing following manufacturer's directions. Cut two 11-1/4" x 14-1/4" rectangles of each background fabric.

A rotary cutter and mat will simplify measuring and cutting the rectangles.

Using heavy scissors or a utility knife and a straight edge, cut four 10" x 11" rectangles of clear vinyl stripping.

Refer to Chapter 2's explanation of machine appliqué on page 13, following whatever combination of techniques gives the best results. Assemble the four faces following the directions below.

Koala Face

1. Cut one Koala Face, two Koala Ear Fronts, and two Koala Ear Backs from the appliqué fabric. Cut one piece of fleece 1/4" inside the face outline and a second piece 1/2" smaller than the face.

2. Working from the wrong-side, cut two Koala Ear Inserts from the 1" fur, matching the direction of the grainline to the fur's nap. Use just the tips of your scissors to snip only the backing of the fur, not the pile. Trim all pile from the inserts' 1/4" seam allowances.

3. Appliqué the nose to the face. Satin stitch the nose's detail lines, continuing to stitch the mouth lines at the same time. Satin stitch the eyes and eyebrows.

4. With rightsides together, pin the Ear Inserts to the Ear Fronts, matching dots and notches. Push all pile away from the seamline. Stitch (Fig. 8.3).

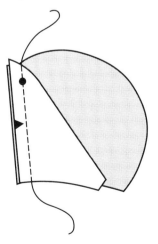

Fig. 8.3 Sewing koala Ear Inserts to Ear Fronts

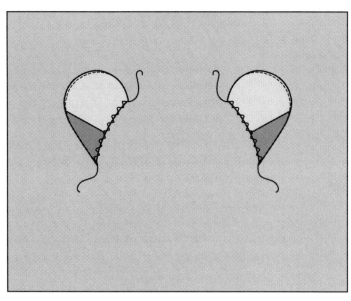

Fig. 8.4 Zigzagging ears to background

5. Pin the Ear Fronts to the Ear Backs, matching dots. Stitch, leaving the bottoms open. Clip curves, turn to rightside. Insert a noise-maker into each ear; baste raw edges together.

6. Center the Koala Face on one layer of the background fabric's rightside. Situate the ears in their proper positions, overlap-ping the face by 1/4". Pin ears only; remove face. Secure with an open zigzag along the ears' raw edges (Fig. 8.4).

7. To pad the face, position the two fleece pieces on the background fabric's right-side with the smaller fleece underneath. Place the face on top, overlapping the ears' raw edges by 1/4"; appliqué.

8. Turn under 1/2" on one short end of each fabric rectangle; press. Trim to 1/4".

9. Pin the two rectangles rightsides together, sand-wiching the face. Stitch in a 1/2" seam on three sides (Fig. 8.5). Trim seams and clip corners. Turn to right-side; press.

10. Topstitch 1" from the closed short side. Apply a 9-3/4" piece of the fastener tape's hook side to the back of the texture pad, centering the tape between the edge and the topstitching (Fig. 8.6).

11. Insert the 10" x 11" vinyl. Match the turned-under edges and edgestitch closed. Topstitch 1" inside this edge, using a zipper foot. Attach the fastener tape's loop side to this front edge (Fig. 8.7).

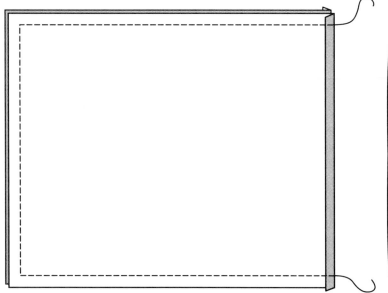

Fig. 8.5 Sewing pad rectangles together

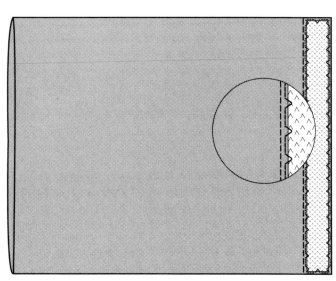

Fig. 8.6 Attaching hook tape to pad's back

Fig. 8.7 Attaching loop tape to pad's front

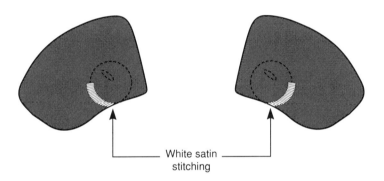

White satin stitching

Fig. 8.8 Whites of the eyes on panda

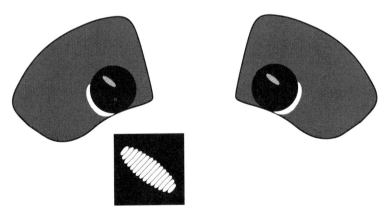

Fig. 8.9 If your machine sews a row of solid ovals, try it for the eye highlights on scraps of your chosen fabrics. Test one pattern repeat using a tight stitch length and a stitch width of 2mm. Otherwise, adjust a regular satin stitch manually from thin to medium to thin again.

Polar Bear Face

12. Cut one Polar Bear Face and four Teddy Bear Ears from the appliqué fabric. Cut one piece of fleece 1/4" inside the face outline and a second piece 1/2" smaller than the face.

13. Satin stitch the mouth lines. Appliqué the nose and eyes. Satin stitch the white eye highlights.

14. Complete the Polar Bear Texture Pad as for the koala, steps 5 through 11.

Panda Face

15. Cut one Panda Face from the light appliqué fabric. From the dark appliqué fabric, cut four Teddy Bear Ears and two eye patches. (Trace the eye patch patterns from the Panda Face.) Cut one piece of fleece 1/4" inside the face outline and a second piece 1/2" smaller than the face.

16. Appliqué the dark eye patches to the face. For the whites of the eyes, make a row of white satin stitches (Fig. 8.8). These stitches can be wider than the pattern because the eyes will cover part of them. If the first pass does not cover the background fabric completely, stitch again.

17. Appliqué the eyes over the white satin stitches, leaving a portion of the white stitches showing. Stitch the eye highlights (Fig. 8.9). Appliqué the nose to the face. Satin stitch the mouth lines.

18. Complete the Panda Texture Pad as for the koala, steps 5 through 11.

Teddy Bear Face

19. Refer to Chapter 2's specific directions for fur appliqué on page 17. Cut one Teddy Bear Face and four Teddy Bear Ears from the main fur with the nap running up. Working from the wrongside, use the tips of your scissors to snip through only the backing of the fur, not the pile. In the lighter color, cut two Teddy Bear Inner Ears with the nap running up and cut one muzzle with the nap running down. (Trace the muzzle pattern from the Teddy Bear Face.) Cut one piece of fleece 1/4" inside the face outline and a second piece 1/2" smaller than the face.

20. Trim all pile from the ears' 1/4" seam allowances. Following page 10's technique, transfer the design lines on the face and muzzle.

Fig. 8.10 Teddy bear's eyes, eyebrows, and eye highlights

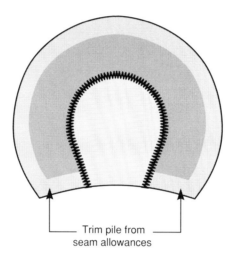

Trim pile from seam allowances

Fig. 8.11 Appliquéing Inner Ear to Teddy Bear Ear

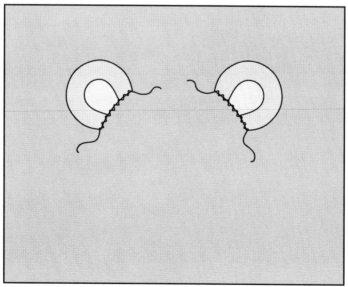

Fig. 8.12 Zigzagging fur ears to background

21. Working on the muzzle only, satin stitch the mouth lines and appliqué the nose. On the face, appliqué the eyes and add the eyebrows and eye highlights (Figs. 8.9 and 8.10).

22. Appliqué the muzzle to the face. Appliqué each inner ear to an ear front (Fig. 8.11). With rightsides together, match an appliquéd ear front to a plain ear back. Pin, tucking all pile to the inside. Stitch the curved outer seam. Repeat for other ear. Turn rightside out.

23. Insert the noisemakers into the ears. Baste the ears to one layer of background fabric along their bottom edges. To reduce bulk, compress the base of each ear by zigzagging along the raw edges (Fig. 8.12).

24. Complete the Teddy Bear Texture Pad as for the koala, steps 7 through 11.

Panda Bib

Any of this chapter's bear faces would make darling bibs—just substitute appropriate colors. If you pick the koala or polar bear, note that their ears are too low; you will need to change to the bib pattern's ear placement.

The directions specify terry cloth. To make this project easier to stitch, you can substitute 100% cotton fabrics. For fabrics other than terry, add three layers of preshrunk diaper flannel between the bib and the lining.

Materials

- 1/2 yd red woven terry velour

Use a nice, thick, woven velour terry cloth, not the lighter-weight stretch terry. If you can't locate a specific color at the fabric shop, investigate washcloths, fingertip towels, or hand towels.

- 1/4 yd white woven terry velour
- 1/8 yd navy woven terry velour

Zigzag or serge the terry cloth's raw edges before preshrinking because they ravel excessively.

- 1/2 yd supple, lightweight outerwear nylon

Outerwear nylon makes a water-resistant lining.

Exploit color here. I backed my bib with vivacious yellow.

- 3/4 yd navy pin dot fabric (100% cotton recommended)
- Remnant of black polished chintz for nose
- Remnant of black shiny vinyl for eyes (or substitute chintz)
- Fusible web (Wonder-Under)
- Stabilizer (Stitch-n-Tear)
- 3" of 1-1/2"-wide red hook and loop fastener tape (Velcro). Substitute 6" of 3/4"-wide tape if you can't find the wider size in red.
- Extra-fine machine-embroidery thread: white, navy, and black
- All-purpose thread: navy, red, and color of lining

Fig. 8.13 Panda Bib

Cutting Directions

Photocopy or trace the Bib pattern pieces on pages 122 and 123. Tape the two sections together where indicated. Placing this single pattern piece on a fold, cut one Bib from red terry and one from the nylon lining. Notice that although the neck extension edges are aligned on the fold, you will cut them apart along the fold at the center back.

Transfer all pattern markings.

Cut two 2-1/2"-wide bias strips from the navy pin dot fabric. Each strip should measure at least 34". Referring to Fig. 5.2 on page 50, seam two short ends together.

Machine Appliqué

Review Chapter 2's explanation of machine appliqué on page 13, paying particular attention to the special terry cloth tips. Treat the smooth, clipped side of the velour as the rightside and the loops as the wrongside.

1. The bib's panda ears are not three-dimensional like the texture pads. You need only two navy terry ears traced from the dashed lines on page 117. Satin stitch the outer edges of the ears to the red terry, but baste the ears' bottom edges, which will be under the face.

2. Appliqué the navy terry eye patches to the white face. For the whites of the eyes, make a row of white satin stitches. These stitches can be wider than the pattern because the eyes will cover part of them.

3. Appliqué two circles of black for the eyes. Highlight the eyes with a satin-stitched oval (Fig. 8.9 on page 113). Appliqué the black chintz nose. Satin stitch the smile lines in black.

4. Appliqué the completed face to the red terry, overlapping the ears by 1/4".

Attaching the Fastener Tape

5. Match the bib's lining to the red terry, wrongsides together. Run a fat zigzag around all raw edges.

6. Following Fig. 2.18's technique on page 16, top-stitch with navy thread around the outer edge of the white appliquéd face.

7. *Skip this step for tape that already measures 1-1/2".*

If you have 3/4" fastener tape, cut each length into two 3" pieces. Place the two loop sections side by side on a tear-away stabilizer and stitch them together with a medium zigzag, width about 2.5mm, length 2 – 2.5mm (10 – 12spi). See Fig. 8.14. Repeat for the hook sections.

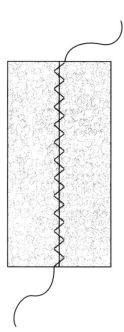

Fig. 8.14 Zigzagging thin fastener tapes together for a wider piece

8. *Position the fastener tape with the hooks up on the bib's rightside. This keeps the rough side away from baby's neck and prevents skin irritation.*

Place the 1-1/2" x 3" hook tape on the rightside of the red terry at the back opening, overlapping the binding stitching lines. Trim one short end to match the angle indicated on the pattern. Thread the machine needle with red and match the bobbin to the lining. Zigzag along the line labeled "hook tape." Baste the tape's remaining three sides along the bib's 3/8" seamlines.

9. Put the 1-1/2" x 3" loop tape on the opposite back edge, with its wrongside *against the nylon lining.* Trim one end to match the line indicated on the pattern. Switch the bobbin thread to red. Zigzag along the line labeled "loop tape." Baste the tape's remaining three sides.

10. Trim both fastener tapes close to the basting stitches.

Binding the Bib

11. With rightsides out, fold the bias binding in half lengthwise and press.

12. Beginning on the outer edge a couple of inches from the center back, pin the binding to the red terry. Keep all raw edges even. Stretch the binding along the neckline; ease binding along the outer arcs. Miter the center back corners at the dots. (See Figs. 5.12 and 5.13 on page 57.) Stitch a 3/8" seam all the way around the bib, ending as shown in Fig. 5.11 on page 57.

13. Turn the binding's folded edge to the bib's lined side, encasing the raw edges. Pin the binding's folded edge to the seam on the bib's lining, folding 45° angles for mitered corners. Slipstitch the binding's folded edge to the lining. Also hand stitch the corner folds and the beginning/ending splice.

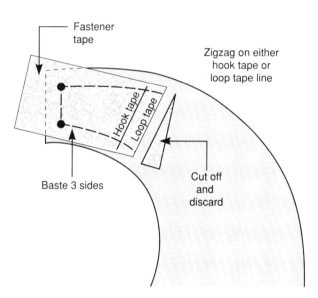

Fig. 8.15 Placement of fastener tape at back neck closure

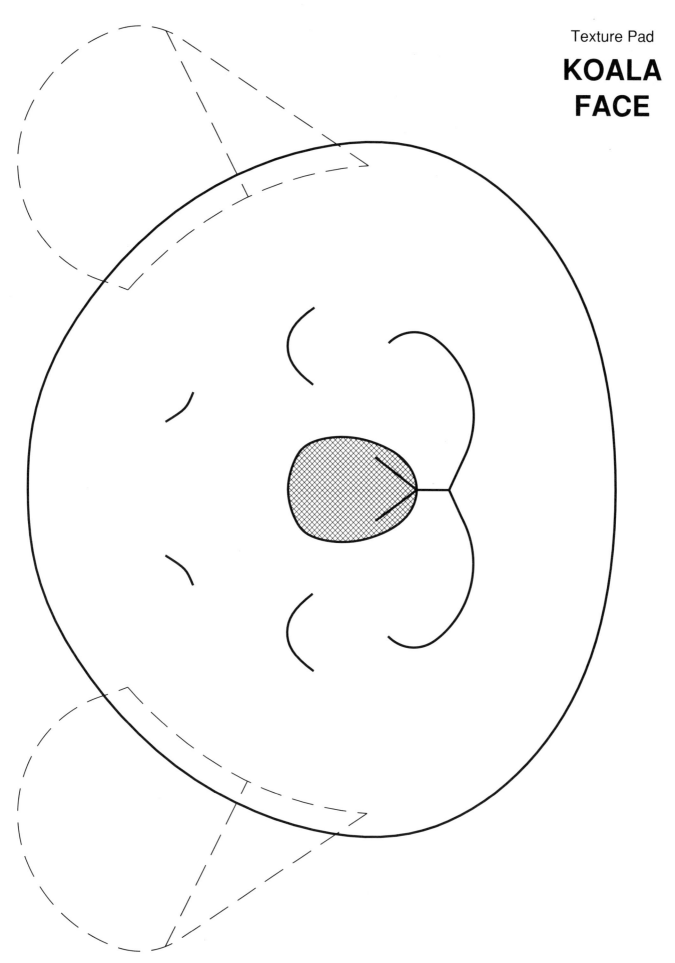

Texture Pad

KOALA
FACE

118 SOFT TOYS FOR BABIES

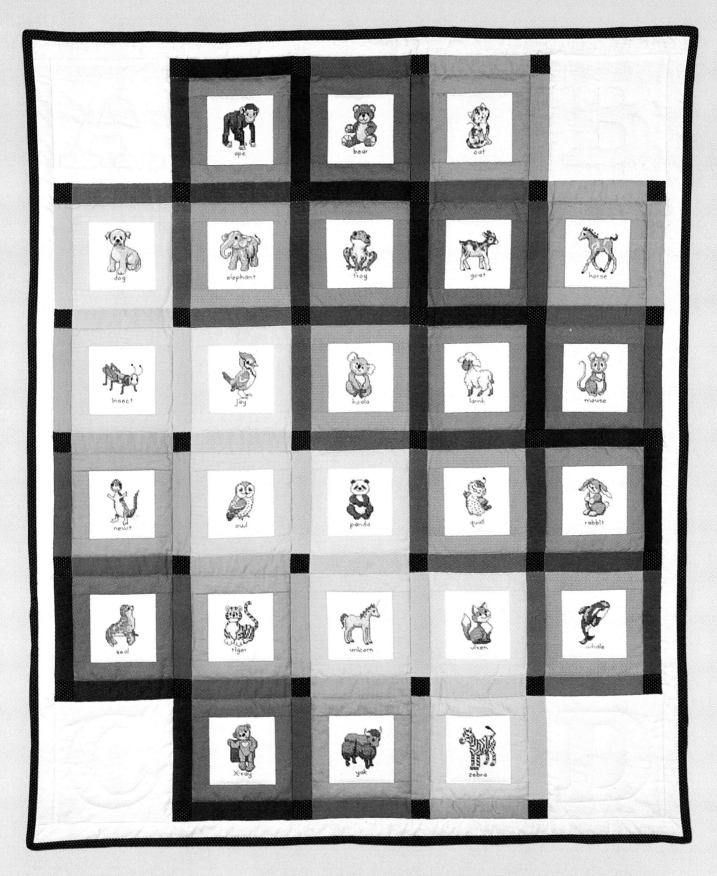

You and your baby will enjoy Chapter 5's AlphaPet Quilt for years. Combining counted cross stitch with quilting, it offers visual stimulation, as well as endless games that teach letters, numbers, colors, and animals.

The bright colors and soft sounds of Chapter 4's Rainbow Cubs Mobile fascinates 2-1/2-month-old Vikramjit Kohli. The Cubs are interchangeable with geometric disks or mylar crinkles.

Hide-and-seek is the classic baby game. In Chapter 10's Peek-a-Pocket, 14-month-old Tara Harrison discovers the eight bear faces playing peekaboo in pockets and doors. A variety of fabrics, textures, and surface embroidery make this an heirloom toy that will last for years.

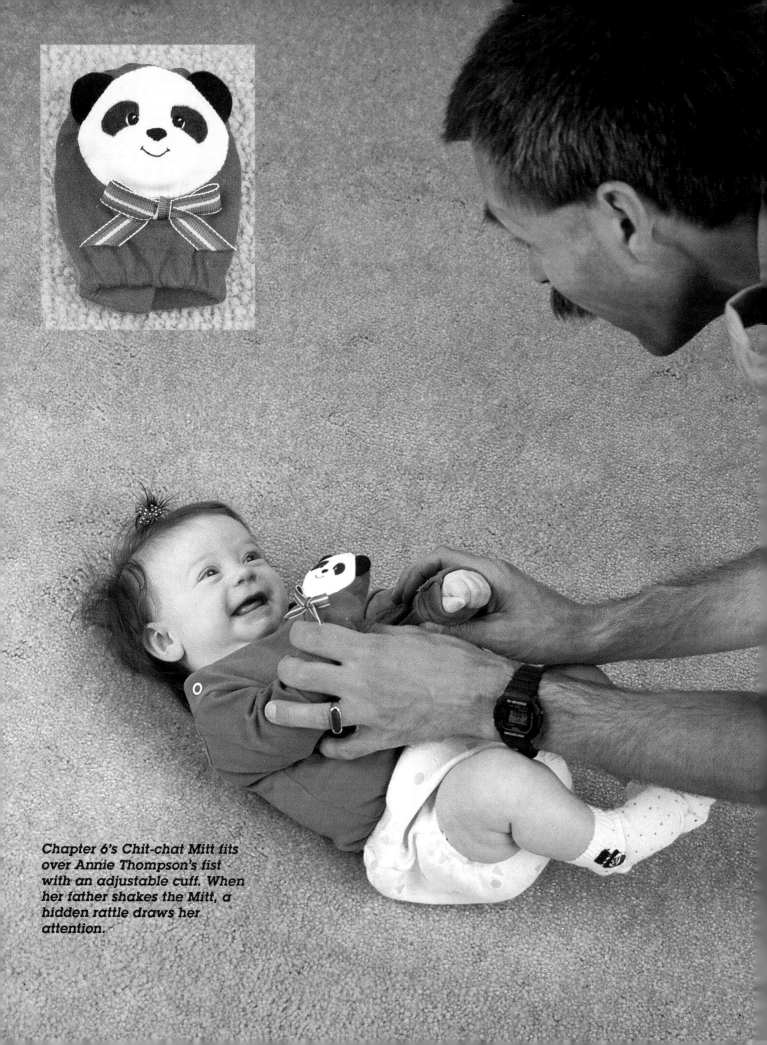

Chapter 6's Chit-chat Mitt fits over Annie Thompson's fist with an adjustable cuff. When her father shakes the Mitt, a hidden rattle draws her attention.

Four-month-old Sean Pacheco is just beginning to reach for one of the three Crib Pals in Chapter 7, Squiggles. Hidden in the legs are jingle bells inside pingpong balls, rewarding a hit with a delightful sound.

Each of the four Texture Pads in Chapter 8 has a different texture and sound. Taylor and Sean Sieling at 8-1/2 months are exploring them flat, but an inner stiffness allows the Pads to stand up in a cube. Their uses as toys are open-ended.

The Teethe-n-Clutch in Chapter 9 allows 11-month-old Hana Raftery to easily grasp it without hurting herself if she falls on it as she learns to walk. Smaller babies can teethe on the strong corded edges.

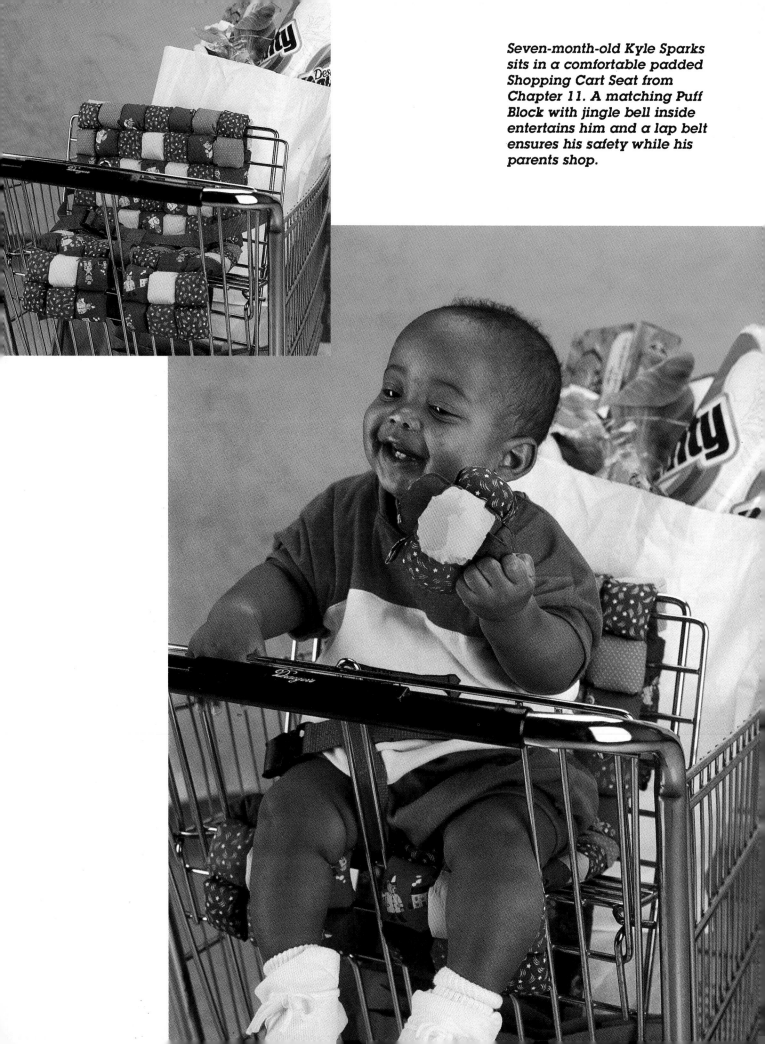

Seven-month-old Kyle Sparks sits in a comfortable padded Shopping Cart Seat from Chapter 11. A matching Puff Block with jingle bell inside entertains him and a lap belt ensures his safety while his parents shop.

POLAR BEAR FACE

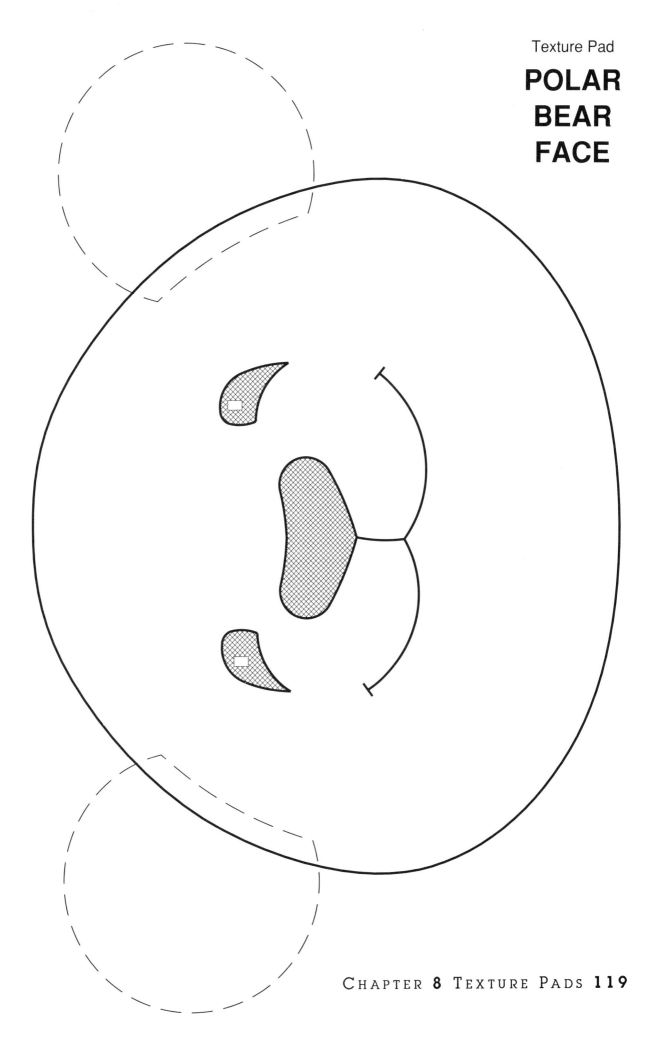

PANDA
FACE

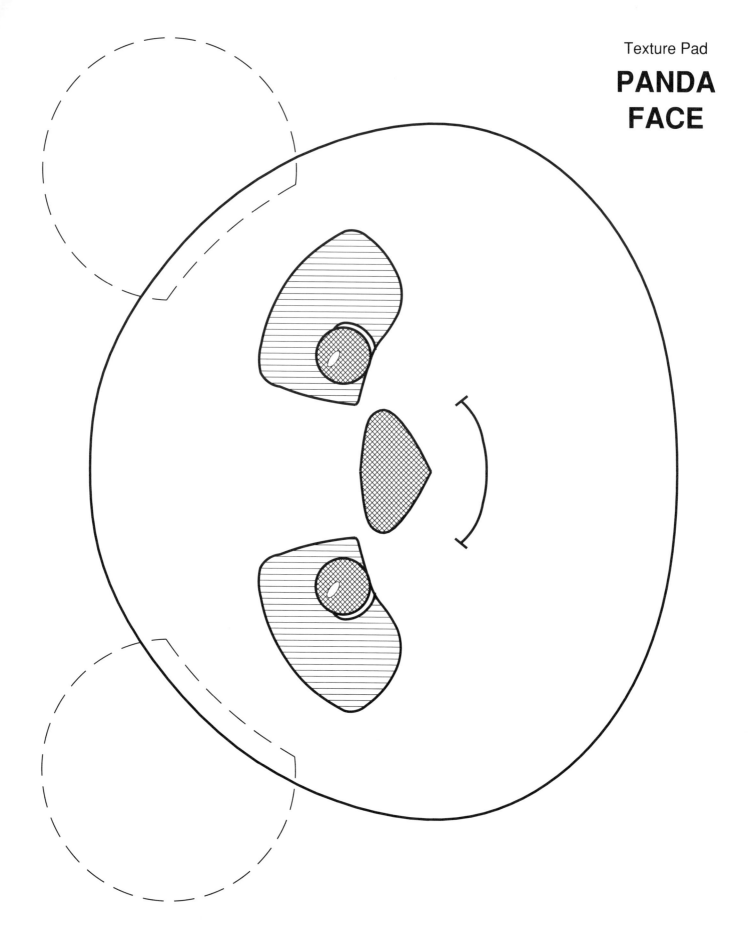

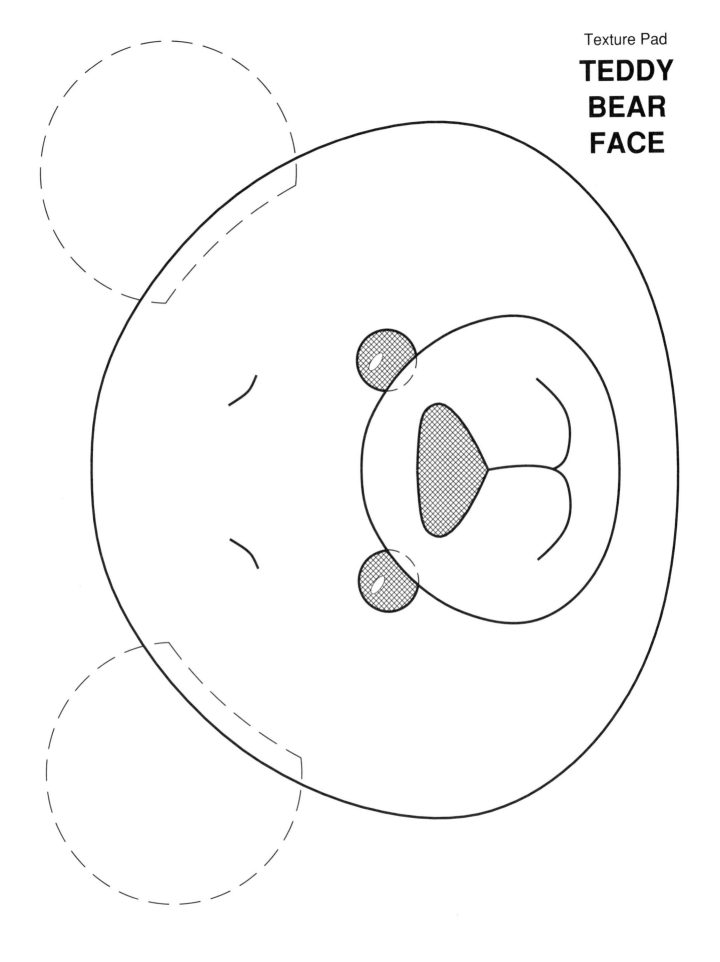

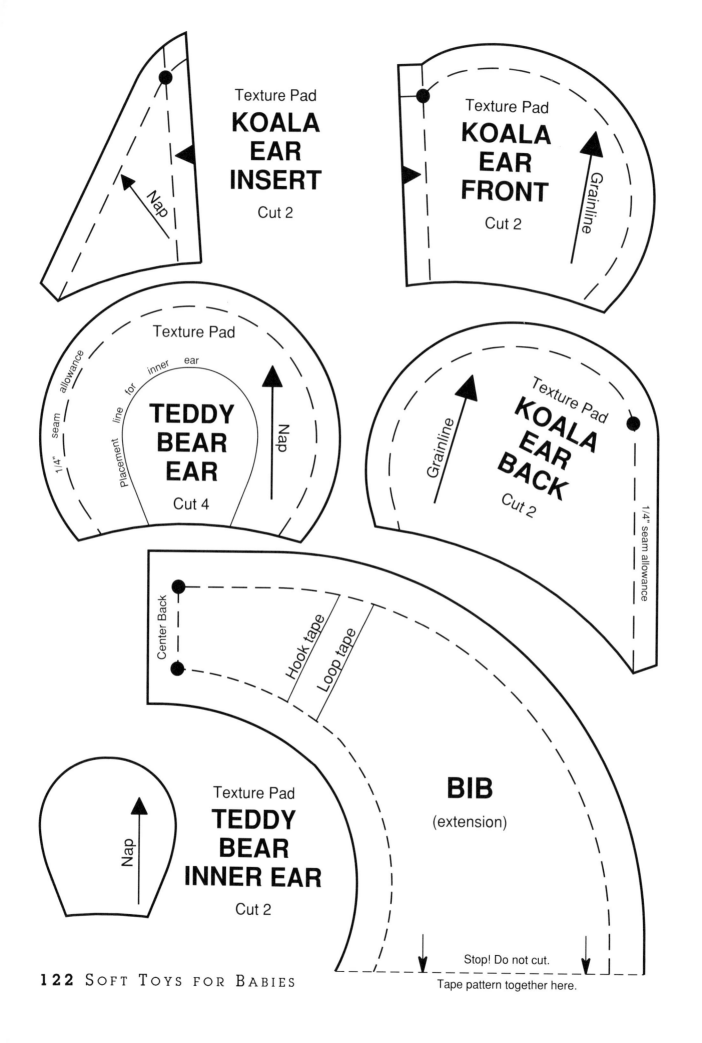

Texture Pad
**KOALA
EAR
INSERT**

Cut 2

Nap

Texture Pad
**KOALA
EAR
FRONT**

Cut 2

Grainline

Texture Pad

1/4" seam allowance

Placement line for inner ear

**TEDDY
BEAR
EAR**

Cut 4

Nap

Grainline

Texture Pad
**KOALA
EAR
BACK**

Cut 2

1/4" seam allowance

Center Back

Hook tape

Loop tape

BIB

(extension)

Texture Pad
**TEDDY
BEAR
INNER EAR**

Cut 2

Nap

Stop! Do not cut.

Tape pattern together here.

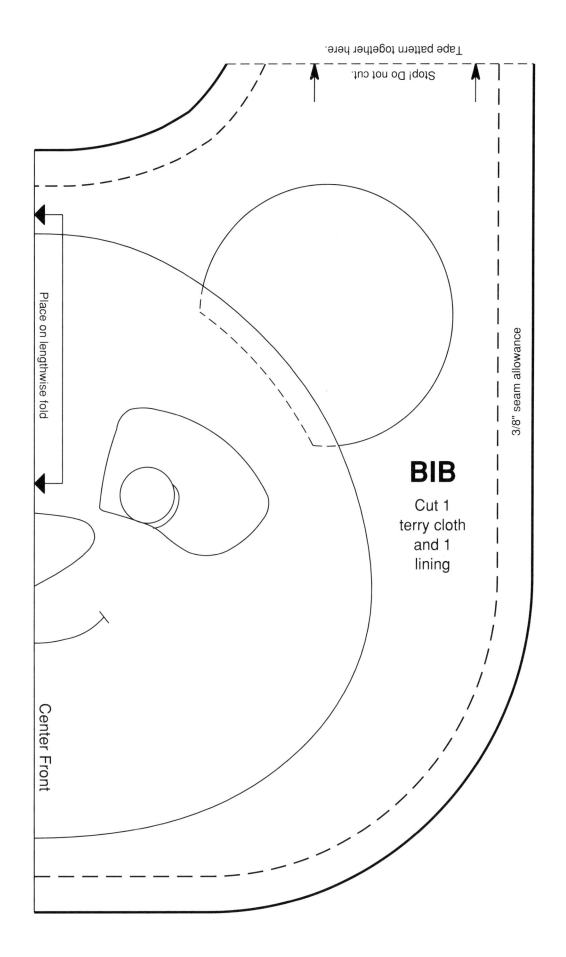

Stop! Do not cut.

Place on lengthwise fold

3/8" seam allowance

BIB

Cut 1
terry cloth
and 1
lining

Center Front

TEETHE-N-CLUTCH PLAY GUIDE

a few suggestions to help you gain the most from this toy

Age Range

Introduce at 3-1/2 to 5-1/2 months; use through 12 months on.

Skills Development

For ages 6 to 9 months, one-piece toys are the best bets, and this ball has many nooks and crannies to investigate. A baby of this age needs practice *transferring an object* from one hand to the other. The Teethe-n-Clutch has the advantage of multiple hand-holds no matter which way it's turned. The Teethe-n-Clutch also makes an excellent toy for a newly crawling baby to chase because it doesn't roll far.

Beginning in the second half of the first year, babies put just about everything they can manage into their mouths. This isn't only during teeth-cutting. Starting at about 5 months, babies use their mouths more than their hands to learn about their surroundings. Through *mouth exploration*, a baby gains some of his most reliable feedback about the properties of objects, their sizes and shapes, their textures and tastes.

As its name implies, the Teethe-n-Clutch has strong, corded edges for *teething.* The toy contrasts nicely with the hard plastic of most commercial rattles. It's also easy to clean—just toss it in the washer and dryer.

Play Suggestions

If you use a foam crib support for 3- to 5-month-olds, suspend the Teethe-n-Clutch within arm's length. When a baby bats and swats at the ball, it will rotate with a colorful display. And the ball's rattle provides an auditory reward for an accurate hit. For variety, attach the Teethe-n-Clutch with plastic toy links to a high chair, car seat, walker, or stroller.

You can also use the ball when a baby is on his stomach. Slowly twirl or roll the ball in front of him, close enough for him to trap. Raising the ball slowly in the air prompts the baby to lift his head and exercises neck and back muscles.

Once a baby in the 4 to 5 months range can grip the ball securely, play a little tug-of-war. Hand him the ball, and offer a little resistance when he grabs it. He'll find this back-and-forth pulling a novel interaction.

The ball can help an older toddler learn to catch. Suspend it in a doorway. (You may already have a suitable hook installed for a baby bouncer, or install a screw eye in the center top of a door jamb.) Tether the ball with a long piece of 100% wool yarn. At rest, the ball should hang close to the floor. Sit on one side of the doorway with your child facing you on the other side. Start by handing him the ball and having him swing it toward you. Hand the ball back to him, slowly following the path the ball would have taken if you had swung it. Once the child can anticipate the path the ball will take, gently swing the ball toward him. The predictable pendulum swing should make catching easier, but even so, catching is an advanced skill that takes lots of practice.

(Remove the ball from the doorway when you're not there. You'll probably need to replace the yarn each play session.)

Safety Considerations

The Teethe-n-Clutch is lightweight and especially easy to carry. It's safe to fall on if a newly walking baby takes a tumble.

Remove the toy from the crib when the baby is sleeping. Untreated materials, especially cotton, are flammable.

To prevent entanglement, do not suspend the ball from a cord, string, or ribbon tied across the crib. Don't leave a cord longer than 12" tied to the ball's loop because it would be a strangulation hazard.

When attaching yarn to the Teethe-n-Clutch, use only wool knitting yarn (4-ply or worsted weight) because it will break under stress. To double-check, pull on the yarn to make sure you can snap it. Do not use acrylic yarns, strong strings, or cords. They would be a serious safety hazard. Even with wool yarn, use adult supervision.

Care Instructions

Machine wash, gentle cycle, warm water, no bleach. Tumble dry low. Remove while still damp; reshape.

*This toy is from the book **Soft Toys for Babies** in Judi Maddigan's **Stitch & Enrich** series.*

CHAPTER 9

TEETHE-N-CLUTCH

From 3 to 14 months, your baby needs:

- Easily held objects
- Teethers
- Soft, padded toys

This toy provides:

- Handholds on each side for hand-to-hand transfer
- Strong, corded edges for teething
- A collapsible ball that's safe for a beginning walker to fall on

Open-ended playthings serve multiple purposes. This category includes blocks and balls, which offer some of the best play value. A crawling baby is not ready for toys with multiple pieces—that's for toddlers—but even a young baby can manage a ball such as the Teethe-n-Clutch.

Like the prior chapter's Texture Pads, this ball adapts to a wide range of developmental stages. For the youngest babies, it delivers splendid color, supple texture, and a rattle. For the oldest, it promotes physical coordination and exercises large muscle groups.

Once a baby gains locomotion, crawling, cruising, and walking become major attractions in themselves. Toys play a less vital role during these stages, but appropriate ones still provide sound learning experiences. The Teethe-n-Clutch answers the mobile child's needs. A newly crawling baby grabs it easily because it doesn't roll far. An advanced crawler spots it across the room and races to retrieve it. An unsteady walker totes it effortlessly and, if he should fall, the ball acts more like a pillow than a problem.

When selecting your fabrics, keep in mind that bright, primary colors attract more attention than pastels. You don't need to stick to solids.

For striking variations, use vivid prints like stripes and polka dots.

Materials

See color pages. The directions assume you have read Chapters 1 and 2. Also check the HelpLine on page 22 when needed.

- 12 fabrics 6" x 6-1/2" each (quilt-weight, 100% cotton recommended)—see Fig. 9.2 for colors
- 18" x 22" fusible, woven, all-purpose interfacing (Stacy Shape-Flex)
- 3-1/4 yd 100% polyester cable cord, Size 200 (9/32" diameter)
- 3-1/2 yd extra-wide bias tape, 1-7/8" wide (or bias strips cut 1-3/4" wide)
- Regular thread to match bias color
- Nylon upholstery thread
- 1 Hide-a-Rattle (3/8"-thick flat plastic rattle, 1-1/2" diameter) available from Aardvark Adventures
- 3/4"-wide masking tape

Cutting Directions

Decide the order of your fabrics. For the book's sample, each main Circle was backed with two facings of different colors (in the order shown in Fig. 9.2) so that facings of adjoining circles match.

Cut one Circle pattern from each of the six main fabric colors (called Circles 1 through 6 in the directions). Label the rightside of each circle with a number written on masking tape (see Fig. 9.2).

Cut two Facings from each of the remaining six fabrics.

Make a main interfacing pattern by drawing a 5" circle or by tracing and trimming the Circle pattern by 1/2". Using this interfacing pattern, cut six interfacing pieces. Center each interfacing on a fabric Circle, wrongsides together, and fuse.

Segment No.	Circle	Left Facing	Right Facing
1	Red	Yellow	Orange
2	Plum	Orange	Pink
3	Purple	Pink	Lavender
4	Blue	Lavender	Turquoise
5	Dk. Green	Turquoise	Lt. Green
6	Gold	Lt. Green	Yellow

Fig. 9.2 Circles and Facings color order

Make a facing interfacing pattern by tracing the Facing pattern. Trim it 1/2" along the semicircular seam, but only trim 1/4" along the entire center back edge. (Check Fig. 9.3.) Using this pattern, cut twelve interfacing pieces. Position each interfacing on the wrongside of a Facing, 1/2" from the semicircular edge, and 1/4" from the center back edge; fuse.

Sewing Directions

1. Clip the seam allowance on each Facing to the small dots. As indicated on the pattern, fold under 1/4" at the top and bottom of each Facing's center back edges (Fig. 9.4); press.

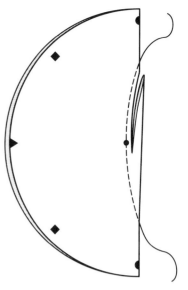

Fig. 9.5 Stitching Circle's dart

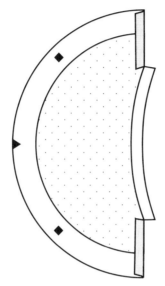

Fig. 9.4 Pressing under Facing's center back edges

2. Make the dart in one Circle (Fig. 9.5). Trim the dart's seam allowance to 1/8".

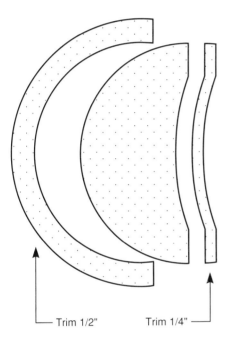

Trim 1/2"   Trim 1/4"

Fig. 9.3 How to make Facing interfacing pattern

Cut six 18-3/8" lengths of cable cord. To form six separate rings, butt each cord (end to end) and fasten with a short piece of masking tape.

Cut six bias strips 18-7/8" long; press flat.

Transfer all pattern markings.

3. Form a bias-strip ring by sewing a 1/4" seam with the short ends of the strip right-sides together (Fig. 9.6). Press seam open.

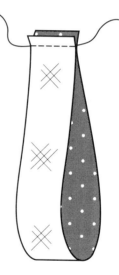

Fig. 9.6 Sewing bias strip into ring

4. To make the piping, fold the bias ring lengthwise (rightside out) over a taped cord, matching the fabric's raw edges (Fig. 9.7). Encase the cord by basting alongside it with a zipper foot. Trim the piping's seam allowance to 1/4".

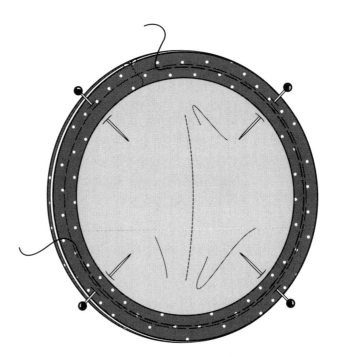

Fig. 9.8 Basting piping to Circle

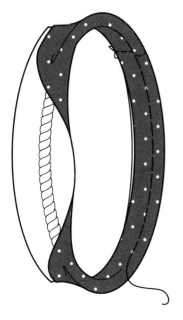

Fig. 9.7 Encasing the cord

5. Quarter the piping. Pin the piping to the Circle's rightside, raw edges even, matching the piping's quarter marks to the Circle's square marks. Baste, using a zipper foot, easing the piping to fit (Fig. 9.8).

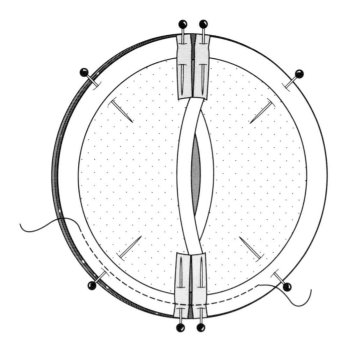

Fig. 9.9 Seaming Facings to Circle

Joining Segments

8. Pin Circle 1's right Facing to Circle 2's left Facing. Stitch this curved seam's two layers from small dot to small dot, leaving open at the top and bottom folded edges; keep the free fabric away from the stitching (Fig. 9.10).

For the book's sample, each Facing was seamed to another Facing of the same color.

6. Consult Fig. 9.2 on page 126. Match appropriate Facings to the Circle. With rightsides together, pin the two Facings to the Circle, matching all pattern markings and sandwiching the piping (Fig. 9.9). With Circle side up and using a zipper foot, stitch around the Circle, following your basting line as a guide.

Grade seam, trimming the piping's seam allowances the shortest. Clip curves. Turn to rightside. Press without flattening the piping.

7. Repeat steps 2 through 6 for each of the remaining five Circles.

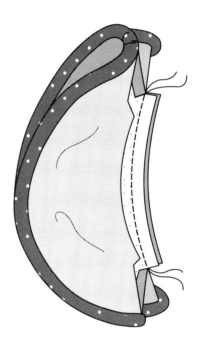

Fig. 9.10 Curved Facing seam

9. Insert the rattle into the pocket formed between Circle 2 and its left Facing. Match Circle 2's dart to the facing seam just completed. Stitch over the dart's previous stitching line, through four thicknesses, to secure the rattle (Fig. 9.11).

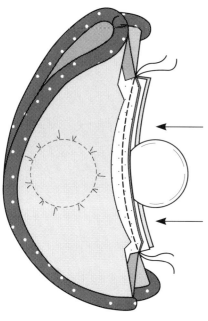

Fig. 9.11 Securing rattle with duplicate stitching

10. Fit Circle 3's left Facing to Circle 2's right Facing; stitch from small dot to small dot. In the same manner, join the Facings of Circles 4, 5, and 6 to the previous ones.

Bar Tacks

11. Fold Circle 1 in half along its dart, rightsides together. Using a button sew-on foot, slide the fabric's main portion behind the foot. Lower the foot at the midpoint of the circle's edge, as close as possible to the piping's seamline. Only the two stacked layers of piping should extend beyond the front of the foot. Bar tack (see HelpLine on page 22) at the notch.

A computerized machine will repeat identical bar tacks; this project has enough to make programming worthwhile.

12. Match Circle 1's right half to Circle 2's left half. Bar tack at both square marks.

13. Repeat steps 11 and 12 in order four times for the remaining Circles. Repeat step 11 once more for Circle 6.

Loop

14. Cut a 3-1/2" piece of bias tape. Fold in half, lengthwise, rightsides together. Stitch 1/4" from the fold. Trim seam and turn strip to rightside. (Use a loop turner or see Fig. 9.12.)

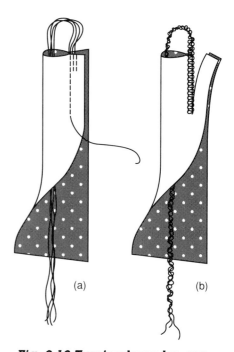

(a)   (b)

Fig. 9.12 Turning loops by conventional machine and serger. (a) For conventional machine: Begin with thread tails about 6" longer than the loop. Take three stitches forward and three reversed through one seam allowance (single thickness, rightside up). Lift foot and draw out thread double the starting tail's length. Lay all six threads on loop fabric as shown. (b) For serger: First chain the length of the loop plus 6". Swing the thread tail around to the front of the machine. For both methods: Fold the loop in half, wrongside out, over the thread tail; serge or stitch. Pull on the enclosed tail to turn rightside out.

15. Bar tack the loop, 1/2" from its end, to the top large dot on the facing side of Circle 3. Bar tack a second time, stitching *through* the piping (Fig. 9.13). In the same manner, bar tack the other end of the loop to Circle 6.

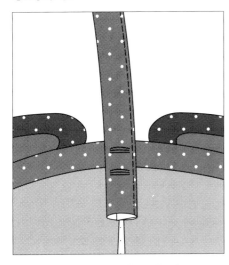

Fig. 9.13 Bar tacking the loop

16. Slipstitch the free facings of Circles 1 and 6 together from small dot to small dot, turning the raw edges under.

17. Bar tack Circles 1 and 6 together at the square marks.

Finishing

18. Thread a long needle with a doubled length of upholstery thread; knot 6" from the ends. Sew the tops of the Circles together by taking a 1/4" stitch at each large dot on the piping seamlines. After stitching through all six large dots, draw the thread up tightly and knot it to the beginning tails (Fig. 9.14).

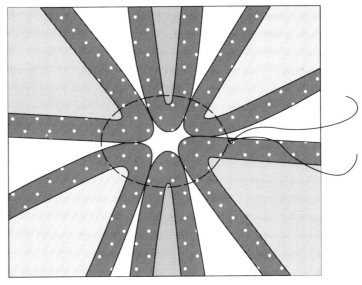

Fig. 9.14 Drawing up and closing the top

19. Stitch around again, this time taking a 1/4" stitch through each segment's piping. Tighten and knot as before.

20. Bury the thread by taking a long stitch through the piping. Clip the thread, then thread the beginning tails on the needle and lose them inside the piping in the same way.

21. Repeat steps 18 through 20, sewing the bottom large dots together.

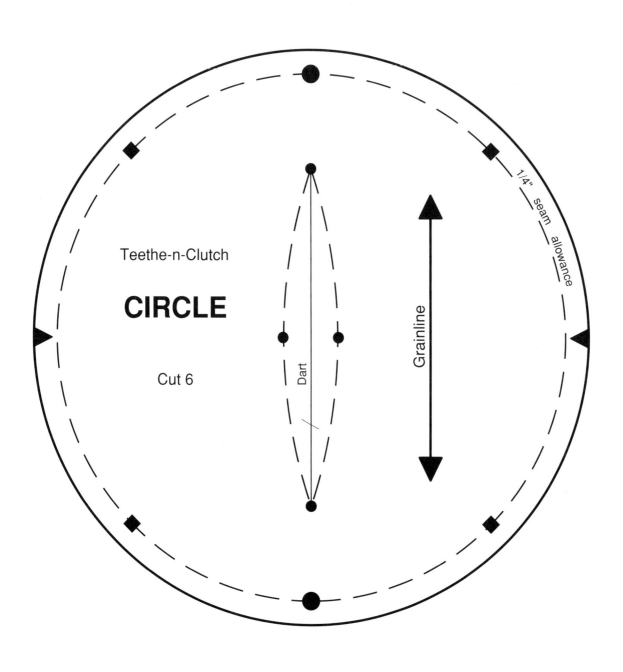

Teethe-n-Clutch

CIRCLE

Cut 6

Dart

Grainline

1/4" seam allowance

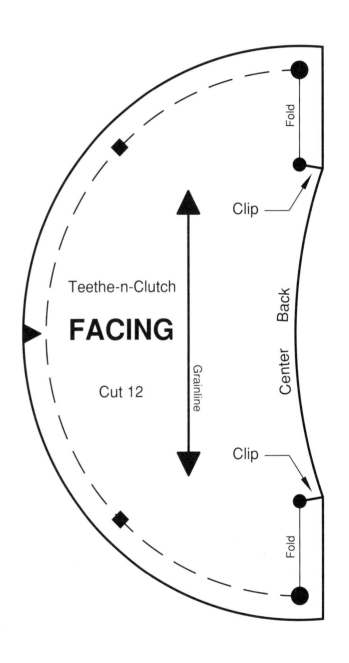

Teethe-n-Clutch

FACING

Cut 12

Grainline

Fold

Clip

Center   Back

Clip

Fold

PEEK-A-POCKET PLAY GUIDE *a few suggestions to help you gain the most from this toy*

Age Range
7 to 18 months and on.

Skills Development

To fully understand their environments, babies need to use all their senses—sight, smell, taste, hearing, touch. Before they crawl or walk efficiently, they can see much more than they can feel. The multiple textures in this toy satisfy this *touch hunger*, letting a baby use other senses besides sight to discover his world.

"Out of sight" to a baby at 6 or 7 months literally means "out of this world." As far as he's concerned, an object no longer exists if he can't see it. And his misconceptions don't stop there. When parents leave the house, their 6-month-old doesn't really know that he can count on their reappearance. (This contributes to the *separation anxiety* often apparent in the second half of the first year.)

Peekaboo games help a baby comprehend that things (and people) still exist even when he can't see them. The Peek-a-Pocket has eight hidden faces that will disappear and reappear, unchanged, as often as the child wishes. By 10 months, most babies understand *object permanence* and can remember where unseen objects are.

This toy also develops *problem solving abilities* from 7 months on. Expect your baby to pull the inserts out of the pockets as early as 7 months, but be prepared to restuff the pockets yourself.

Fully inserting the bears into the pockets will take another year for him to perfect. He will operate the doors and pop-ups well before that time, and might try inserting other toys into the pockets, too.

At 12 to 15 months, babies begin to handle objects with a *pincer-grasp*, matching the tips of their thumbs to their fingers. Manipulating the Peek-a-Pocket cultivates this movement. It develops *manual dexterity* and *fine motor skills.*

Play Suggestions

The way you play with your child and the Peek-a-Pocket is the most exciting part. Initially, let your baby absorb the toy without interference. Don't concern yourself if he doesn't operate all the pop-ups and doors right away. It's much more important for him to turn the object around in his hands and taste all that can fit in his mouth. (Remember that tongues are as important as fingers at this stage.)

After he's familiar with the toy, carry the concept of *object permanence* one step further. Hide the entire toy and have your 8- or 9-month-old find it. At first, cover the toy with a pillow, blanket, or towel, but leave a corner of the toy showing. Ask the child to find the toy, and applaud him when he succeeds. Later, you can find more concealing hiding places.

For an older child, the Peek-a-Pocket provides a non-threatening way to discuss feelings and emotions. Psychologists use games picturing different expressions as a way to open communi-

cation channels to better understand a young child's concerns. You can do the same, in a less structured way, by having your preschooler tell you stories about what one of the bears did that made him look that way. Ask him if he ever feels like this bear or that one. This line of questioning can lead to intriguing insights. It is most useful if you approach the game as a listener, not as a judge.

You can also use the Peek-a-Pocket to teach colors and counting. Have your preschooler point to a color you name, then have him name the colors. Count the bears, starting on the side that only has three bears. Gradually work up to all eight.

Safety Considerations

Remove the Peek-a-Pocket from a child's crib while he sleeps. Untreated fabrics, especially cotton, are flammable.

Check periodically to confirm that all the parts are firmly attached. Repair or replace worn pieces.

Care Instructions

Hand wash the Peek-a-Pocket in lukewarm water with mild soap. Rinse thoroughly, blot between terry towels. Stand upright, accordion style, to air dry.

*This toy is from the book **Soft Toys for Babies** in Judi Maddigan's **Stitch & Enrich** series.*

CHAPTER 10

P E E K - A - P O C K E T

In the first year and a half, your baby likes:

- Toys to touch and feel
- Hinged objects
- Hide-and-seek toys

This toy provides:

- A variety of fabrics, textures, and surface embroidery
- Flaps and pop-ups to open and explore
- Eight teddy bears that play peekaboo in pockets and doors

Let's see what a 7-month-old does with a Peek-a-Pocket. He picks it up. *Oh, something new!* He turns it around in his hands and sticks a corner in his mouth. *Gosh, it feels nice on my gums. It's spongy.* He's caught in a dilemma: He can't see it and mouth it at the same time, and he wants to do both.

When curiosity takes over, he stops gumming and starts investigating. *I wonder what it does . . . .* He runs his fingers along a corduroy pocket and snags a handle. Out pops—*A winking teddy bear!* He realizes that if his new toy had one surprise, it might have more. It opens. It has doors and (yes!) more teddies jumping up to say "Hi."

The Peek-a-Pocket goes one step beyond ordinary baby toys. Yes, it does give the typical fingering, grasping, pulling, and nibbling experiences. Besides that, it hides eight teddies that convey emotions, such as surprise, worry, anger, contentment, and happiness.

The point behind the expressions is that psychologists use drawings of different emotions in story-telling and role-playing games. In a similar way, parents can help their children express and resolve difficult issues through conversations sparked by the Peek-a-Pocket.

When your 7-month-old is old enough to talk, he will enjoy making up stories about the bears, and you'll enjoy the insights into his thoughts. But any way you look at it, it's fun.

Materials

See color pages. The directions assume you have read Chapters 1 and 2. Also check the HelpLine on page 22 when needed.

- 1/4 yd muslin
- 1/4 yd poplin to back muslin
- 1/4 yd denim
- Imitation suede scraps (Ultrasuede or Facile) for bear faces
- Four corduroy remnants for doors and pockets
- Lining material remnants to match corduroy
- Remnants of four cotton fabrics for pocket inserts and Pop-up
- 1/8 yd strong, iron-on adhesive (Heat N Bond) for bear faces
- 5/8 yd fusible web (Wonder-Under) for muslin
- 2/3 yd cable cord, Size 100 (7/32" diameter)
- 1" navy 3/4"-wide hook and loop fastener tape (Velcro)
- 2" white 3/4"-wide hook and loop fastener tape (Velcro)
- One foam-backed plastic kitchen place mat approximately 12" x 18"
- Six flexible plastic lids as from margarine tubs or coffee cans: four 6" or larger and two 4" or larger.

(You can substitute a double layer of quilter's template plastic.)
- Ultra-fine point *permanent* black marking pen (Pilot)
- White paint pen or white embroidery floss
- Disappearing pen (optional)
- Extra-fine rayon machine-embroidery thread (Sulky), (optional)
- Assorted 1/8" ribbons (optional)
- Jeans 14 (90) sewing machine needle recommended

Machine Embroidery (Optional)

If your machine does decorative stitches, experiment with the four corduroy pockets and doors. Cut the fabric about an inch outside the pattern's cutting lines. Work on top of a stabilizer like Stitch-n-Tear. For my plaids, I played with thin satin ribbons and narrow satin stitching, working a couple of patterns over them in Sulky 40 thread (colors 1109, 1122, 1023, and 1078).

Alternately, embellish this project with free-machine embroidery or serger flat-locking. The embroidery is an optional step—leaving the corduroy plain is fine, too.

Cutting Directions

Cut squares and rectangles grain-perfect.

Fuse the poplin to the muslin using Wonder-Under. Cut one rectangle measuring 6-3/4" x 20-1/4".

From the denim, cut one 6-3/4" x 14" rectangle and one 6-3/4" square.

Cut one Pocket/Door in each of the four corduroy remnants, or trim the previously embroidered squares to size. Cut one Pocket/Door in each of the four corresponding linings.

In one of the cotton fabrics, cut two Hidden Squares and four Pop-ups. Cut two Hidden Squares in the second cotton fabric. For each of the remaining two cotton fabrics, cut two Pocket Inserts and one Bias Guide.

Transfer all pattern markings.

Cut three 5-3/4" squares from the place mat.

Use a pencil to draw the cutting lines on the place mat's wrongside. A permanent black marker will work on the plastic lids.

From the smaller plastic lids, cut two Pocket Insert Templates. Cut two Door Templates and two Pop-up Templates from the larger lids.

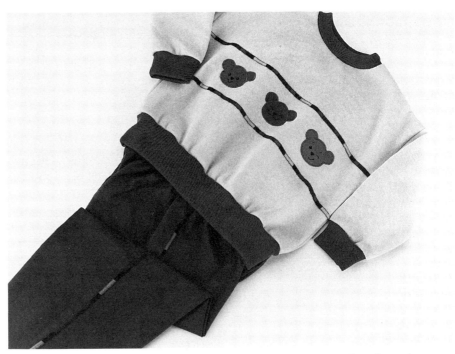

Fig. 10.2 This chapter's eight teddy bear faces also make charming appliqués for children's clothing. Serger flatlocking with variegated, texturized woolly nylon thread highlights this outfit.

Bear Faces

These directions use no-sew appliqué, but you can substitute any of the machine appliqué techniques from Chapter 2 on page 13. Stitching enhances the project's durability.

1. Trace eight bear face outlines (page 147) to the paper side of Heat N Bond.

2. Place the Heat N Bond, paper side up, on the suede's wrongside. Press three seconds with a medium temperature iron. Cut out the designs; peel off the paper backing.

The first time I used Heat N Bond, I mistakenly peeled off the paper backing before cutting out the designs. Conveniently, I discovered you can reattach the paper by pressing a few seconds.

3. Position the faces on the cotton fabric's rightside as follows: Place one face on one Pocket Insert (the front) in the location indicated on the pattern. For the matching back insert (same color), place another face in a corresponding location but *upside down.* See Fig. 10.3.

4. Repeat the previous step for the second pair of Pocket Inserts.

5. Center a face on each of two different colors of Hidden Squares.

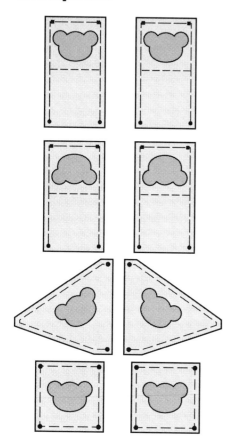

Fig. 10.3 Placement of eight faces

6. Referring to the pattern, place one face on each of two Pop-ups. Make these pieces mirror images as in Fig. 10.3.

7. Adhere each face to the fabric by covering the rightside with a dry press cloth and pressing for seven seconds. Flip the fabric over and press for seven seconds from the wrongside.

8. Draw the bears' expressions following the book's examples, or sketch your own freehand. You may practice with a disappearing pen. After you have captured the look you want, trace the lines with the permanent black marker.

Instead of drawing, faces can be hand-embroidered in black floss. Use tiny stitches of white for eye highlights.

Also trace the outline of the head and draw the ear lines. For the eye highlights, make a tiny stitch with white floss or dot the eyes with a spot of white paint pen. If you highlight too much, simply cover the unwanted white with the black marker.

9. To set the marker, cover the appliqués with a dry press cloth and press for five seconds with an iron set on "cotton."

Avoid pressing the completed appliqués during later construction steps.

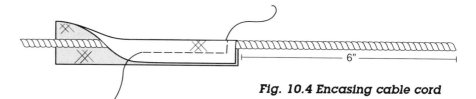

Fig. 10.4 Encasing cable cord

Pocket Inserts

10. Encase the cable cord as follows: Leaving 6" free cord, fold the bias strip rightsides together over the cord. Stitch across one end and along the cord using a zipper foot (Fig. 10.4). Trim seam. Pull on the excess cord to turn the bias rightside out. Cut off the stitched end. Pull on the free cord to slip the cut end 3/8" inside. Scrunch the other bias edge down and clip the excess cord so that end will also be 3/8" inside the fabric tube.

11. Baste the ends of the bias tube inside the upper corners of one Pocket Insert at the square markings (Fig. 10.5). The cord will loop over the face.

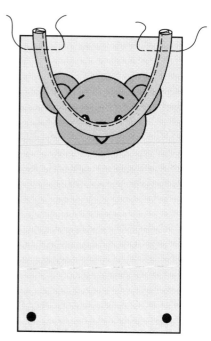

Fig. 10.5 Basting covered cord to Pocket Insert

12. Pin the two Pocket Inserts, rightsides together, sandwiching the piping. Check that both bear heads are at the top (one is upside down). Using a zipper foot, stitch three sides; leave open between dots (Fig. 10.6). Use care not to catch the cord in the stitching. To reinforce bias ends, stitch again over first stitching. Press stitching flat (avoid cording). Trim seams and corners. Turn to rightside; press.

13. Push a plastic template into the pocket insert. Topstitch along the line indicated on the pattern, trapping the plastic at the top.

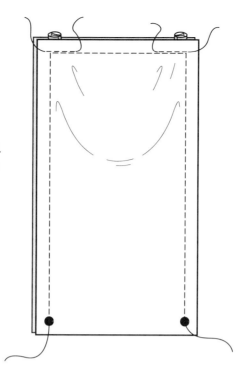

Fig. 10.6 Seaming Pocket Inserts

14. Repeat the previous directions for the other pair of Pocket Inserts.

15. Mark the dots diagramed in Fig. 10.7 on the denim square and the muslin rectangle. Pin the prepared pocket inserts in place, matching the dots. Stitch from dot to dot. Zigzag over the raw edges to prevent ravels.

Muslin Rectangle

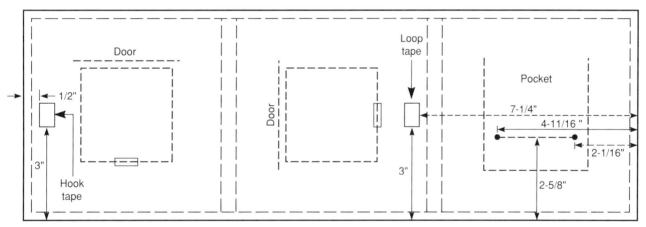

Denim Rectangle

Denim Square

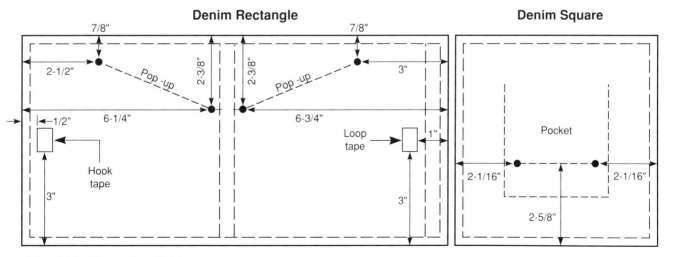

Fig. 10.7 Measuring dot locations

Hidden Squares

16. Pin two matching Hidden Squares rightsides together. Stitch around all four sides. Press stitching lines. Clip corners; grade seams. Slit only the backing square horizontally for 1-1/2". Turn rightside out through the slash; press. Repeat for the second Hidden Square.

17. Center the first Hidden Square horizontally and vertically on the muslin rectangle (Fig. 10.7). Edgestitch

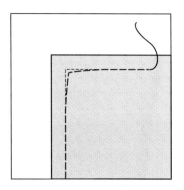

Fig. 10.8 For an accurate square, creep inside the stitching lines by one or two fabric threads as you approach and exit each corner. This will prevent "cat-ears" (acute, too-sharp corners).

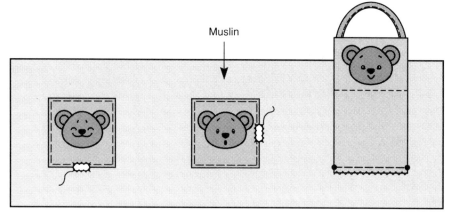

Muslin

Fig. 10.9 Zigzagging small loop tapes

all four sides. Place a 1/4" x 3/4" piece of white loop tape centered along the square's right edge (Fig. 10.9).

Double-sided basting tape will hold small hook and loop pieces in position.

Zigzag around the tape's four sides.

18. Position the second Hidden Square 1-7/8" from the muslin rectangle's left edge and centered vertically (Fig.10.7). Edgestitch as before. Zigzag a 1/4" x 3/4" piece of white loop tape centered along the square's base (Fig. 10.9).

Closures

19. Zigzag four 1/2" x 3/4" pieces of hook and loop tape in the locations shown in Fig. 10.7. Use navy tape on the denim and white tape on the muslin.

20. Center a 1/4" x 3/4" piece of hook tape along one side of a Door lining, 3/8" from the raw edge (Fig. 10.10); zigzag. Repeat for the second Door lining.

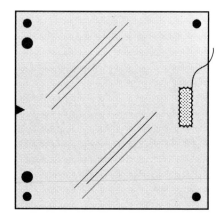

Fig. 10.10 Zigzagging hook tape on Door lining

Pop-ups

21. On each of the four Pop-ups, press under 1/4" along the straight edge that will be left open. With rightsides together, seam one appliquéd Pop-up to its back along the remaining sides. Repeat for the second Pop-up.

22. Press stitching flat. Clip corners; trim seams. Turn to rightside and press again.

23. Mark the denim rectangle with dots corresponding to Fig. 10.7. Match the Pop-ups' small dots to the denim's marks (Fig. 10.11). The Pop-ups will extend above the denim. Topstitch each Pop-up in place, stitching from small dot to small dot. Fold each Pop-up down and press along topstitching lines.

Pockets and Doors

24. For all Pocket/Doors and their linings, press under 1/4" along the notched edge. For the two door linings, this side is directly opposite the fastener tape. Open out the pressed folds.

25. Match each Pocket/Door to its corresponding lining. Seam three sides, leaving the notched edges open between the large dots.

Notice both pockets' openings are along the bottom edge, but one door lifts upward and the other swings left.

Grade seams and trim corners. Turn to rightside; press, turning under along previously pressed folds.

26. Insert a plastic template into each of the two doors.

Bow the template so it fits through the opening, and flatten it once inside.

Turn under the notched edges along the previously pressed lines. Hand baste about 1/8" from the fold to keep the plastic away from the edge.

27. Center each door over its hidden square, fastening the hook and loop tape (Fig. 10.12). Using a zipper foot, topstitch the notched edges only, backstitching 1/2" at both ends. Check that the stitching caught the lining's folded edge. If necessary, slipstitch any gaps.

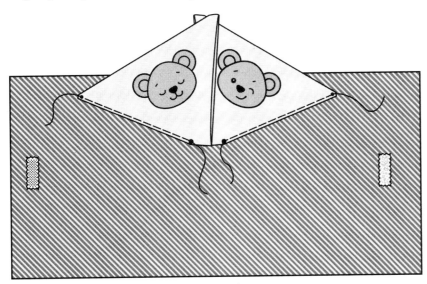

Fig. 10.11 Positioning Pop-ups on denim

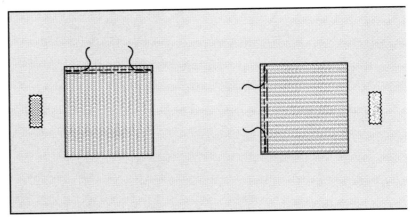

Fig. 10.12 Positioning doors

28. Place the pockets over their pocket inserts following Fig 10.13. Topstitch, reinforcing the upper corners as shown in that figure. Remove all basting.

Assembling the Peek-a-Pocket

29. With rightsides together and both Pop-up and pocket opening upward, machine baste the denim square to the right edge of the denim rectangle (Fig. 10.14). Press seam toward rectangle.

gle and square. Turn to rightside through this opening; press, staying clear of plastic templates. Edgestitch all four sides using a bulky overlock, edgestitch, or zipper foot.

31. Insert one place mat piece into the Peek-a-Pocket, snugging it against the denim rectangle's outer

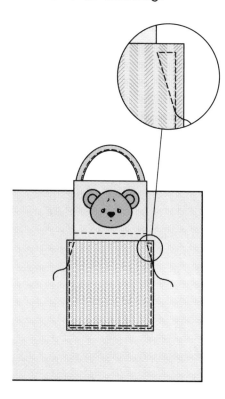

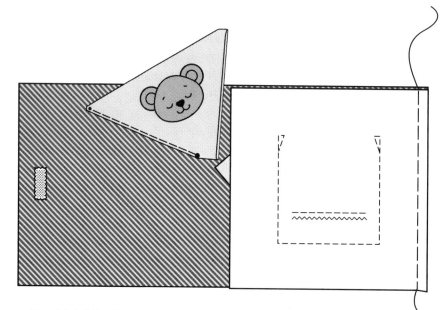

Fig. 10.14 Basting denim square and rectangle together

30. Pin the denim and muslin rectangles, rightsides together, keeping the tops oriented consistently. Stitch all four sides (Fig. 10.15). Trim seams and corners. Press stitching lines only. Remove the basting between the denim rectan-

three sides. Topstitch vertically 6-3/16" from the denim's left edge, and again 1/2" from the first stitching (Fig. 10.16). Don't catch the Pop-ups in the stitching.

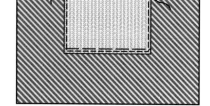

Fig. 10.13 Placement and topstitching for pockets

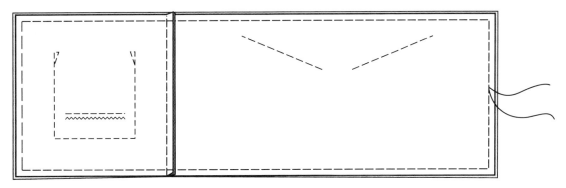

Fig. 10.15 Seaming denim and muslin rectangles

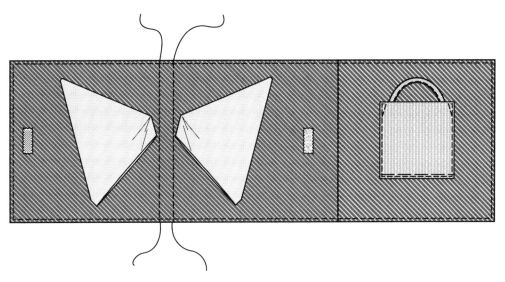

Fig. 10.16 Topstitching between pages

32. Work the second place mat piece under the denim square, and slide the third place mat piece into the middle section. Check that both place mats are fully inserted against previous stitching. Topstitch the opening closed, and topstitch 1/2" away from this stitching (Fig. 10.17).

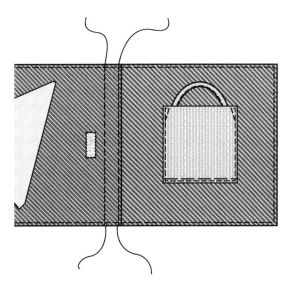

Fig. 10.17 Two final topstitching lines

Finishing the Pop-up

33. Insert a plastic Pop-up Template into each Pop-up, pushing it as far as possible away from the opening. Hand baste the edges closed about 1/8" away from the folds to keep the plastic away from the edges (Fig. 10.18).

34. Folding the Peek-a-Pocket back on itself, match both Pop-ups' basted edges with the bears facing out. Edgestitch along the folds through all thicknesses from dot to dot, backstitching at both ends (Fig. 10.19).

35. Remove basting. If part of the Pop-up eluded the first stitching, stitch a second time from the underside.

36. Push the Pocket Inserts into the pockets to show only the cord handles. Close the Peek-a-Pocket accordion style, folding the Pop-up down. The fastener tapes will keep the Peek-a-Pocket compact until a child is ready to explore.

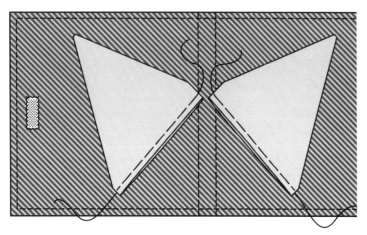

Fig. 10.18 Hand basting Pop-ups

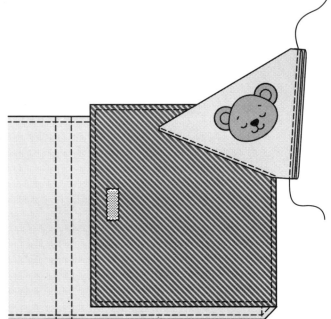

Fig. 10.19 Edgestitching Pop-ups together

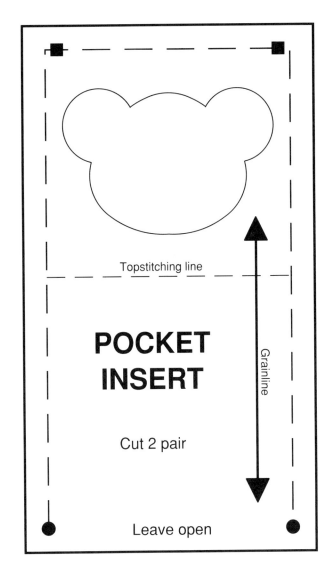

Topstitching line

POCKET
INSERT

Grainline

Cut 2 pair

Leave open

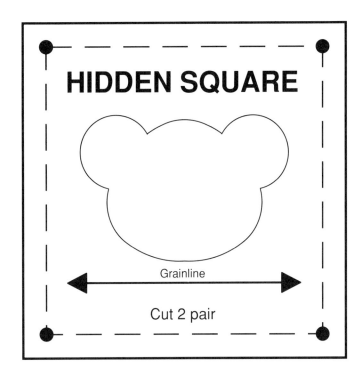

HIDDEN SQUARE

Grainline

Cut 2 pair

POCKET
INSERT
TEMPLATE

Cut 2 in plastic

Grainline

1/4" seam allowance

POCKET/DOOR

Cut 1 each of 4
corduroys and 4 linings

Leave open

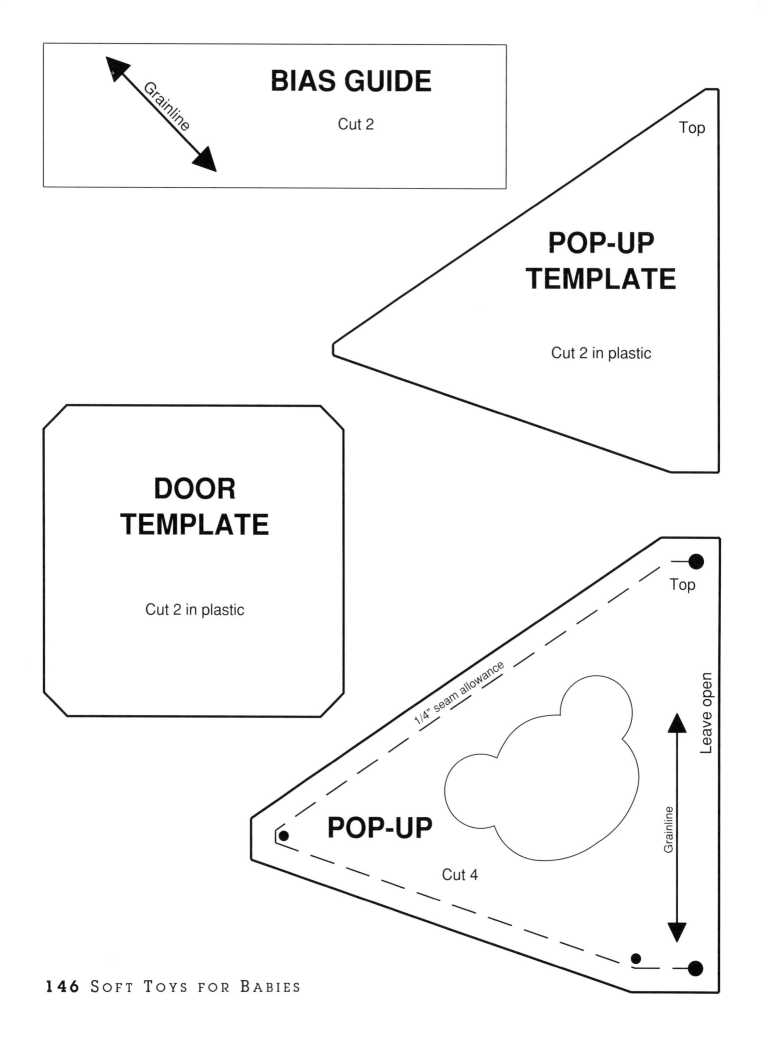

BIAS GUIDE

Cut 2

Grainline

POP-UP TEMPLATE

Top

Cut 2 in plastic

DOOR TEMPLATE

Cut 2 in plastic

1/4" seam allowance

Top

Leave open

Grainline

POP-UP

Cut 4

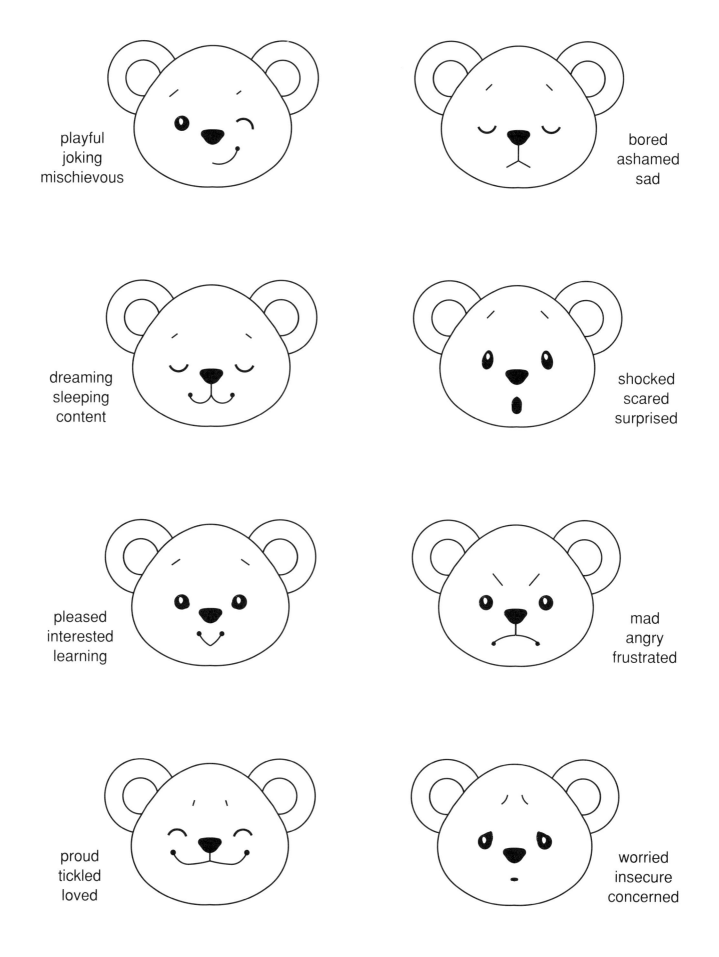

playful
joking
mischievous

bored
ashamed
sad

dreaming
sleeping
content

shocked
scared
surprised

pleased
interested
learning

mad
angry
frustrated

proud
tickled
loved

worried
insecure
concerned

SHOPPING CART SEAT WITH PUFF BLOCK PLAY GUIDE

a few suggestions to help you gain the most from this toy

Age Range

6-1/2 or 7 months on. Prerequisite skill: stable sitting without support.

Suggestions

A shopping trip can frustrate a child. He cannot touch all the enticing items he sees. This seat's safety belt has snap tape for attaching toys. That way, while the parent shops, the child can manipulate safe objects. Attached toys are especially useful for babies still in the mouthing stage (under 12 months).

Keep a baby interested in the toys by saving them exclusively for the store. Rotate them often, storing extras in the zippered pouch. Likely toys include rattles, teething rings, plastic toy links, shower curtain rings, and any soft toy with a loop. The child will outgrow the need to have a teething toy before he outgrows the seat.

Remember that you can turn a simple shopping trip into a learning experience. A grocery store provides all sorts of opportunities, including the following:

1. Practice counting: 3 oranges in a bag, 4 puddings in a package, 12 eggs in a dozen.

2. Teach colors: yellow bananas, green broccoli, orange carrots, purple eggplant.

3. Compare sizes: lemons are smaller than grapefruit, cataloupe is smaller than watermelon, a gallon of milk is bigger than a quart of juice.

4. Classify and sort: soups go with cans, crackers go with boxes, grapes go with produce.

5. Play alphabet games: apple starts with A, bread starts with B, chicken starts with C.

Puff Block

If you use a foam crib support for 3- to 5-month-olds (see Chapter 7), suspend the Puff Block within arm's length. When a baby bats and swats at the block, it will rotate and jingle, rewarding an accurate hit.

You can also use the Puff Block when a baby is on his stomach. Slowly twirl or roll the block in front of him, close enough for him to trap. Raising the block slowly in the air prompts the baby to lift his head, which exercises neck and back muscles.

Once a baby in the 4 to 5 months range can grip the block securely, play a little tug-of-war. Hand him the block, and offer a little resistance when he grabs it. He'll find this back-and-forth pulling a novel interaction.

For 6 to 9 months, play a fishing game. Sit at a table with the baby on your lap. Tie a piece of wool yarn to the block's loop. Set the ball at the far side of the table and give the baby the free yarn end. Within a few days the baby will learn to pull on the yarn to snare the toy. Once he gets the idea, surprise him. Put an open box on a chair on the opposite side of the table so that the baby can't see inside. Hide a couple of lightweight toys in the

box, each with yarn attached. Have the baby pull on each yarn and see what he reels in.

The toy provides six easy handholds, so it's perfect for practice transferring an object from one hand to the other (6 to 9 months). It's light, safe to fall on, and easy to tote. In fact, a newly crawling baby might decide to carry it in his mouth. The Puff Block also makes an excellent toy for a crawling baby to chase because it doesn't roll far.

For variety, use plastic toy links to attach the Puff Block to a high chair, car seat, walker, or stroller.

Safety Considerations

Although the cart seat's straps provide some degree of restraint, they are not fail-safe. Never leave a child un-attended in a shopping cart.

When not in use, store the seat out of reach. A baby could become entangled in the straps.

When attaching yarn to the Puff Block, use only wool knitting yarn (4-ply or worsted weight) because it will break under stress.

Care Instructions

Machine wash the Shopping Cart Seat or the Puff Block, gentle cycle, warm water, no bleach. Tumble dry low. Remove while still damp; reshape.

*This toy is from the book **Soft Toys for Babies** in Judi Maddigan's **Stitch & Enrich** series.*

CHAPTER 11

SHOPPING CART SEAT WITH PUFF BLOCK

In a shopping cart, your baby needs:

- A safety restraint
- Secure toys
- A comfortable seat

This project provides:

- Lap belts that fasten with a quick-release buckle
- Snap tape for a Puff Block or other toy
- A cushion to pad baby's legs

What a tantalizing place, the grocery store. It's hard for a child to sit patiently in a cart. This safety-belted seat will remind him not to climb out.

Besides safety, comfort is a concern. Shopping carts are hot in summer, cold in winter, and wet in sleet or rain. They can also be hard, spiny, and downright dirty. No wonder a youngster fusses and fidgets in one.

For shopping comfort, quilt this special seat with padded extensions for the child's legs. It even has snap tape for attaching toys like the matching Puff Block. A zippered pouch stores extra toys or Mom's wallet, keys, sunglasses, whatever.

The cushion uses a technique called "biscuit" quilting. (This is an advanced technique; previous quilting experience is recommended.) Assembly-line methods speed the piecing, but be prepared for time-consuming pinning.

Pressed for time? You can create a seat in prequilted fabric quickly. Just substitute 7/8 yd for the biscuit quilt part.

Shopping Cart Seat

Materials

See color pages. The directions assume you have read Chapters 1 and 2. Also check the HelpLine on page 22 when needed.

- 1 yd main fabric, 44" wide, 100% cotton recommended (called "fabric E" in these directions).

Obvious one-way designs, stripes, and plaids are not appropriate.

- 1/4 yd of each of five fabrics, 100% cotton recommended (fabrics A, B, C, D & F)

You will need a 7-1/2" x 42" crosswise strip of five fabrics. A quarter yard provides only 1-1/2" extra. For yardage that needs extensive straightening or a print that suggests specific placement, you should purchase 3/8 yd.

- 1/2 yd muslin
- 1-5/8 yd 1"-wide polypropylene or cotton webbing (as used for belts)

In a hardware store, I found the perfect luggage strap. The 6' strap already had the correct type of buckle attached—at a price comparable to buying the webbing and buckle separately.

- One 1" plastic quick-release buckle (Fastex, available in fabric stores). This two-piece buckle pinches to unfasten and is sometimes called a "slide release."
- 1 package Dritz snap tape, 100% cotton (the 18" tape has plastic snaps)
- 14" x 28" woven, fusible, all-purpose interfacing (Stacy Shape-Flex)
- 1/8 yd 3/4"-wide hook and loop fastener tape (Velcro) to match fabric E
- 9" zipper
- Fine monofilament nylon thread
- Soft polyester fiberfill such as Dacron II. (Test fiberfill by clenching a handful. The fibers should spring back and not pack down.)
- Fabric marking pen or pencil
- Double (twin) sewing-machine needle (optional)
- 250 straight pins. (No, that's not a typo. You'll need several hundred pins—preferably with glass heads.)
- 100 quilting pins
- Masking tape
- Seam ripper

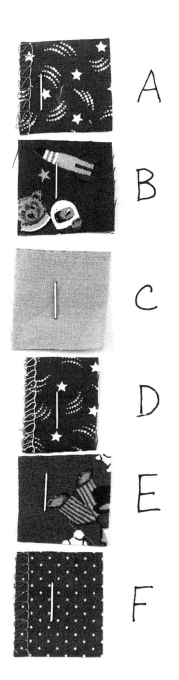

A

B

C

D

E

F

Fig. 11.2 Plan your color placement and assign each fabric a
letter from A to F. (Remember
that the main fabric is "E.")
Label a swatch card for easy
reference.

Cutting and Marking

Straighten one crosswise edge of each cotton fabric. Cut two full crosswise 3-3/4"-wide strips from each of the six cotton fabrics.

A rotary cutter and mat speed this step. Check the cutting techniques in Chapter 2 on page 11.

Cut one grain-perfect 16" x 30" rectangle from muslin. Beginning 1-1/2" from the edge, draw a grid of 1-3/4" squares on the muslin rectangle. The grid needs 7 columns across and 15 rows down, with a border on all sides. The overall dimensions should measure 12-1/4" x 26-1/4".

Draw a parallel line 1/4" above the top horizontal line and another line 1/4" below the bottom horizontal line. Mark a parallel line 1/2" beyond the leftmost vertical line. See Fig. 11.3. For the leg notch, draw a vertical line through the two center squares in rows 14 and 15, placing it 1/2" inside the center column's right edge. (This 3-1/2" line will be 5-3/4" inside the grid's right edge.) Draw a short, horizontal line 1/4" below row 13, in the center column. Cross out the remaining portions of the two center bottom squares because they will be removed later.

Row 10 needs less stuffing than the other rows because the seat folds there. As a reminder, label this row in the muslin's margin.

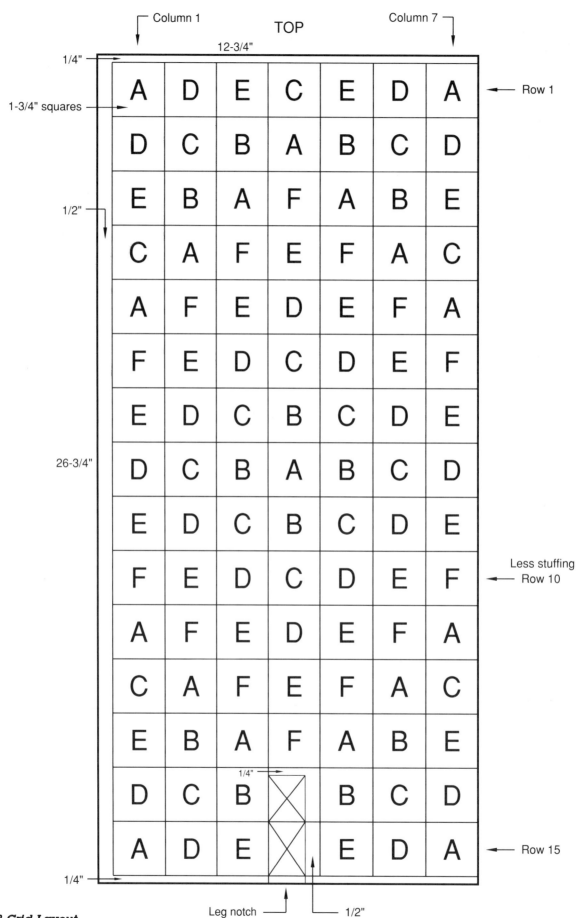

Fig. 11.3 Grid Layout

Machine Piecing

Use 1/4" seam allowances throughout.

This design combines a traditional quilting pattern called Around the World (the center section) with Nine Patch corner blocks. Alternately, you could piece 3-3/4" squares randomly into six 15-square strips and one 13-square strip, or develop your own pattern of 103 squares.

Columns 2 - 6:

1. First, strip-piece fabrics for the 6-square strips in Fig. 11.4. Join the first set of six different crosswise strips as follows: With rightsides together, seam a long edge of strip D to strip E. Seam the other long edge of strip E to strip F. Add strips A, B, and C in order, always adding the new strip to the free edge of the most recent strip. Press seams open.

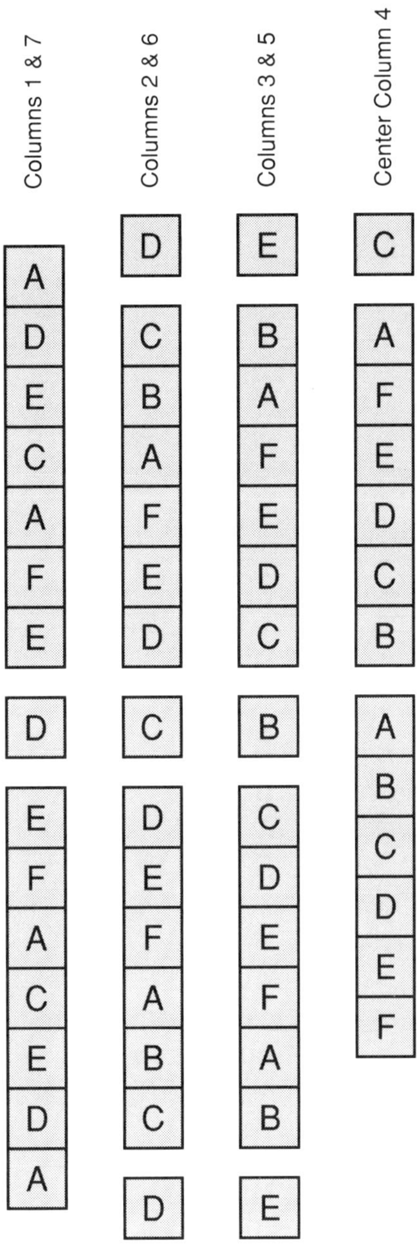

Columns 1 & 7

A
D
E
C
A
F
E

D
E
F
A
C
E
D
A

Columns 2 & 6

D

C
B
A
F
E
D

C

D
E
F
A
B
C

D

Columns 3 & 5

E

B
A
F
E
D
C

B

C
D
E
F
A
B

E

Center Column 4

C

A
F
E
D
C
B

A
B
C
D
E
F

Fig. 11.4 Strips and single blocks

2. Remove selvedges, cutting perpendicular to the seams. Cut four 3-3/4"-wide strips perpendicular to seamlines (Fig. 11.5). Stack these strips, label them "Col. 2 & 6," and set aside.

I use a small, stick-on note (Post-it) to temporarily label the fabrics. Masking tape would also serve.

3. Form a tube with the remaining 6-strip piece by seaming the free edges of strips C and D, rightsides together. Press seam open. Flatten the tube and slice it into six 3-3/4" rings (Fig. 11.6).

4. For one ring, rip the stitching between squares F and A; on a second ring, rip between squares A and B. Label these two strips "Col. 4" and set aside. For the remaining four rings, rip between squares B and C. Label these strips "Col. 3 & 5."

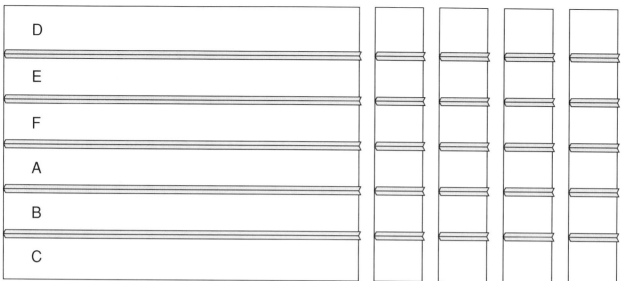

Fig. 11.5 Slicing first 6-piece strips

Columns 1 and 7:

5. For the second set of crosswise strips, cut one 16" length of fabrics C, D, and F, and two 16" lengths of fabrics A and E. Join the long sides of these strips in this order: E, F, A, C, E, D, A. Press seams open. Remove selvedges. Perpendicularly slice this piece into four 3-3/4" strips; label "Col. 1 & 7," and set aside.

Individual squares:

6. From the excess crosswise strips, cut the following number of separate 3-3/4" squares: two from fabric B, three from C, four E (you'll need extra fabric here), and six D.

7. Referring to Fig. 11.4, complete piecing the previously labeled strips in the following manner: Seam one C square to the D end of one 6-piece strip labeled Col. 2.

Fig. 11.6 Slicing tube into rings

Seam the opposite side of the new C square to the D end of the second 6-piece strip. Join one D square at each end of the strip, making it 15 squares long. Repeat this step for column 6.

8. Complete columns 3 and 5 in the same manner, seaming one B square to the C end of each pair of 6-piece strips (refer to Fig. 11.4 for strip orientation). Finish each long strip with an E square.

9. For column 4, seam the two 6-piece strips to each other by joining the B end of the AFEDCB strip to the A end of the other strip. Join a C square to the A end of the long strip.

10. For column 1, seam one D square to each E end of the 7-piece strips. Repeat this step for column 7.

11. Press all new seams open. Lay out the finished strips to double-check the pattern. (Due to the leg notch, the center column should end two squares above the others.) After verifying, number each strip with a label at its top.

Assembling Columns 1 – 3

12. Pin strip 1 to the gridded muslin with *both rightside up.* Match the strip's raw edge to the far left vertical line. Pin all 14 seamlines to the horizontal grid lines (Fig. 11.7). At this stage, the strip's excess fabric will ripple. Pin the strip's top and bottom raw edges to the first and last horizontal lines.

13. To distribute the excess fabric along the pinned edge, form a 3/8" pleat at both left sides of each square. Pin each pleat's fold 1/8" inside the seamline (Fig. 11.8), forming a fat box pleat in every square. Machine baste a scant 1/4" from column 1's left edge, removing pins as you reach them.

14. Match the strip's opposite raw edge to the vertical line that defines the right boundary. Using quilting pins, attach each seam to the corresponding horizontal line and pin the top and bottom edges even with the outer grid lines.

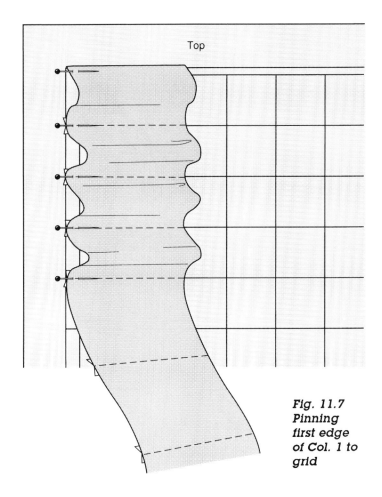

Fig. 11.7 Pinning first edge of Col. 1 to grid

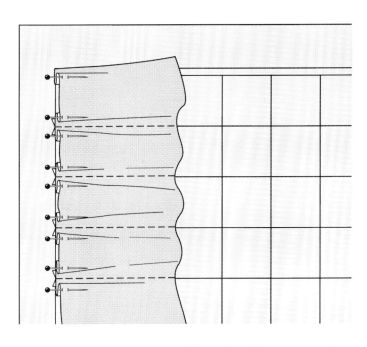

Fig. 11.8 Pinning first box pleats

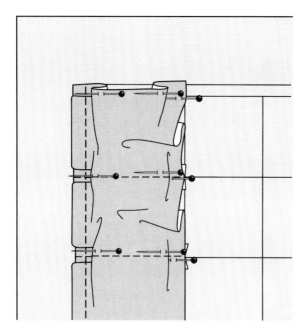

Fig. 11.9 Pinning vertical pleats on seamlines

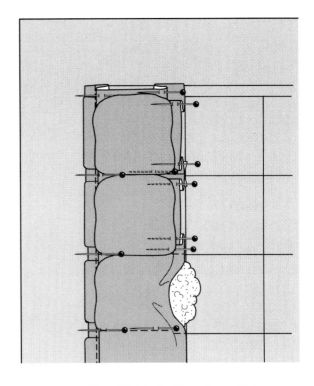

Fig. 11.10 Stuffing fiberfill into biscuits

15. Form two 3/8" *vertical* pleats in each of the strip's seamlines, with the pleats' folds 3/8" in from the raw edges (1/8" in from the seamlines). Skewer each pleat with a regular pin placed on the seamline (Fig. 11.9). *Important: Insert all pins on horizontal rows 1 through 7 pointing from right to left. Pins for rows 8 through 15 point from left to right. Maintain this orientation for all horizontal pins throughout the seven columns. Also pleat the top* and bottom edges, placing pins 1/4" in from the strip's raw edges.

Keep all vertical pleats pinned until after attaching column 7.

16. Stuff a loose ball of fiberfill (about the size of a lemon) into each biscuit, tucking it away from the opening (Fig. 11.10). Put less fiberfill in row 10's square because the seat folds on that row.

17. Use quilting pins to close the strip's open side, forming pleats as in step 13 (Fig. 11.10). (Machine basting at this point is optional—I did not.) After pleating on both sides of each seamline, remove the seamline quilting pin inserted in step 14.

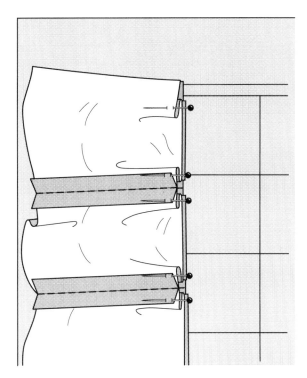

Fig. 11.11 Adding and pleating Col. 2

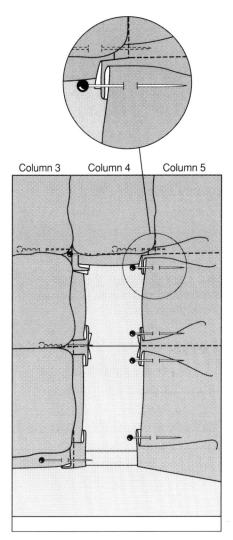

Fig. 11.12 Detail of leg notch, Col. 5

18. Pin strip 2 on top of strip 1, *rightsides together.* First match the horizontal seamlines. This will be your only chance, so check where it counts: a quarter inch inside the raw edges. After pinning all seamlines, form *inverted* pleats right on top of the pinned pleats (Fig. 11.11).

Notice that because the second strip is wrongside up, the pleats fold the opposite way.

Reuse the same pins from the previous step, one by one.

19. Stitch a 1/4" vertical seam. (The stitching line will offset 1/4" left of the grid's line.) Open out strip 2.

20. Repeat steps 14 through 19 for the next two columns, using the next two grid lines.

Assembling Column 4

21. Construct the fourth column in the same manner as the previous three. Notice, however, that this strip has only 13 squares and its bottom edge extends to the grid's short, horizontal leg notch line. (This is 1/4" below row 13's bottom seamline.)

Assembling Columns 5 – 7

22. In column 5's pre-pieced strip, rip the left seam allowance's stitches for 1/4" between rows 13 and 14. Following step 18's technique, pin the left edge of column 5, rows 1 through 13. Pleat these 13 rows as in step 18; stitch, stopping at row 13's bottom pin.

23. Unfold the strip, opening out the seam allowance on rows 14 and 15. Pin the left edge of these two rows to the grid's shorter vertical line, pleating and basting as in step 13 (Fig. 11.12).

24. From here on out, the assembly follows the same procedure as for the early rows. End by pinning the pleats in column 7's right edge. Baste column 7 a scant 1/4" from its right edge.

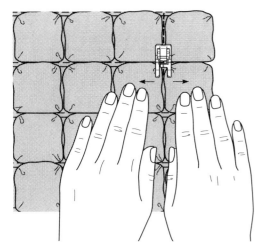

Fig. 11.13 With fingers on both sides of the seam, spread the biscuits apart to make room for the presser foot.

Horizontal Stitching

25. Thread monofilament nylon thread in the machine's needle; keep all-purpose thread in the bobbin. Ditch-stitch between rows 1 and 2, starting at the edge the sharp end of the pins point toward (Fig.11.13). Remove each pin when the presser foot crowds it.

If you used normal pins rather than glass-headed, a small pair of needle-nosed pliers or tweezers will facilitate removal.

26. Use the same method to ditch-stitch all horizontal rows *except* between rows 4 and 5, rows 9 and 10, and rows 13 and 14. For now, leave the pins in those three rows. As you work toward the center rows, roll the material to the right of the foot so that it fits under the machine's head. When you reach row 8, turn the seat 180° so the finished bulk is to your left.

27. Machine baste the top and bottom edges, and baste the bottom edge of column 4. Check that any remaining pins clear the stitching lines.

Pouch (optional)

28. Cut one 10-1/4" x 28-1/2" rectangle and one 10-1/4" x 4" rectangle from fabric E. Fold the larger rectangle in half, crosswise, wrongsides together; press. Attach two 2" x 3/4" loop fastener tapes following Fig. 11.14's placement. Fold the other rectangle in half, lengthwise, wrongsides together; press.

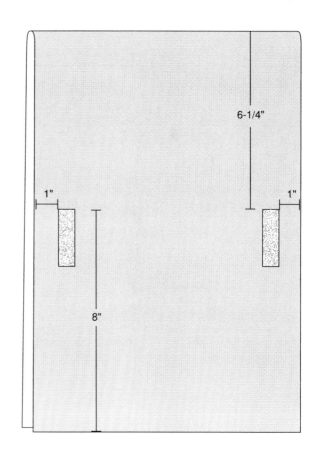

Fig. 11.14 Location for loop tape on pouch

29. For an exposed zipper application, twin-needle topstitch the zipper tapes between the two folds.

Topstitching with a twin needle is a nice touch, but you can substitute single stitching or a decorative stitch if you prefer.

Some zipper feet will not accommodate a twin needle. To apply the zipper with a normal foot, open the zipper. Twin needle topstitch one side halfway and stop with the needle down. Lift the foot and slide the zipper pull past the foot. Lower foot and continue. Stitch second side.

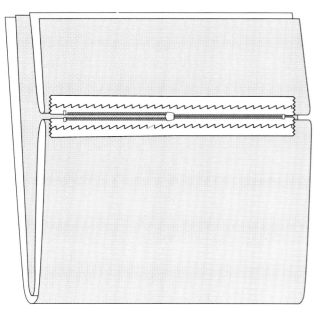

Fig. 11.15 Folding pouch inside out

tape. Sear (Fig. 11.16) or zigzag all cut webbing ends.

31. Separate the snap tape and cut it, following Fig. 11.17, leaving the maximum amount of tape possible at each end of the cut pieces. With the snaps' back sides facing each other, join a male and female tape together with a flat-fell seam (using a 1/2" seam allowance). Hem the free end of the male tape by turning up 1/4" twice and topstitching.

Keep the loop tapes and the zipper pull on the topside. Unzip the zipper about half way. Fold the pouch inside out as shown in Fig. 11.15. Stitch 1/2" side seams through four layers. Trim and finish the seam allowances (zigzag or serge). Turn the pouch rightside out; press. Baste the top edges together.

Webbing

Fusing will not seal the ends of cotton webbing. So, add 1" to webbing A & B when cutting cotton webbing. Turn the additional 1" under the box-lock stitch.

30. Cut three webbing pieces as follows: 12" for webbing A (crotch strap), 17-3/4" for webbing B (female buckle side), and 25-1/4" for webbing C (male or slide buckle side). Temporarily label the webbings with a piece of masking

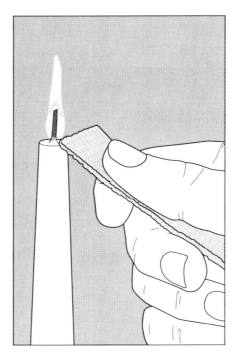

Fig. 11.16 To heat-seal polypropylene webbing, hold a cut edge next to—but not in—the base of a candle flame. The fibers will melt precisely along the edge to prevent fraying. (Be sure to have adequate ventilation for this procedure.)

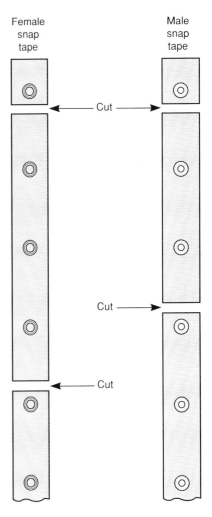

Female snap tape

Male snap tape

Cut

Cut

Cut

Fig. 11.17 Cutting male and female snap tapes

32. Sew the female snap tape to webbing C: Face the snap tape working side down as shown in Fig. 11.18. Stitch a 1/4" seam.

Whenever you need to sew over uneven webbing thicknesses or near snaps, prop the presser foot with a shim.

Fold the snap tape back on the stitching line. With a straight-stitch foot (keeping its narrower side toward the snaps) or a zipper foot, top-stitch following Fig. 11.19. Use an automatic reinforced stitch or add backstitching near the two snaps.

33. Fold under the extra webbing 3/4" twice. Stitch crosswise in the middle of this folded end to secure. (The resulting 3/8" flap will prevent removal of the slide buckle.) Thread the male buckle onto webbing C (Fig. 11.20).

34. Fold one end of webbing A under 3", forming a loop. Secure the end with a box-lock stitch (Figs. 11.21 and 2.29 on page 22).

35. Thread webbing B through the female buckle (Fig. 11.20). Fold back 1-3/4"; stitch a box-lock.

Keep the stitching at least 1/2" away from the buckle so the foot doesn't interfere. Set the webbings aside.

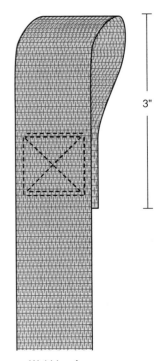

Webbing A

Fig. 11.21 To prevent drawing the beginning thread tails into the bobbin case, clip them after stitching two sides of the box-lock stitch.

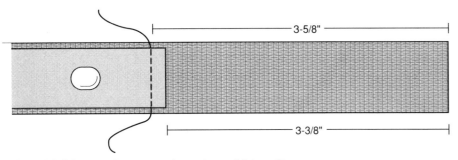

3-5/8"

3-3/8"

Fig. 11.18 Seaming snap tape to webbing C

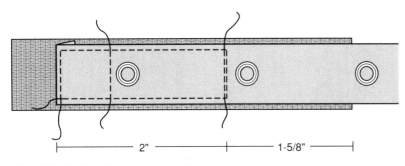

2"   1-5/8"

Fig. 11.19 Reinforcing snap tape

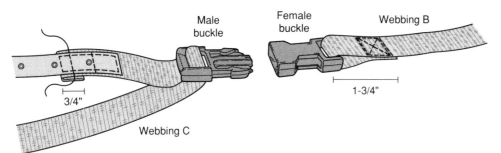

Male buckle

Female buckle

Webbing B

3/4"

Webbing C

1-3/4"

Fig. 11.20 Threading male and female buckles on webbing

Joining the Backing

36. Trim the seat's muslin 1/8" outside the biscuits' raw edges. Cut a rectangle from fabric E larger than the seat. Fuse interfacing to the rectangle's wrongside.

37. Place the interfaced fabric E, rightside down, on a table. Center the seat, rightside up, on top of it. Trim the backing fabric even with the seat's muslin.

38. Center the pouch along the backing's top edge; the pouch's loop tapes should face fabric E's rightside. Baste 1/4" from the raw edges (Fig. 11.22).

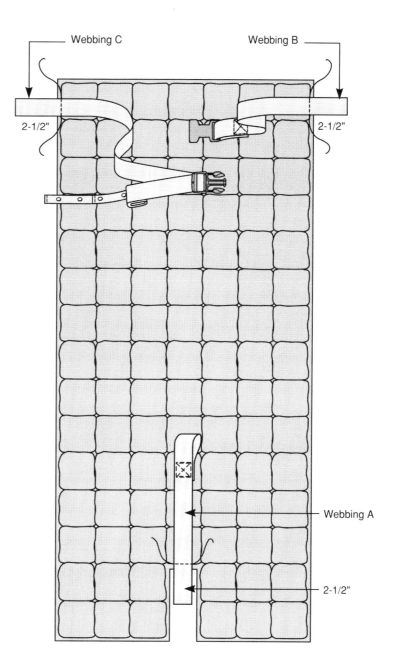

Fig. 11.23 Placement of webbings on seat

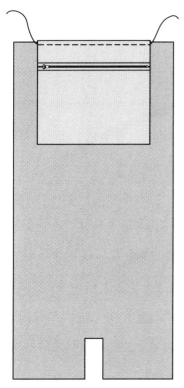

Fig. 11.22 Basting pouch to backing

39. Position two 2" x 3/4" hook tapes on fabric E's rightside, directly under the pouch's loop tapes. Zigzag the hook tapes to fabric E.

40. Following Fig. 11.23's placement, pin the webbing pieces to the seat. Center each webbing on its corresponding biscuit; baste.

41. Use quilting pins to match the seat to fabric E, rightsides together. Stitch the seat's entire perimeter, leaving one side open between rows 5 and 11 for turning (Fig. 11.24).

Since this is a tricky seam, you don't need to sew it all at once. One solution is to pin and sew the leg notch first, then the bottom seams, then the top, and finally the side seams.

Work with the backing up and the muslin toward the feed dogs. The 3/8" seam should fall just inside the prior basting lines. Stitch again over first stitching at each webbing and along the leg notch's inner corners.

42. Trim outside corners; clip inner corners to stitching. Turn seat to rightside. Press the backing's opening edge under 3/8". Slipstitch the opening closed.

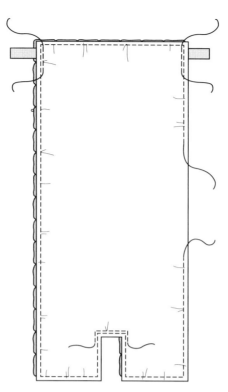

Fig. 11.24 Sewing perimeter and reinforcing webbing

43. Thread the machine's needle with monofilament nylon thread. Open the pouch out of the way. To reinforce the webbings, catch the webbing's 2-1/2" tails by topstitching vertically between columns 1 and 2 of row 1, vertically between columns 6 and 7 of row 1, and horizontally between rows 12 and 13 of column 4 (Fig. 11.25).

44. Complete the biscuits by topstitching between rows 4 and 5, rows 9 and 10, and rows 13 and 14 through all layers. Double-check that all pins have been removed.

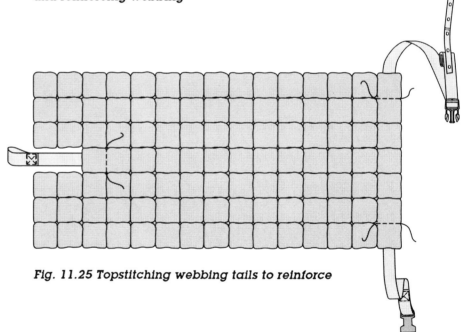

Fig. 11.25 Topstitching webbing tails to reinforce

Puff Block Materials

If you made the shopping cart seat, you have plenty of extra material for this project.

- 3-3/4" squares of six different cotton fabrics (a couple of inches more of one fabric)
- 5" x 8" muslin
- Polyester fiberfill
- One Hide-a-Rattle (flat plastic rattle, 1-1/2" diameter—see page 174) or one pingpong ball rattle made according to Chapter 7's directions on page 96
- Quilting thread

Cutting Directions

Cut one Side and two Ends from muslin. Using either a rotary cutter and mat or the pattern, cut one 3-3/4" Square from each of six different fabrics (called Squares 1 through 6 in these directions). Cut one Loop from cotton fabric.

Transfer all pattern markings.

Fig. 11.26 Puff Block

Sewing Directions

1. Pin the wrongside of Square 5 to one End. Form a large box pleat in the *middle* of each of the four sides (Fig. 11.27). Machine baste inside the 1/4" seam allowance along all sides. Repeat for the second End with Square 6.

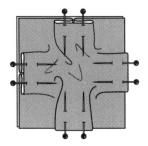

Fig. 11.27 Pinning box pleats on End

2. With rightsides together, seam Squares 1 and 2 along one side from dot to dot. Repeat for Squares 3 and 4. Pin these two pair of Squares together to form one 4-square strip. Join Square 2 to Square 3, stitching for 1/2" from outer square marking to inner square marking twice and leaving center open (Fig. 11.28). Press seams open, also pressing under 1/4" along the center opening's edges.

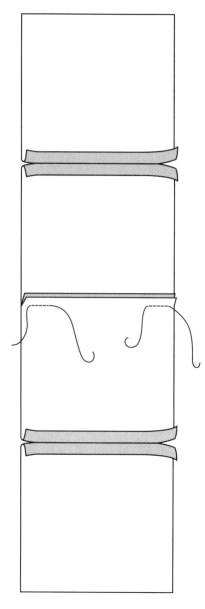

Fig. 11.28 Seaming four Squares

3. With both rightsides up, pin the four-square strip to the Side, matching dots at seamlines and raw edges. Form a big, horizontal box pleat in the middle of each Square along both the left and right edges (Fig. 11.29); stitch just inside the 1/4" seam allowances.

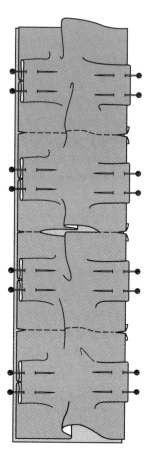

Fig. 11.29 Pinning horizontal box pleats

4. Clip the Side's seam allowances to the six inner dots (Fig. 11.30).

5. Pin vertical box pleats on the seamlines of Squares 1 and 2 and Squares 3 and 4; ditch-stitch. Pin vertical box pleats along the free edges of Squares 1 and 4.

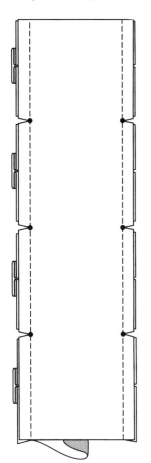

Fig. 11.30 Clipping to dots

Baste a scant 1/4" from the raw edges.

6. Fold the Loop in half, lengthwise, rightsides together. Stitch the long edge. Trim the seam and turn rightside out. (Use a loop turner or check Fig. 9.12 on page 130.) Press Loop.

7. Fold the Loop in half, crosswise. Center it on one of the top End's box pleats with raw edges even and loop extending toward middle; baste.

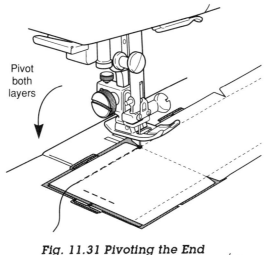

Pivot both layers

Fig. 11.31 Pivoting the End

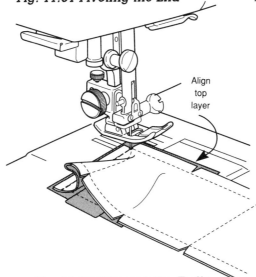

Align top layer

Fig. 11.32 Aligning the End's second side

8. Align the top End right-sides together to the top edge of the Side. Start machine stitching at a dot, with the End toward the feed dogs. Stitch across one edge of the End, dropping the needle at the next dot (at the start of the second Square). Lift the presser foot and pivot the End 90° to align the second side (Fig. 11.31). Pull the Side's free end toward you to match the edge of the second Square with the End's next side. See Fig. 11.32.

9. Stitch the second side of the End, once again stopping at the next dot and pivoting. Align and stitch the third and fourth Squares to the remaining sides of the End. The stitching should meet at the beginning dot.

10. Attach the bottom End to the Side's opposite edge, *but stitch only three of the four sides.*

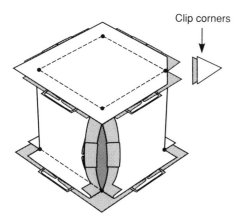

Clip corners

Fig. 11.33 Trimming the corners

11. Trim the Ends' corners (Fig. 11.33). Carefully cut a 1-1/4" slit in the top End's muslin layer only. Working through this slash, stuff the top biscuit (Fig. 11.34). Close the slash with a catchstitch (Fig. 2.31 on page 23).

12. Turn the Puff Block to the rightside. Find the opening between Squares 2 and 3's square markings. Stuff these two Squares. Slipstitch between the markings. Box pleat this seam and pin to muslin. Ditch-stitch by hand using a backstitch.

Fig. 11.34 Stuffing top biscuit through slash

13. Gain access for stuffing the bottom End and Squares 1 and 4 by removing basting threads along the open edges. Stuff the three biscuits, repleat, and rebaste by hand.

14. Working from the bottom opening, stuff the block's top four interior corners. Add the rattle. Complete the stuffing, paying particular attention to all corners.

15. Turn the raw edges under 1/4" and close the openings by hand with quilting thread. Knot securely several times along the way. Hide the thread ends inside. Remove basting threads. Double-check that you have removed all pins.

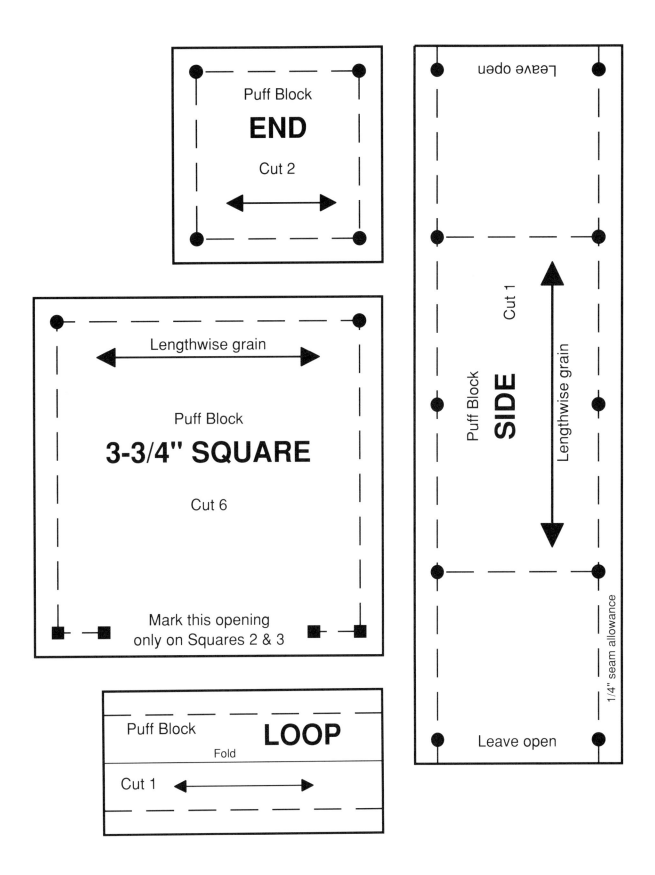

Puff Block
END

Cut 2

Leave open

Lengthwise grain

Puff Block

3-3/4" SQUARE

Cut 6

Mark this opening
only on Squares 2 & 3

Cut 1

Puff Block **SIDE**

Lengthwise grain

1/4" seam allowance

Leave open

Puff Block **LOOP**

Fold

Cut 1

CHAPTER 12

CONCLUSION

Even if you've made only one toy from this book, you've begun a great tradition. If you've made several of these toys, you've given your baby powerful learning tools. But we know we can't stop here. Your child will soon be ready to tackle more advanced tasks, and the *Stitch & Enrich* series of books will be there for him. In the second book, we'll cover exciting toys for toddlers; the third will continue with educational toys for ages three to five.

In playing with children, the adult learns as much as the child. Whenever you and your baby have the chance to play together, you owe it to yourself to grab it. The paperwork from your job will wait. The housework will wait. The gardening, the plumbing, the mopping, the dusting, the computer will wait. The baby won't.

Life won't wait for you to find the time to do all the things you hope to do, either. The secret to finding time for toymaking is to decide what's most important, to set your goals, and to go after them. My final messages might help. One is especially for new parents who find it difficult to set aside even a little time for sewing. The second is for grandparents, aunts and uncles, and friends of the family who already have some free time and love to spend it sewing.

To New Parents:

Bringing up a child is a full-time job, and the burdens on the modern family make it even more demanding. There never seem to be enough hours in the day. Being a single parent, having two or more young children, or tending a "high needs" baby compounds the stress.

To handle that strain, you may find this advice useful. It comes from Kay Dunbar, a nurse in maternity at a large hospital, and I've heard it from others many times since. Kay always sent her new parents home with these words: *Take time each day to nurture yourself.*

If you don't take the time to nurture yourself, you won't have the reserves to care for anyone else. Kay didn't specify whether nurturing meant soaking in a bubble bath, or spending some uninterrupted time reading, or merely daydreaming. Your particular form of nurturing doesn't matter as long as it is something all for yourself.

Sewing is a marvelous way to pamper yourself. Manipulating thread and fabric frees tension and provides a sense of satisfaction and accomplishment. The process of making is just as important as the finished product. Once you set sewing as a priority, you'll find the time.

If you choose reading as your reward, a good place for a busy person to start is **Get It All Done and Still Be Human, A Personal Time-Management Workshop** *by Tony & Robbie Fanning (Kali House, 1990)—see last page for ordering information.*

To Other Sewers:

While new parents have their hands full sewing for their own baby, you might have the luxury of extra time to sew. You could share your valuable sewing skill with others. When you buy the materials to make a toy for your family, you'll likely have enough extra to make a second one. All it costs is your time. For that matter, the second time through, you're faster and experienced.

Perhaps you'd consider making an extra toy and donating it to a needy family. If you don't know an appropriate charity, call your local office of the United Way. (They're listed in the Yellow Pages under Social Service Organizations.) The United Way can refer you to community service agencies and non-profit organizations in your area. They will also have contacts for Christmas gift programs like Toys for Tots. These organizations would be thrilled to have your hand-crafted toy. You'll probably never meet the lucky baby who receives it, but rest assured that your efforts can have far-reaching consequences.

Think of the next generation of children. Think what it would mean if each child were given stimulating toys and a loving adult to guide him. Think what it would mean to our future.

These are lofty goals for one home sewer. But our combined strength is awesome. Imagine if you made just one extra toy for a needy child. Imagine if several of your neighbors did the same thing. Imagine if hundreds of sewers around the world sewed toys for the neglected thousands of babies each year . . . .

Okay. Feet back on the ground. So we can't change the world overnight. But you can change one child's life.

Whether that child is your own or not, whether you're a new mom or dad or a great-grandma, your toymaking can make a difference. When you give a child a handmade educational toy, you start him on the path toward a lifetime of learning. You show him that you care about his future and that you think he's worth your efforts. Who knows where it might lead?

And it all starts with one stitch.

BIBLIOGRAPHY

Child Development Books

Aston, Athina. **Toys that Teach Your Child: From Birth to Two.** Charlotte, NC: Fast & McMillan, 1984. Recommends toys by various manufacturers.

Berne, Patricia H., and Louis M. Savary. **Building Self-Esteem in Children.** New York: Continuum, 1989.

Brazelton, T. Barry. **What Every Baby Knows.** Reading, MA: Addison-Wesley, 1987. This is the companion volume for Dr. Brazelton's television series by the same name. The author has written many books that all reflect his gentle, relaxed, reassuring parenting philosophy. Enjoyable reading, highly recommended.

Burck, Frances Wells. **Babysense.** New York: St. Martin's Press, 1979.

Dodson, Fitzhugh, and Ann Alexander. **Your Child: Birth to Age 6.** New York: Simon & Schuster, 1986. Comprehensive guide to child development. Down-to-earth attitude. Recommended.

Dunford, Jill W. **Teach Me Mommy: A Preschool Learning Guide.** Cincinnati: Writers Digest Books, 1985.

Einon, Dorothy. **Play With a Purpose.** New York: Pantheon Books, 1985.

Eisenberg, Arlene. **What to Expect the First Year.** New York: Workman Publishing, 1989. Easy, relaxed style with practical, up-to-date information. Very good.

Elkind, David. **Children and Adolescents: Interpretive Essays on Jean Piaget.** New York: Oxford University Press, 1974.

Fisher, John J. **Toys to Grow With.** New York: Perigee Books, 1986. Author is a co-creator of the Johnson & Johnson line of development toys. Excellent text for making easy, home-made toys. Includes play ideas.

Gordon, Ira J. **Baby Learning Through Baby Play.** New York: St. Martin's Press, 1970.

Kaban, Barbara. **Choosing Toys for Children.** New York: Schocken Books, Inc., 1979.

Kelly, Paula. **First-Year Baby Care.** Deephaven, MN: Meadowbrook Press, 1983.

Lally, J. Ronald, and Ira J. Gordon. **Learning Games for Infants and Toddlers.** Syracuse: New Readers Press, 1977. Sixty-five practical games requiring few props. Recommended.

Leach, Penelope. **Your Baby & Child: From Birth to Age Five.** New York: Alfred A. Knopf, 1989. The new edition, revised and enlarged, is beautifully illustrated and produced. An excellent, all-purpose reference.

Lovell, K. **An Introduction to Human Development.** Glenview, IL: Scott, Foresman & Co., 1971.

Madaras, Lynda. **Child's Play.** Culver City, CA: Peace Press, 1977. Games, toys, and playgroups.

Munger, Evelyn Moats, and Susan Jane Bowdon. **Childplay: Activities for Your Child's First Three Years.** New York: E.P. Dutton, Inc., 1983. Tip-oriented tidbits.

Princeton Center for Infancy. **The Parenting Advisor.** Edited by Frank Caplan. New York: Anchor Press/Doubleday, 1977.

Rogers, Fred, and Barry Head. **Mister Rogers' Playbook.** New York: Berkley Publishing Group, 1986. Analysis of what is normal for play. Biting, tantrums, sharing, etc. Homemade, craft-type toys.

Segal, Marilyn M. **Your Child at Play: One to Two Years.** New York: Newmarket Press, 1985. How to play with toys rather than how to make them.

Sinker, Mary. **Toys for Growing: A Guide to Toys That Develop Skills.** Chicago, IL: Year Book Medical Publishers, Inc., 1986. Recommends toys for both disabled and non-disabled children.

Sutton-Smith, Brian, and Shirley Sutton-Smith. **How to Play With Your Children.** New York: Hawthorn Books, Inc., 1974.

Time-Life Books. **Playtime.** Alexandria, VA: Time-Life Books Inc., 1987.

Sewing Books

De Sarigny, Rudi. **How to Make and Design Stuffed Toys.** New York: Dover, 1971.

Fanning, Tony, and Robbie Fanning. **The Complete Book of Machine Embroidery.** Radnor, PA: Chilton, 1986.

———. **The Complete Book of Machine Quilting.** Radnor, PA: Chilton, 1980.

Geiger, Jennifer. **See Me Learn Toys.** New York: Sedgewood Press, 1988.

Griffin, Barb. **Petite Pizzazz.** Radnor, PA: Chilton, 1990.

Maddigan, Judi. **Learn Bearmaking.** Menlo Park, CA: Open Chain Publishing, 1989.

Perrone, Lisbeth. **Handmade Baby Clothes.** S. Yarmouth, MA: Allen D. Bragdon Publishers, Inc., 1985.

Reader's Digest. **Complete Guide to Sewing.** Pleasantville, NY: Reader's Digest Association, 1978.

Saunders, Jan. **Teach Yourself to Sew Better: A Step-by-Step Guide To Your Sewing Machine.** Radnor, PA: Chilton, 1990.

Sunset. **Soft Toys and Dolls.** Menlo Park, CA: Lane Publishing Co., 1977.

Booklets, Pamphlets and Catalogs

Be Sure It's Safe for Your Baby. Juvenile Products Manufacturers Association, Inc., P.O. Box 955, Marlton, NJ 08053.

Product Safety Fact Sheet No. 47: Toys; The Safe Nursery, A Buyer's Guide; Tips for your Baby's Safety; Which Toy for Which Child: A Consumer's Guide for Selecting Suitable Toys: Ages 0-5. U.S. Consumer Product Safety Commission, Washington, DC 20207. For the latest information on toy safety and product recalls, call the CPSC toll-free at (800) 638-2772. Recorded messages are available from a touch-tone phone.

Childswork/Childsplay: A Catalog Addressing the Mental Health Needs of Children and Their Families Through Play. The Center for Applied Psychology, 3rd Floor, 441 N. Fifth Street, Philadelphia, PA 19123.

Choking Prevention and First Aid for Infants and Children; Learning Disabilities and Children: What Parents Need to Know; Your Child's Growth: Developmental Milestones. American Academy of Pediatrics, Department of Publications, P.O. Box 927, Elk Grove Village, IL 60009.

Play It Safe! Trial Lawyers of America, Box 3717, Washington, DC 20007.

Toy Safety for Consumers. Oregon State Public Interest Research Group, 027 SW Arthur Street, Portland, OR 97201.

Parenting Magazines and Newsletters

Child. The New York Times Company Magazine Group, 110 Fifth Avenue, New York, NY 10011.

Growing Child, Growing Parent, and *Growing Child Playthings.* P.O. Box 620, Lafayette, IN 47902. Monthly newsletters timed to your child's birthdate.

Parenting. Parenting Magazine Partners, 501 Second Street, San Francisco, CA 94107.

Parents Magazine. Gruner & Jahr USA Publishing, 685 Third Avenue, New York, NY 10017.

Working Mother Magazine. McCall's Publishing Co., 230 Park Avenue, New York, NY 10169.

SUPPLIERS

- **Aardvark Adventures**
P.O. Box 2449
Livermore, CA 94551-0241

  (415) 443-2687;
orders: 1-800-388-ANTS

  Hide-a-Rattles (flat, plastic rattles, 1-1/2" diameter, 3/8" thick), flat squeakers, Fine Fuse, Easy Way Appliqué pressing sheets, threads and machine-embroidery supplies. $2.00 catalog (refundable).

- **Aleene's Division of Artis, Inc.**
85 Industrial Way
Buellton, CA 93427

  1-800-825-3363

  Offers a complete line of nontoxic glues including Tacky Glue and Stop Fraying. General craft supplies. Free catalog.

- **The An-Ser**
P.O. Box 20296
San Jose, CA 95160

  (408) 296-9110

  Counted cross stitch supplies, Aida, DMC floss.

- **Bernina of America, Inc.**
534 W. Chestnut
Hinsdale, IL 60521

  (708) 654-4136

  Sewing machines and accessories.

- **Carver's Eye Co.**
P.O. Box 16692
Portland, OR 97216

  (503) 666-5680

  Safety eyes and noses with metal lock washers as used in Chapters 4 and 7.

- **Cabin Fever Calicoes**
P.O. Box 550106
Atlanta, GA 30355-2506

  (404) 873-5095;
orders: 1-800-762-2246

  Cotton quilt-weight fabric and quilting notions.

- **Clotilde**
1909 S.W. First Avenue
Fort Lauderdale, FL 33315

  (305) 761-8655

  Top quality invisible nylon thread for machine quilting, snap tape, clear elastic, No More Pins, Ensure Quilt Wash, Orvus Quilt Soap, template plastic, Teflon pressing sheets, a variety of fusible webs including Heat N Bond, Fine Fuse, Jiffy Grip, and Wonder-Under.

- **Edinburgh Imports, Inc.**
P.O. Box 722
Woodland Hills, CA 91365

  (USA): 1-800 EDINBRG;
(CA): (818) 703-1122

  Top quality, woven synthetic furs; squeakers; stuffing sticks; Bunka brushes.

- **G Street Fabrics**
11854 Rockville Pike
Rockville, MD 20852

  (301) 231-8998;
orders: 1-800-333-9191

  Wide selection of fabrics including Ultrasuede and Facile. Numerous sample charts available for $10.00 each (refundable).

- **Intercal Trading Group**
P.O. Box 11337
Costa Mesa, CA 92627

  (714) 645-9396

  Top quality, woven synthetic furs.

- **Keepsake Quilting**
P.O. Box 1459
Meredith, NH 03253

  (603) 279-3351

  Specializes in 100% cotton quilt-weight fabric and quilting notions. Prepackaged kit, the "Stitch & Enrich Medley," is available for the 12 solid fabrics in Chapter 5's AlphaPet Quilt. Free catalog.

- **Judi Maddigan**
P.O. Box 700158
San Jose, CA 95170-0158

  Mobile and crib gym warning labels available for $0.25 each plus a self-addressed, stamped envelope.

- **Nancy's Notions**
P.O. Box 683
Beaver Dam, WI 53916

(414) 887-0690;
orders: 1-800-765-0690

General sewing supplies including 100% cotton batiste, template plastic, clear elastic, Stitch-n-Tear, fusible webs, Jiffy Grip, and non-stick pressing sheets.

- **The Perfect Notion**
566 Hoyt Street
Darien, CT 06820

(203)968-1257

General sewing and serging supplies. Free catalog.

- **Sea-Bark Teddies**
P.O. Box 2840
Alameda, CA 94501

(415) 865-0485

Top quality upholstery velvet.

- **Sewing Emporium**
1079 Third Avenue
Chula Vista, CA 92010

(619) 420-3490

Rotary cutters and mats, sewing machine accessories, wide selection of notions and supplies. Their informative catalog, normally $2.95, will be sent free if you mention this book.

- **Speed Stitch**
3113-D Broadpoint Drive
Harbor Heights, FL 33983

(813) 629-3199;
orders:1-800-874-4115

Sulky rayon and metallic threads, books and supplies for machine embroidery.

- **Tomorrow's Treasures**
19722 144th Avenue N.E.
Woodinville, WA 98072

(206) 487-2636;
orders: 1-800-882-8932

E-Z Stitch solid oak and hardwood needlework frames.

- **Toys to Grow On**
P.O. Box 17
Long Beach, CA 90801

(213) 603-8895

Catalog of educational toys. Send $1.00 for No-Choke Testing Tube.

- **Treadleart**
25834 Narbonne Avenue
Lomita, CA 90717

(213) 534-5122;
orders: 1-800-327-4222

Music boxes, sewing supplies.

- **The Unicorn**
1304 Scott Street
Petaluma, CA 94954

(707) 762-3362

Sewing and craft books. Free catalog.

ABOUT THE AUTHOR

Judi Maddigan, an award-winning designer, uses state-of-the-art Computer-Aided Design programs to create sewing projects filled with charm and personality. She began her writing and teaching career with a B.A. in Art from U.C. Berkeley. Her feature articles and advice columns have appeared in many magazines, including *Teddy Bear and friends*, *Lady's Circle*, and *Woman's Day*. Her first book, **Learn Bearmaking**, has become widely recognized as one of the best books on teddy bear making. Judi lives with her husband, Joe, and teenaged daughter, Laura, in San Jose, California, where she continues to pursue her lifelong love of sewing. She is a member of the American Sewing Guild, the Authors Guild, and the Society of Craft Designers.

Also by Judi Maddigan: *Learn Bearmaking*. From bearmaking basics to professional finishing details, this 168-page step-by-step text teaches you to create your own adorable teddy bears. Full-sized patterns for six bears (graded by skill level) and complete directions for counted cross stitched, quilted, and knitted accessories. Softbound copies are available from Open Chain Publishing, Inc., for $18.50 postpaid ($20 California residents).

GIFT TAGS

INDEX

P	p	Q	q
R	r	S	s
T	t	U	u
V	v	W	w

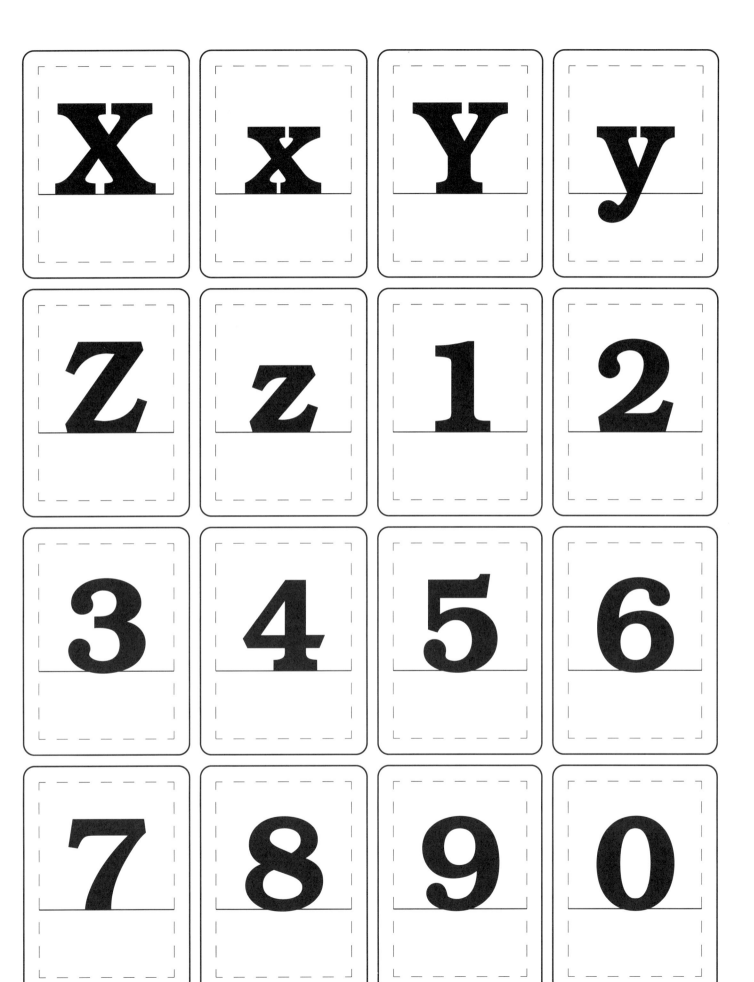

OPEN CHAIN PUBLISHING, INC.

About future books in the Stitch & Enrich Series

If you would like information about **Soft Toys for Toddlers** and **Soft Toys for Preschoolers**, write Open Chain Publishing, Inc., at the address below.

We would like to hear about your experiences with these toys. Do you have suggestions for improvements? Did your baby love what you made? Write Judi at the address below—and send us a snapshot of your baby with your toy to cheer up our office wall.

Additional softbound copies of **Soft Toys for Babies** are available from:

Open Chain Publishing, Inc.
PO Box 2634-B
Menlo Park, CA 94026

(415) 366-4440
fax (415) 366-4455

$20.50 postpaid
($22 California residents)

Wholesale inquiries and bulk orders welcome.

We publish other good books, like **Learn Bearmaking**, **Jane Asher's Costume Book**, **The Busy Woman's Sewing Book**, **Quick Napkin Creations**, and **Get It All Done and Still Be Human**.

Please write for a free list and a sample of our quarterly newsletter, "The Creative Machine." Meanwhile, hug your sewing machine.